D1695212

Real Time Programming
Languages, Specification and Verification

Real Time Programming
Languages, Specification and Verification

R K Shyamasundar
Tata Institute of Fundamental Research, Mumbai

S Ramesh
Indian Institute of Technology, Bombay

NEW JERSEY · LONDON · SINGAPORE · BEIJING · SHANGHAI · HONG KONG · TAIPEI · CHENNAI

Published by

World Scientific Publishing Co. Pte. Ltd.
5 Toh Tuck Link, Singapore 596224
USA office: 27 Warren Street, Suite 401-402, Hackensack, NJ 07601
UK office: 57 Shelton Street, Covent Garden, London WC2H 9HE

British Library Cataloguing-in-Publication Data
A catalogue record for this book is available from the British Library.

REAL TIME PROGRAMMING: LANGUAGES, SPECIFICATION AND VERIFICATION

Copyright © 2010 by World Scientific Publishing Co. Pte. Ltd.

All rights reserved. This book, or parts thereof, may not be reproduced in any form or by any means, electronic or mechanical, including photocopying, recording or any information storage and retrieval system now known or to be invented, without written permission from the Publisher.

For photocopying of material in this volume, please pay a copying fee through the Copyright Clearance Center, Inc., 222 Rosewood Drive, Danvers, MA 01923, USA. In this case permission to photocopy is not required from the publisher.

ISBN-13 978-981-02-2566-7
ISBN-10 981-02-2566-0

Desk Editor: Tjan Kwang Wei

Printed by FuIsland Offset Printing (S) Pte Ltd, Singapore

Preface

The concept of process control has made *Embedded Systems* all pervasive. The applications range from home appliances (video pumps, cameras, set-top boxes, games), personal telecom and multimedia, medical therapy systems, process control systems, automobiles, avionics, tactical Control, nuclear industry etc. If one considers the processors by numbers or volume, it is of interest to note that only 1% of the total number of processors manufactured are used for general purpose computers (say desktop etc); the rest are all used in embedded systems. While general purpose processors is essentially a dedicated general purpose computational system, an embedded system is a complex system consisting of a package of hardware and software systems that can include a range of mechanical systems interfaced with the real-world to realize repetitive monitoring/actuating of the environment. Its' purpose is a dedicated function rather than general purpose computing. Hence, in embedded systems the focus is on the control logic that governs the interaction of the system with the real world. In other words, the challenges in the design of embedded systems lies in interfacing with the real-world meeting concurrent real-time constraints, and stringent safety considerations to augment component (sensor/actuator) interfaces. Thus, challenges towards the specification, design and realization of embedded systems can be summarized as follows:

1. Rigorous design and verification methodologies for embedded software. The grand challenge advocated by David Harel in this direction can be summarized as follows:

    - Devise frameworks for developing complex reactive systems providing means for describing and analyzing systems with the understanding that the structure be driven and propelled by *behaviour* of the systems. Needless to say tools play a vital role in the realization of such a dream.

2. Software Plays an important role in the design of embedded systems. A study shows that at least 60% of development time spent is spent on software coding. This has made a paradigm shift from hardware to software. This is also necessitated by the need to include late specification changes, shorter lifetime of embedded systems, and the need for the reuse of previous design functions independent of the platform. Thus, the main challenge is to invent design structures that match with the application domain. Developing a language independent platform to support such designs is another serious challenge.

In this book, we shall be focussing on the first goal.

Embedded control applications are concurrent and often real-time in nature: a controller runs concurrently with the physical system being controlled and is required to respond to the changes in the physical system state not only correctly but at the right times. For instance, a brake-by-wire subsystem of a car needs to brake the wheels of the car within a few milliseconds after detecting the pressing of the brake pedal. The development of real-time concurrent systems is many orders of magnitude more difficult than conventional data processing applications due to simultaneous evolution of concurrent components.

An emerging methodology of development of embedded control applications is *model-based development*. One of the main features of model based development paradigm is the use of models which are high level abstractions of software (and systems) and can be easily developed from requirements and are executable; the models can be automatically translated into low level code which can be mapped to target platform and integrated. Executable models help in early debugging of design leading to shorter and fast design cycle.

Synchronous programming methodology is one of the successful model based development methodologies of real-time embedded applications and hardware. This methodology was developed at around the same time by three French groups. An important feature of this methodology is a simplified and elegant abstraction of real-time: the synchrony hypothesis. According to this hypothesis, the reaction time of the controller implemented in software is zero. The validity of this assumption stems from the fact that the controllers are executed by powerful micro-controllers and processors which are quite fast compared to the slow physical system being controlled. The synchrony hypothesis greatly simplifies the design and verification of real-time systems as it reduces the number of interleaved executions of concurrent systems. Synchronous programs can also be efficiently translated into low level code that can run on a variety of platforms. Recently these techniques have been commercialized into a number of tools that are being used in the aerospace and process control industries.

Spurred by the success of the synchronous methodology in many important industrial control applications, and due to the power and relative unawareness of this technology, we decided to devote this monograph to this methodology. In this monograph, we focus on the basic elements of synchronous methodology and include a detailed description of three synchronous languages: ESTEREL, Lustre and Argos.

Synchronous Languages are suitable for centralized, single processor and sequential applications. But many complex real-time embedded systems are often implemented over distributed platforms. Recently, the authors of the monograph have extended the synchronous methodology to such applications, developing modeling languages like Communicating Reactive Processes (CRP), Multi-clock ESTEREL and Communicating Reactive State Machines (CRSM). We discuss aspects of these formalisms and illustrate applications of the same.

Organization of the Monograph

The organization of the monograph is as follows. Chapters 1 - 4 discuss the general aspects of real time and reactive systems. Chapters 5 - 10 contain detailed descriptions of the ESTEREL language. While Section 5 gives in detail all the important constructs of ESTEREL, Chapter 6 gives a number of small case studies highlighting the features and tools of ESTEREL. Chapters 7 and 8 are concerned with advanced constructs of ESTEREL. Chapter 9 discusses a large case study in ESTEREL while the formal aspects of ESTEREL are given in Chapter 10. Chapters 11 - 12 deal with the other synchronous language, Lustre. While Section 11 introduces the features of Lustre, Section 12 discusses the modeling of Time Triggered Protocol in Lustre followed by a discussion of graphical language Argos motivated from Statecharts in Section 13. Chapter 14 discusses the verification methods used for ESTEREL and followed by observer based verification for Lustre.

While many reactive systems can be described using synchronous languages, large distributed applications demand a more flexible approach of combining both synchronous and asynchronous features. Chapter 16 introduces Communicating Reactive Processes (CRP), one of the earliest approach to combining synchrony and asynchrony. The semantic challenges of CRP is described in chapter 17 along with a formal semantics of CRP.

Chapter 18 discusses a pictorial variant of CRP, called Communicating Reactive State Machines Chapter 19 demonstrates how real time systems can be captured within the synchronous framework of ESTEREL . Multi-clock ESTEREL is a generalization the basic ESTEREL and is discussed in Chapter 20; multiclock ESTEREL permits modeling subsystems with different clocks. Chapter 21 summarizes the topics covered with a few important observations.

Dependence of the chapters

For the convenience of the reader, the dependence of the chapters are given below, where $a \to b$ denotes that Chapter b requires reading of Chapter a
$1 \to 2 \to 3 \to 4 \to 5 \to 6 \to 7 \to 8 \to 9$
$5 \to 6 \to 10, 5 \to 11 \to 12 \to 13$
$7 \to 12, 5 \to 14, 5 \to 15, 11 \to 16$
$5 \to 17 \to 18, 17 \to 19, 5 \to 20, 5 \to 21$

The intended audience for the monograph include advanced graduate students and researchers interested in synchronous languages and embedded software engineering; practicing engineers involved in embedded software development would also benefit from the book. The monograph would also provide useful material for part of a graduate course on embedded systems.

Acknowledgement

It is great pleasure to thank the inventors of synchronous languages ESTEREL (Gerard Berry), LUSTRE (Paul Caspi, Nicolas Halbwachs), SIGNAL (P. Le Guernic , Albert Benveniste), Statecharts (David Harel, Amir Pnueli), and ARGOS (Florence Maraninchi), with whom the authors had close collaborations and discussions. We also thank the Synchronous Programming Community (the authors have gained a lot in their participation in the yearly Synchronous Programming Workshops) with whom we have had a long association.

The major part of the work was done while the authors were with Tata Institute of Fundamental Research, Mumbai, and Indian Institute of Technology Bombay, Mumbai respectively. We gratefully acknowledge the generous support of these Institutions. Many of the joint works in the area came through the projects under Indo-French Centre for Promotion of Advanced Research (IFCPAR), New Delhi. It is pleasure to thank IFCPAR for the generous support. Professor R.K. Shyamasundar thanks IBM India Research Lab., New Delhi, with which he was affiliated during 2005-2008 and Prof. S. Ramesh thanks India Science Lab General Motors R&D Bangalore, with which he is currently affiliated, for the support and permission to use the resources towards the finalization of the material.

Thanks go to a large number students and collaborators who worked with us. Specially we thank Basant Rajan, Tata Institute of Fundamental Research who mainly worked and developed the multiclock Esterel. A special thanks goes to K Kalyanasundaram who developed and tested examples on Lustre and TTP, and Prahladavaradan Sampath, General Motors R&D Bangalore for reading the entire draft and giving very useful comments that improved the presentation of the monograph.

The authors would like to express their sincere appreciation for the patience and understanding shown by the publishers without which this monograph would not have seen the light of the day.

Contents

PART I: Real Time Systems — Background   1

1 Real Time System Characteristics   3
    1.1 Real-time and Reactive Programs 4

2 Formal Program Development Methodologies   9
    2.1 Requirement Specification 10
         2.1.1 An Example 12
    2.2 System Specifications 13

3 Characteristics of Real-Time Languages   17
    3.1 Modelling Features of Real-Time Languages 19
    3.2 A Look at Classes of Real-Time Languages 22

4 Programming Characteristics of Reactive Systems   25
    4.1 Execution of Reactive Programs 26
    4.2 Perfect Synchrony Hypothesis 26
    4.3 Multiform Notion of Time 27
    4.4 Logical Concurrency and Broadcast Communication 27
    4.5 Determinism and Causality 28

PART II: Synchronous Languages   29

5 ESTEREL Language: Structure   31
    5.1 Top Level Structure 31
         5.1.1 Signals and Events 32
         5.1.2 Module Instantiation 33
    5.2 ESTEREL Statements 34
         5.2.1 Data Handling Statements 36
         5.2.2 Reactive Statements 36

		5.2.3 Derived Statements	41
	5.3	Illustrations of ESTEREL Program Behaviour	43
	5.4	Causality Problems	45
	5.5	A Historical Perspective	46

6 Program Development in ESTEREL — 49
- 6.1 A Simulation Environment 49
- 6.2 Verification Environment 52

7 Programming Controllers in ESTEREL — 55
- 7.1 Auto Controllers 55
  - 7.1.1 A Very Simple Auto Controller 55
  - 7.1.2 A Complex Controller 56
  - 7.1.3 A Cruise Controller 58
  - 7.1.4 A Train Controller 61
  - 7.1.5 A Mine Pump Controller 63

8 Asynchronous Interaction in ESTEREL — 67

9 Futurebus Arbitration Protocol: A Case Study — 71
- 9.1 Arbitration Process 71
- 9.2 Abstraction of the Protocol 72
- 9.3 Solution in ESTEREL 74

10 Semantics of ESTEREL — 79
- 10.1 Semantic Structure 79
- 10.2 Transition Rules 81
  - 10.2.1 Rules for `Signal` Statement 84
- 10.3 Illustrative Examples 87
- 10.4 Discussions 89
- 10.5 Semantics of Esterel with `exec` 90

PART III: Other Synchronous Languages — 95

11 Synchronous Language LUSTRE — 97
- 11.1 An Overview of LUSTRE 97
- 11.2 Flows and Streams 97
- 11.3 Equations, Variables and Expressions 98
- 11.4 Program Structure 99
  - 11.4.1 Illustrative Example 101

	11.5	Arrays in LUSTRE	102
	11.6	Further Examples	103
		11.6.1 A Very Simple Auto Controller	103
		11.6.2 A Complex Controller	103
		11.6.3 A Cruise Controller	104
		11.6.4 A Train Controller	106
		11.6.5 A Mine Pump Controller	107

12 Modelling Time-Triggered Protocol (TTP) in LUSTRE   111
    12.1 Time-Triggered Protocol 111
         12.1.1 Clock Synchronization 113
         12.1.2 Bus Guardian 114
    12.2 Modelling TTP in LUSTRE 115

13 Synchronous Language ARGOS   123
    13.1 ARGOS Constructs 123
    13.2 Illustrative Example 125
    13.3 Discussions 128

PART IV: Verification of Synchronous Programs   133

14 Verification of ESTEREL Programs   133
    14.1 Transition System Based Verificationy of
         ESTEREL Programs 133
         14.1.1 Detailed Discussion 134
    14.2 ESTEREL Transition System 135
         14.2.1 Abstraction and Hiding 136
         14.2.2 Observation Equivalence Reduction 137
         14.2.3 Context Filtering 139
    14.3 Temporal Logic Based Verification 140
    14.4 Observer-based Verification 141
    14.5 First Order Logic Based Verification 143

15 Observer Based Verification of Simple LUSTRE Programs   145
    15.1 A Simple Auto Controller 145
    15.2 A Complex Controller 146
    15.3 A Cruise Controller 146
    15.4 A Train Controller 147
    15.5 A Mine Pump Controller 148

PART V: Integration of Synchrony and Asynchrony 151

16 Communicating Reactive Processes 151
- 16.1 An Overview of CRP 151
- 16.2 Communicating Reactive Processes: Structure 153
  - 16.2.1 Syntax of CRP 154
  - 16.2.2 Realizing Watchdog Timers in CRP 155
- 16.3 Behavioural Semantics of CRP 156
- 16.4 An Illustrative Example: Banker Teller Machine 157
- 16.5 Implementation of CRP 160

17 Semantics of Communicating Reactive Processes 165
- 17.1 A Brief Overview of CSP 165
- 17.2 Translation of CSP to CRP 166
- 17.3 Cooperation of CRP Nodes 168
- 17.4 Ready-Trace Semantics of CRP 168
- 17.5 Ready-Trace Semantics of CSP 168
  - 17.5.1 Semantic Definition 170
  - 17.5.2 Semantics of Parallel Composition 170
  - 17.5.3 Semantics of 'send' Action 170
  - 17.5.4 Semantics of 'receive' Action 171
  - 17.5.5 Semantics of Assignment Statement 171
  - 17.5.6 Semantics of Sequential Composition 171
  - 17.5.7 Semantics of Guarded Selection 171
- 17.6 Extracting CSP Ready-trace Semantics from CRP Semantics 172
  - 17.6.1 Behavioural Traces of CRP Programs 172
- 17.7 Correctness of the Translation 174
- 17.8 Translation into MEIJE Process Calculus 176

18 Communicating Reactive State Machines 181
- 18.1 CRSM Constructs 182
- 18.2 Semantics of CRSM 183

19 Multiclock ESTEREL 187
- 19.1 Need for a Multiclock Synchronous Paradigm 187
- 19.2 Informal Introduction 189
  - 19.2.1 Latched Signals 191
  - 19.2.2 Expressions 192
  - 19.2.3 Multiclock ESTEREL Statements 193

	19.2.4	Informal Development of Programs in Multiclock ESTEREL	194
19.3		Formal Semantics	197
	19.3.1	Specification of Clocks	197
19.4		Embedding CRP	212
19.5		Modelling a VHDL Subset	218
19.6		Discussion	219

20 Modelling Real-Time Systems in ESTEREL   **221**
   20.1   Interpretation of a Global Clock in terms of `exec` 222
   20.2   Modelling Real-Time Requirements in ESTEREL 222
         20.2.1   Deadline Specification 222
         20.2.2   Periodic Activities 223
         20.2.3   Guaranteed Activities 224

21 Putting it Together   **231**

Bibliography   **235**

Index   **243**

Part I: Real Time Systems: Background

Summary

In the next four sections, we shall provide (i) an overview of the general characteristics of real-time systems and reactive systems, (ii) a general discussion on formal development methodologies for real-time systems, (iii) characteristics of real-time languages and (iv) programming characteristics of reactive systems and the synchrony hypothesis.

Chapter 1

Real Time System Characteristics

Real-Time systems are designed to cater to many applications ranging from simple home appliances and laboratory instruments to complex control systems for chemical and nuclear plants, flight guidance of aircrafts and ballistic missiles. All these applications require a computational system (including both the computer and software) interacting with physical equipments like sensors and actuators. Such systems are often referred to as *embedded systems*.

An important feature of many of these systems is the ability to provide *continual* and *timely* response to unpredictable changes in the state of the environment. Hence, these systems have relatively rigid performance requirements. Further, these systems have to satisfy stringent *fail-safe* reliability requirements as failure in many of the applications will result in economic, human or ecological catastrophes. For these reasons, these systems are called *safety-critical* or *time-critical* systems.

In general, the interface between a real-time system and its environment tends to be complex, asynchronous, and distributed. This is due to the fact that the environment of the system consists of a number of physical entities that have autonomous behavior and that interact with the systems asynchronously; it is probably the complexity of the environment that necessitates computer support in the first place. Such systems can be extraordinarily hard to test. The complexity of the environment interface is one obstacle, and the fact that these programs often cannot be tested in their operational environments is another. It is not feasible to test flight-guidance software by flying with it, nor to test ballistic-missile-defense software under battle conditions. In summary, some of the important characteristics of real-time systems are:

- The environment that a system interacts with, is highly nondeterministic and often consists of asynchronous distributed units; there is no way to anticipate in advance the precise order of different external events.

- High speed external events may affect the flow of control in the system easily.

- Responses to external events should be within strict bounded time limits.

- They tend to be large, complex and extraordinarily hard to test.

- In some real time applications, the mission time is long and the system, during its mission time should not only deal with ordinary situations but also must be able to recover from some exceptional situations.

In view of the above characteristics, the design of real-time systems poses serious challenges. There is a definite need for systematic methods and methodologies for designing them. In the design of quality software, high level programming languages and abstract models have a major role to play. The focus of this monograph is on some of the high level programming abstractions that have been found to be useful in designing provably correct real-time programs.

1.1 Real-time and Reactive Programs

There are many dichotomies of programs such as determinism/non determinism, synchrony/asynchrony, off-line/on-line, virtual time/ real-time, sequential/concurrent. However, depending on the way they interact with their environment, programs can be classified into the following three broad kinds[9]:

1. *Transformational Programs:* These programs compute outputs given the input; programs interact with their environment once at the beginning to get inputs and once at the end to give outputs. Compilers are examples belonging to this category.

1.1. Real-time and Reactive Programs

2. *Interactive Programs:* These are programs that interact at their own speed with users or with other programs; time-sharing operating systems are typical examples of this category.

3. *Reactive Programs :* These programs maintain a continuous interaction with their environment, but at a speed which is determined by the environment (and not by the programs). In other words, the output may affect future inputs due to the *feedback* inherent with continual interactions. Real-time programs are sub-classes of reactive programs wherein hard-clock sensor values are needed and the correctness of the programs depends on the speed of the sensors and processors.

Traditional programs like data processing application programs and numerical computations are transformational in nature, as they describe transformations of values of variables (in discrete steps). Any processor implementing these transformations takes a nonzero finite amount of time. These programs, by their very definition, are time independent and hence, designed such that the computed results are independent of the execution speed of their processor(s). In other words, time considerations are completely irrelevant for the functional behaviour of these programs and their correctness; it is only relevant for questions of efficiency.

A typical example of an interactive program is a time-sharing operating system. An operating system consists of a number of sequential programs called processes that run concurrently and interact with each other. Some of these processes interact with I/O devices while some others execute user programs. The rate at which different processes are executed depend, besides processor speeds, upon the process scheduler. A process involving a lot of I/O will be slow compared to a process which does pure computation. Also, the processes executed at different rates may need to interact; for instance, a user program sending a sequence of inputs to another process that stores these inputs onto a disk. A naive design of such systems would take into account explicitly the speeds of different processes. But such a design is not desirable as it will not be robust to the changes of the processors or the schedulers or even a change in a specific algorithm being used in a process. Consequently, the design of interactive systems has always proceeded by abstracting the execution speed (or time) of processes with the result that correctness of programs is not dependent upon the processor speeds and hence time; of course, a price to be paid in such an abstraction is that programs exhibit nondeterministic behavior.

A classic example of a reactive system is the quartz digital watch. In a digital watch, quartz vibrations and button pressures (i.e., the environment) determine the watch behaviour; the environment plays a vital role in reactive programs as cómpared to interactive programs. As an aside, it is important to note that interactive programs have reactive components. For example, the terminal driver in an operating system is a reactive program.

For real-time systems, it is not necessary to use clock-times. For example, consider the description of a braking system of a train. One could say

> when brakes are applied the train should come to halt within 200 meters.

In fact, the above specification is more acceptable than the following clock-time based specification:

> when brakes are applied the train should come to halt within 2 sec.

In the latter specification, one has to verify whether the specification is meaningful in the context of trains with different speeds.

The most important reason for considering time explicitly is in modelling some physical processes wherein the internal laws that define the *natural* behaviour of the physical process are functions of *physical time*. It is in this context one enters the field of real-time programming. In recent times, *hybrid* systems which are a combination of discrete and continuous systems have become important. In these systems, the reference to global clock-time is again important. Wirth showed in [90], that there is a need to consider explicit time/speed even in some concurrent programming situations wherein all the logical processes cannot be physically mapped onto processors due to some hidden assumptions on synchronization.

From the design point of view, transformational and interactive programs have similar characteristics and their behaviour can be described by mathematical functions. Reactive systems are quite different from these two classes. In real-time systems, timely execution of requests and responses by the controllers is critical to the successful operation of both the physical systems and the computer itself. That is, in addition to the normal functional requirements, it is necessary that any response to an input (from the environment) must happen in a given interval of time, called its *deadline*.

Deadlines are classified into hard- and soft-deadlines. A deadline in a program or a system is said to be *hard* if it is mandatory for the program/system to meet the deadlines. In other words, violating the deadlines leads to failure. A deadline is said to be *soft* if missing the deadline does not compromise the correctness of the program but possibly degrades the

1.1. Real-time and Reactive Programs

performance of the system. Systems with hard (or soft) deadlines are called hard (or soft) real time systems . Our emphasis in this monograph is on the development of correct hard real time systems.

The need for robustness and fail-safeness calls for a sound and systematic methodology for the design of reactive programs. In fact, one of the main hurdles in the development of a sound methodology is that the well-known principle of *separation of concerns*, is difficult to follow. For example, even a small real-time system, say, a tactical embedded system for an aircraft might be simultaneously maintaining a radar display, calculating weapon trajectories, performing navigation functions etc. In these systems, one sees that:

1. the software implementing the various tasks are mixed together and it is difficult to determine which task is performed by a part of the code

2. the timing dependencies between tasks are such that changing the timing characteristics of one task may affect other unrelated tasks meeting their deadlines.

In real-time systems, the functional and timing requirements are interwoven. In view of this, the classical approaches of software development cannot be relied upon. We suggest the use of rigorous formal methods for the various phases of software development ranging from specification to realization. The monograph addresses some of these aspects.

Chapter 2

Formal Program Development Methodologies

Formal methods are characterized by their use of mathematically sound and rigorous techniques for developing correct programs. All these methods involve at least the following steps for correct program development:

1. Clear and unambiguous specification of requirements of the program being developed using a formal language, called *requirement specification language*.

2. Detailed design of the system using precisely defined high level abstract models/languages models, called *system specification languages*.

3. Rigorous verification of the design against the specification; use of mathematical techniques is very essential for this step.

4. Implementation of high level designs by low-level code that can run directly on the computational platform.

The use of formal approach to software development has been advocated by many even for traditional programs [23, 36, 47]. As per these works, there are two distinct approaches to development of correct programs:

- Refinement-based methodology: In this approach, the development of a program and its correctness verification are carried out *hand-in-hand*. Starting from the requirement specification of a system, first a correct design at a very high level is obtained. This is then systematically subjected to a series of *refinements* until a design that can be readily implemented is obtained. Each refinement step involves a transformation of one design to another. The crucial aspect of the approach is that each transformation is proved valid during the development. A transformation is valid if the transformed program is equivalent to the original one. As a result, once the initial design has been verified then the series of transformations coupled with their proofs of validity ensures the correctness of the final design.

- *Develop-and-Verify Methodology*: In this methodology, as the name suggests, first the entire system is developed which is then verified to guarantee correctness constraints. Obviously, in this approach, the verification step is rather elaborate requiring examination of the entire final design.

The refinement based methodology has obvious advantages:

1. The task of verification becomes manageable as the task is split into the task of verification of validity of refinements.

2. If there is an error in the design, it is easier to go back one or more steps and redesign.

Because of these obvious advantages, refinement based methods have been suggested for program development [89, 36, 23, 56, 57]. However, refinement methodology is effective provided there is a rich collection of valid and useful refinement rules; the above works describe a number of refinement rules that are found to be useful for *programming in the small*, i.e., for small academic-size programs. More research efforts are required to find a large collection of rules that can be used for developing large industrial-size programs. Also, only a small set of these rules are applicable to real-time programs. Researchers are working at finding useful refinement rules for real-time programming. In the absence of a reasonable set of refinement rules, methodologies being used currently for real-time programming are of the *develop-and-verify* type.

In the rest of this chapter, we give a brief overview of the issues involved in the design of requirement and system specification languages for general as well as real time systems; we also discuss the issues behind verification.

2.1 Requirement Specification

This is perhaps the closest to the conceptual understanding of the problem and hence the earliest stage in the design. In a sense, this could be viewed

2.1. Requirement Specification

as the basis for a contract between a customer who orders the system, and a representative of the team implementing the system. The important parts of a requirement specifications are the *static part*, which identifies the interface between the system and its environment, and the *dynamic part*, which specifies the behaviour that the customer expects to observe on the identified interface.

The static part describes the interface of the system being specified. This interface determines the kind of interaction that could take place between the component and the rest of the system. The dynamic part specifies in detail the behavior of the system under all possible states and behavior of the rest of the system. An important feature of the dynamic part of the specification is that it is logical in nature. That is the specification merely lists down the properties of the systems and it is natural to use a logical language for specification. New properties/functionality could be added/deleted. It is straightforward to add/delete properties from a requirement specification.

Another important aspect of requirement specification is that it should be *consistent* and preferably *complete*. An inconsistent system cannot be realized. An incomplete system may be developed into an implementation not having desirable behavior.

A third aspect of requirement specification is that it provides a very abstract specification of the system. An abstract specification provides more lee-way for implementation; looser the specification, richer is the set of all allowed implementations.

The requirements of systems could be classified broadly into two: *safety* requirements and *liveness* requirements. A safety requirement or property states that nothing bad happens, e.g., when an elevator is moving, it has a weight less than the overweight specified. A liveness property states that something good eventually happens, e.g., any request for going down/up in an elevator will be served in a finite time. In addition, real-time systems could have real-time requirements like: the elevator door is open for 30 seconds unless the open button is pressed..

In traditional methods, the requirements are written in natural languages. Formal approaches, emphasizing on precision and unambiguity, recommend precise languages with a well-defined syntax and semantics. such languages are called *requirement specification languages*. There are many proposals for requirement specification languages. All these languages are based upon symbolic logic studied by meta-mathematician and logicians for precise formulation of mathematical reasoning. Some examples of requirement specification languages are B [92], Z [91], Temporal logic [51].

2.1.1 An Example

We shall now explain the requirement specification scheme using a simple example.

A Mission Control Computer

This is a simplified control unit which forms a part of a generalized avionics system; this example has been inspired by the description in [63, 46]. This control unit, upon external request (by the pilots), provides certain crucial aircraft flight data like altitude, external pressure, ground speed, air speed etc. There is a device corresponding to each data and the appropriate device reading is read by the control unit upon a request. The control unit stores the previous data so that if the requested device is broken then it calculates the required data of sufficient accuracy based upon previous data. There is a flash unit corresponding to each device which is controlled by the control unit. A flash unit is *lit* whenever the corresponding device is broken thereby indicating that the data given is calculated data and that the device needs repair/replacement. The flash unit can be switched off by the pilots after the repair.

We shall now attempt to give a requirement specification of this control unit. First, we shall develop the static part of the specification. As mentioned earlier, the static part decides the interface between the unit under specification and its environment. Let us employ an event-oriented approach to the specification; in this approach, abstract events are used for exchange of information between the unit and its environment.

Let *req* be the event generated by the pilots indicating the request for data. Further, let *data* be the response event to the request by the control unit; for the purpose of illustration, we shall ignore the values carried by various events. In addition, let *on* and *off* be the events indicating the switching on and *off* of the flash init; note that *on* is generated by the control unit while *off* is issued by its environment.

Now we can state the requirements of the control unit as follows:

- Every *req* event is followed by a *data* event and every *data* event is preceded by a *req* event.

- A *data* event may be accompanied by the flash unit getting lit, indicating that the device is broken and needs repair.

- The flash light is switched off when the off signal is issued from the environment.

As one can see, the above specification specifies the *temporal* relationship between the various events happening in the system. In this sense, the chosen example exemplifies reactive systems whose behavior can be specified as temporal relationship among the various events. Also, the specification is *logical* in nature as it is a logical conjunction of the three constraints stated above each of which by itself is logical in nature. Because of these reasons, logical languages like first order logic and temporal logics have been used for formal specification of reactive systems. A spectrum of temporal logic languages for specifying reactive systems have been developed [51, 61, 58].

One of important features of this type of specification is that it is not very detailed; it specifies only *what is necessary and nothing more*. It leaves a lot of freedom for the implementor; for instance, how the control unit infers the working state of the device is left out of the specification as it is part of the implementation.

2.2 System Specifications

In contrast to requirement specification, this is a more detailed description of the system as it describes how requirements can be realized. A system specification contains the complete architecture of the system, being specified, detailing all the constituent modules or sub-systems, their interconnections and the behavior of the all subsystems. It is an intermediate level specification lying between requirement specification and actual implementation. It is more detailed than the requirement specification but reasonably abstract to allow plausible freedom for implementation.

System specification needs to be precise and unambiguous for two reasons:

- It should be possible to develop concrete implementations from it.
- It should be possible to verify the satisfaction of the requirements of the system.

This feature necessitates a precise language/model for expressing the system specifications.

One of the earliest system specification languages used for specifying detailed behavior of reactive systems (especially hardware), is the state transition systems. In this language, the entire set of system states and the various transitions that are possible between states are described. The set of states is usually finite (could be infinite) e.g., sequential circuits. Transition between states are effected because of external events.

14   Chapter 2. Formal Program Development Methodologies

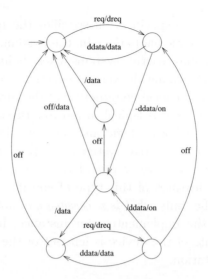

Figure 2.1: **FSM Specification**

The main advantage of transition system specification is its simplicity and ease of specification. It is very intuitive, does not require any special training and describes, the complete details of the system. The implementation is also straightforward.

For instance, let us consider the mission control computer discussed earlier. The behavior of this system can be described by the state-transition specification shown in Figure 1.

One of the main disadvantages of this formalism is that it has absolutely no structure. System specifications are sufficiently detailed and hence the state transition descriptions may blow-up and become unmanageable and error-prone. Hence, all later attempts to provide languages for system description incorporate a rich set of structuring primitives. Some important primitives that have been found to be useful are given below:

1. **Concurrency:** It is natural to view systems, especially large ones, as a collection of concurrent subsystems each having its own behavior with few interactions among them.

2. **Encapsulation:** This primitive provides facilities for hiding away details of subsystems and thus, helping in hierarchical development. It would be desirable to have a hierarchical encapsulation mechanism that would allow one to develop/view systems at different levels with different degree of details.

2.2. System Specifications

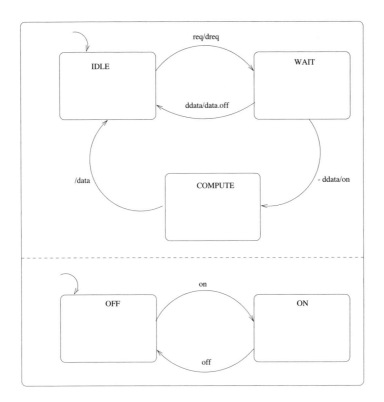

Figure 2.2: **A Statechart Specification**

3. **Nondeterminism:** This is less of a structuring primitive than an abstraction primitive that enables to express specifications with open-ends which are completed during the course of implementation. These open-ends are details which are not of importance to the user of the system but required for the implementation.

Figure 2.2 illustrates the usefulness of these structuring primitives by describing the behavior of the mission computer in a language called Statecharts [40]. this description is much more compact than the original flat finite state description.

Like Statecharts, many languages have been proposed for system specifications. This include abstract modelling languages like CSP [44], CCS [53] and Petri-nets [73]. and more concrete languages like ADA [6] and SDL [24].

Chapter 3

Characteristics of Real-Time Languages

As mentioned earlier, real-time systems are special classes of reactive systems. Hence, many real-time languages adopt the response-stimulus model of reactive systems: any system is an infinite reactive process waiting for certain events to happen in its environment; when these events happen it responds within some specified deadlines, by possibly generating new events. Pictorially, this is described in Figure 3.1.

Real-time languages have to take into account many aspects which include:

- *Concurrency*: It is natural to view a reactive process as a collection of concurrent tasks each monitoring and generating distinct components of the environment. Since the correctness depends upon the speed of the underlying processors, it is necessary to a provide a clear execution model.

- *Timing Constraints*: In order to describe time-bound responses, various abstractions for specifying timing constraints are required. Naturally, one needs to arrive at some notions of *expressiveness/completeness* for arriving at various abstractions.

- *Determinism vs Nondeterminism*: Though nondeterminism is essential in specification, it is important to have deterministic response from a system.

- *Preemption*: Preemption is the process of controlling the life and death of processes. In the context of a reactive process, it is very easy to

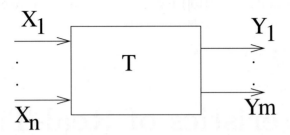

A. Transformational Program

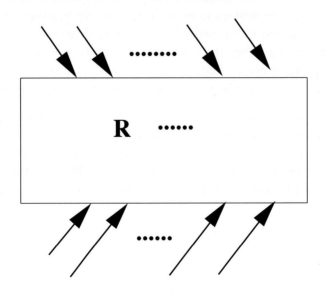

B. Reactive Program

Figure 3.1: **Structure of Transformational and Reactive Programs**

find the need for preemption; imagine undoing the command/action done by mistake. Berry ([10]) has argued the need of preemption as an orthogonal feature for reactive systems.

- *Priority*: In a typical reactive/real-time application, scenarios must be predictable. Since the environment is invariably nondeterministic, it is essential that priority among the simultaneously plausible events be specified without any ambiguity.

- *Verification*: Needless to say that the need for high confidence makes it mandatory to have good methods of verification and tools supporting them. The very fact that the programs have to be formally proved correct makes it imperative that the language should have a formal semantics. Further, programming discipline in the language is based on a few orthogonal features for writing good programs capable of ensuring good source-code quality.

Traditionally, real-time systems were designed at assembly level with these features being supported indirectly by the underlying operating systems. The recent trend is to use high level languages that have abstractions supporting the above features. Advantages of directly supporting these aspects are:

- system developers are able to express the concurrency inherent in the problem more naturally thereby reducing the chance of errors.

- with the addition of verification and simulation facilities, the correctness and performance of the system can be analyzed even before the system is installed.

- Portability of the system is enhanced as the design would be less dependent on the characteristics of the platform.

We shall give a very brief review of the various real-time programming language categories that are in use.

3.1 Modelling Features of Real-Time Languages

Languages for reactive programming or real-time systems have been generally categorized based on the underlying model for concurrency, specification of timing constraints and verifiability. First, let us look at these broad features of languages in some detail.

Concurrency:

Two distinct models of concurrency followed in reactive/real-time programming are the *asynchronous model* and the *synchronous model*.

The asynchronous model is a classical model of concurrent programs: It is also called the interleaved model of concurrency, introduced by Dijkstra [23]. In this model, the concurrent components of a program, called processes or tasks are executed in an interleaved fashion with no assumption being made on the speed of the processes except that the speeds are nonzero and finite. The underlying implementation of this model has a scheduler for scheduling the processes for execution (i.e., mapping the logical processes onto physical processors). The speed-independence assumption corresponds to the fact that the behavior of the program is independent of the scheduler and the architecture of the system from the correctness point of view.

The asynchronous approach for real-time programs employs a model of concurrency that is the natural extension of the above classical model. In this extension, processes are associated with deadlines within which they should be scheduled. The schedulers are expected to follow these constraints. Using maximal parallelism model, a compositional semantics for Ada like real-time languages was first proposed in [49] and elaborated for different broadcast communications models in [74]. While isolated formulations of concurrency, real-time, exceptions etc satisfied good properties, these studies established the problems (and partial solutions) when these features are integrated. Also the studies related to the problems of uncertainty in clock synchronization.

The synchronous[1] approach, in contrast, is based on a new programming paradigm that assumes that a reactive program produces its outputs in no *observable time*; this is often referred to as the *zero delay hypothesis*. This paradigm has been the basis of reactive languages such as Esterel[11], Lustre[20], Signal[38] etc. and Statecharts [41] in a larger sense.

The zero delay hypothesis coupled with the logical concurrency has two important consequences:

1. The (timing) analysis of programs is simplified as there is no need for keeping track of the various communication costs.

2. The behavior of the implementation is exactly the same as the original high level design as there are no additional run-time overheads.

---

[1] The term differs from the same term used in Statechart models.

3.1. Modelling Features of Real-Time Languages

The exact correspondence between the design and implementation is very useful because any analysis carried out on the design directly carries over to the implementation. Considering the criticality of many real-time applications, the exact correspondence between the implementation and design aids in achieving the reliability by analyzing the high level design. No extra analysis needs to be done taking into account the run-time system as has to be done in the case of classical models.

While zero-delay hypothesis is useful for many embedded applications, there are applications (distributed reactive controllers) for which this hypothesis may not hold. There are a few attempts to have an integrated single model that can capture both asynchrony and synchrony. We shall more details of these later.

Time Constraints:

The main task of a reactive program is to provide the *right reaction at the right time*. Thus, a straightforward way of incorporating a notion of time is to associate with each event, the physical-time at which the event takes place. One question that arises: Is it always necessary to associate physical time? Recalling that a reactive program must be fast enough react to the environment without loosing any input, it may be observed that it is possible to do away with physical time as long as it is not necessary for the functional model. Such an abstraction will have the additional benefits of designing programs that can be refined to several situations rather than that particular situation. Further, the approach also makes reasoning simpler. The same example of the *brake* for train illustrates this aspect. These forms of time are often referred to as *multi-form notions of time*. The perfectly synchronous languages mentioned earlier follow this approach.

Verifiability:

Verification ensures the correctness of the proposed design by checking whether a designed system meets its requirements or not. Once formal techniques are used for specifying the requirements and designs, then the verification problem becomes a mathematical problem and can be solved rigorously. This increases the confidence in the correctness of the system being designed.

The specific approaches used for verification varies depending upon the languages used for specifying requirements and design. One can classify these approaches into two kinds: One Language approach and Two Languages approach.

In the *one language approach*, the requirements and design are expressed in the same language and consequently the task of verification amounts to showing the equivalences of the two expressions in the same language. The main technique used for verification is based upon *bisimulation equivalence* introduced by Milner [53]. There are various verification systems that have been built using this technique such as AUTO [17] and Concurrency Workbench[72].

The *two-language-approach* as the name suggests, assumes that the requirements and design are expressed in two distinct languages, the former in a logical language like temporal logic. The techniques used for verification using this approach are based upon symbolic logic. Two distinct techniques referred to as *deductive* and *model-theoretic* are widely used for verification analysis:

Deductive techniques require axiomatization of system specification languages. The problem of verifying a design then consists of stating that the design satisfies the given requirements in logic and proving (using theorem provers or manually) that it is indeed the case using logical deduction in the axiomatic system.

Model-theoretic techniques, in contrast, are more algorithmic in nature. Given a design, it directly checks whether the design satisfies its requirements or not.

3.2 A Look at Classes of Real-Time Languages

There are many languages having many of the above mentioned features. Typical languages such as Ada, Modula and Java have been designed keeping in view the general computational requirements as well as real-time requirements; Ada caters to shared memory as well as distributed architectures and Java and Modula caters to shared variable architectures. Both these languages provide concurrency constructs and use the asynchronous model of communication. No special constructs are provided for specifying preemption. Instead, processes can be assigned priorities. These languages can be called *general purpose languages*, as they include all the constructs required for general computation; they have additional support for specifying real-time constraints.

In contrast to these general purpose languages, there are some special purpose languages that are designed specifically for describing real-time computations. ESTEREL, Lustre, Signal and Statecharts are of this kind. They

3.2. A Look at Classes of Real-Time Languages

have limited constructs for specifying features like preemption, watch-dog constructs and traps; they often rely on a standard general purpose language like C, C++, Java for realizing standard computational requirements They are all based on the synchronous model of concurrency.

These two classes of languages take two extremes: either purely asynchronous or purely synchronous. But there are applications, where one would like to have a combination of both synchronous and asynchronous paradigms. Such applications are distributed control programs and large hardware systems involving multiple cycles. One of the earliest languages for describing such computations is Communication Reactive Processes (CRP) [13]. In CRP, programs consist of interacting synchronous processes that communicate using asynchronously.

The rest of the book will mainly describe the synchronous paradigm and synchronous languages. Some recent attempts to generalize the synchronous paradigms like CRP and CRSM would also be discussed. Important issues like programming, semantics, verification and application would be the focus of the discussion.

Chapter 4

Programming Characteristics of Reactive Systems

A reactive system has three main components:

- An *interactive interface*.
- A *reactive kernel*.
- A collection of *data processing* modules.

The interface handles the environment reading/acquiring inputs and generating output. Typically, it will consist of a number of device drivers, one for each class of devices which transforms physical signals into logical inputs to the reactive kernel; they also convert logical outputs generated by the kernel into physical signals and output to external devices. The data processing modules perform the traditional computations involving data. These two components are classical in nature and standard programming languages and practices can be followed for developing them.

The reactive kernel is the component of our interest. It is responsible for analyzing the inputs and deciding on appropriate control actions and generating appropriate outputs. Synchronous languages that form the core of this monograph are designed to program reactive kernels. They are not general purpose languages as they have primitives for programming the logic of reactions and limited facilities for data handling; the latter are left to traditional languages (called host languages) like C, ADA etc. Due to this reason, synchronous languages always come with one (or more) host language and programs are compiled into host language programs. This makes the reactive kernel independent of the interface handling the environment and hence, can be ported across different platforms with relatively more ease.

4.1 Execution of Reactive Programs

In the view of synchronous languages, a reactive system is executed as follows. The interface modules are either executed periodically polling for inputs or driven by interrupts caused by physical inputs. The data processing modules are under the control of the reactive kernel, invoked by the latter to perform some computations. The execution of the reactive kernel takes a bounded amount of time without any waits nor any unbounded loops. The kernel is said to perform a *reaction* each time it is executed. It is called upon to execute at definite (often periodic) points of time. When it executes, it produces appropriate outputs for the given inputs depending upon the internal state of the kernel. The execution of the kernel is wait-free in the sense that it does not wait for some inputs to arrive or for some outputs to be transferred out. Also no inputs during the execution of the kernel can influence its execution. This has been made possible because of two reasons: the kernel deals purely with logical signals and it is executed after making sure that all the relevant inputs are registered.

4.2 Perfect Synchrony Hypothesis

In view of the high priority nature of the kernel the *reaction time* (the time taken for a reaction to be completed) should be as small as possible. In order to make the programming task easier, synchronous languages make an idealization by assuming the reaction time to be *zero*! That is, a synchronous program (hereafter whenever we mean program we refer to the kernel written in a synchronous language) reacts *instantaneously* to its inputs. This is referred to as the (perfect) synchrony hypothesis. This idealization is achievable in practice by making the reaction time negligible compared to the time of arrival of input events. Though, in principle, inputs can arrive at arbitrary rates, the hardware devices are in general slow (compared to the CPU) and can process the inputs only at a finite rate much larger than the speed with which CPU can compute the reactions.

With the above idealization, we can consider an execution of a program to be a discrete sequence of *reaction instants*. In each instant, the program reacts to inputs by generating outputs. If one considers the input as an infinite flow of inputs then the kernel can be considered as a flow transformer transforming the input flow into an infinite output flow. In fact, this view is taken in some of the synchronous languages like Lustre and Signal.

4.3 Multiform Notion of Time

Besides the synchrony hypothesis and the novel structure imposed by the synchronous approach on real-time systems, another novelty of synchronous languages is its handling of time. In these languages, time is treated as a periodic signal like any other signal that can be input to the system. This overcomes differences between the clock-time and other events and thereby, provides a uniform view of events. By viewing time as any other event, there is no need to talk about actual physical time. In many real-time applications, there is actually no need for referring to real-time. The following standard example illustrates this. Consider a rail-road crossing gate controller. One of the requirements of the controller using explicitly the physical time is given below:

> The closed gate may open 100 seconds after train started crossing the gate.

Now, let us consider the following statement:

> The gate may open after the last carriage of the train crossed the gate.

The latter statement is preferable to the first one, as the safety of the first requirement depend upon the speed of the train. By giving equal status to time and events, it is indeed possible to write specifications independent of physical time – this is indeed a good practice. This feature can be effectively used to verify the synchrony assumptions relative to the exact timings as illustrated in [84].

4.4 Logical Concurrency and Broadcast Communication

Synchronous languages offer concurrency constructs using which programs can be structured as a collection of concurrent modules. But the concurrency is *logical* in the sense there is no correspondence between the concurrency that exists in the source program and the object program. In the translation process, concurrency is compiled away to get a purely sequential code. The reasons for this is many-fold: Concurrency is a structuring construct that enables easy understanding of the source program. There is no need for this structure to exist at the object level which is not meant for human consumption. Another important reason is that keeping the object code as a collection of concurrent tasks require special task management strategies. These strategies involve delays unseen at the source level as they depend upon scheduling policies. With the result that any property, especially real-time properties that one can claim at the source level may not hold at the object level. Synchronous approach prefers to have a tighter correspondence of real-time properties between the source and object codes rather than of their structures.

Such a model of concurrency should be distinguished from the more traditional approach to concurrency. In the traditional approach, like the one followed in ADA, OCCAM, concurrency is physical in the sense that object programs would contain a number of tasks which needs to be scheduled.

Concurrent components of a synchronous program interact by means of signals that are broadcast simultaneously to all the concurrent units. That is, a signal emitted by one concurrent unit can be observed *simultaneously* by *all* the other units. Since all the units are simultaneously active, they can in addition to observing the presence of signals can also observe *absence* of signals. It should be noted that the above kind of seemingly impossible instantaneous communication is an abstraction at the source level; in the actual implementation, there are no concurrent units and hence, its interaction can be easily implemented.

4.5 Determinism and Causality

Synchronous languages reconciles concurrency with determinism. They allow only those programs that have deterministic reactions. The role of deterministic behaviors in the case of safety-critical application hardly need emphasis. All conventional sequential languages are deterministic. Languages supporting traditional models of concurrency are, however, nondeterministic.

Part II: Synchronous Languages

Summary

Several synchronous languages have been proposed in the literature. The principal languages of the family of synchronous languages that have been founded on the *perfect synchrony hypothesis* are ESTEREL, LUSTRE and SIGNAL. ESTEREL is an imperative language that has its origin in catering to explicit control applications. LUSTRE has been founded on a data flow model, whereas SIGNAL is a relational model that has its origin in the specification of feedback control systems. In a sense all these languages are equally powerful with the exception that SIGNAL is more expressive from the specification point of view. Statecharts is a visual formalism that can in fact be included in the family of synchronous languages considered from the perspective of specifying robust reactive systems. Statcharts are not strictly based on the synchrony hypothesis even though formally it has been defined with respect to asynchronous and synchronous models. Argos is another synchronous language that is based on visual formalism similar to Statecharts based on synchrony hypothesis. It must be noted that all these languages have found significant usage in various industries like Avionics, CAD, Nuclear plant control, Telecom, Automobile etc. In this part (next six chapters), we shall discuss the following languages structure, methodology, semantics and programming of typical reactive real-time systems in ESTEREL.

Chapter 5

ESTEREL Language: Structure

ESTEREL is an *imperative* synchronous language having a textual syntax somewhat along the lines of Pascal. It's distinguishing feature (among other synchronous languages) is the rich set of signal handling constructs useful for reactive programming. In this section, we shall discuss the programming concepts, rationale and informal semantics of the ESTEREL language. Our discussion is based upon version 5 and the main source of reference is version 5.0 [34].

5.1 Top Level Structure

The basic unit of programming in ESTEREL is called *module*. Any application written in ESTEREL is structured as a collection of modules. Each module has two parts: a declaration and a body. The declaration defines the signal interface between the module and its environment. The declaration lists down a list of signals that are inputs or outputs to the module. Each signal has a name and optionally the type of values that can be carried by the signal. A signal without any type declaration is called a pure signal.

The body of a module is an ESTEREL statement. Here is an example of a typical module:

```
module tel-exchange:
    input on_hook,digit_dialled(integer),serve_user(user_id);
    output check_number(string);
    inputoutput give_busy_tone(user_id);
    Statement-body
end module
```

5.1.1 Signals and Events

Signals are the means of communications between different ESTEREL modules and between a module and its environment. Signals can be pure or valued. Following our discussion in a previous section, a program or a module has a sequence of reactions each of which involves sensing the presence of input signals and possibly checking the values they carry and generating output signals. Due to the synchrony hypothesis, outputs are generated at the same instant inputs are observed. The inputs as well as the generated outputs are available (and broadcast respectively) to all the modules instantaneously. ESTEREL has statements that can sense the presence of signals and that can generate output signals. There are statements and scope rules that can limit the regions of statements or modules which can sense the signals generated in other concurrent modules or in the environment.

A signal declaration may include the name of the data type of values carried by the signal when it is emitted (ESTEREL buzzword for *generated*). ESTEREL has a few built-in data types which includes integer and boolean. Arbitrary data types can be defined by the user but these definitions appear outside ESTEREL, in declarations in the host language.

The declaration in the module `tel-exchange` given above, defines `on_hook`, `digit_dialled` and `serve_user` to be *input* signals with the first signal being a pure signal (not carrying any value) while the other two signals carry the value that is of type integer and user_id. Of these two types, integer is defined in the ESTEREL language while user_id is a type defined by the user and its definitions need to be included in the host language program accompanying the ESTEREL program.

The above declaration declares `check_number` to be an output signal carrying values of type string, which is again user-defined. The signal `give_busy_tone` is declared to be an inputoutput signal which means that certain modules of the associated ESTEREL program can input this signal while certain other modules can output this signal.

A signal can be emitted simultaneously by several modules. If the signal is pure then the result is the presence of the signal. If the signal is valued, the values of the different emissions can be different and these values are *combined* using a combination operator that may be specified in the declaration of the signal-value data types. Also, there are default combination operators for the built-in data types of ESTEREL. For instance, for integer values the default combination operator is addition.

There is a special signal called `tick` that is always present at any reaction instant. This signal is typically used to delay reactions.

5.1.2 Module Instantiation

Modules, in general, are generic units that can be instantiated. The command for reuse is the 'run' command. A typical example of this command is:

```
run tel-exchange[on_hook/on_hook1,serve_user/serve_user1]
```

The effect of this command is to copy the *body* of the module tel-exchange in the place of the run command, renaming all occurrences of the signals on_hook, serve_user in the body by on_hook1, serve_user1 respectively; thus parameters are *bound by capture*.

Structure of another typical module is illustrated below:

```
module tel-user:
    %type definitions
    type user_id,time_units;
    %constant definitions
    constant first_digit_limit;
    %input signals
    input
    on_hook,digit_dialled(integer),serve_user(user_id);
    input valid_number,invalid_number;
    %output signals;
    output check_number(string);
    output set_time_limit(time_units);
    %input-output signals
    inputoutput give_busy_tone(user_id);
    %procedures
    procedure connect()(user_id,user_id);
    procedure set_call_forward()(user_id,user_id);
    %functions
    function add_digits(string,integer):string;
    %tasks
    task printlog (integer) ();
    return fin;
    relation invalid_number # valid_number;
    statement-body
end module
```

The above example illustrates typical declarations given in an ESTEREL module. As the name of the module suggests, the above fragment could be part of a module that handles telephone users. This module makes use of data values that are of type user_id and time_units. These two types are user defined in the host- language program that accompanies this module. In this module, on_hook, digit_dialled and serve_user are *input* signals with the first signal being a pure signal (not carrying any value) while the other two signals carry the value that is of type integer and user_id.

The above declaration declares `check_number` and `set_time_limit` to be output signals carrying values of type string and time_units respectively. The signal `give_busy_tone` is declared to be an inputoutput signal which means that certain modules of the associated Esterel program can input this signal while certain other modules can output this signal.

The module may call two procedures `connect` and `set_call_forward` and a function `add_digits`. The exact specification of the numbers and types of the arguments and results are given in the declaration. Procedures and functions may have two lists of arguments, one containing those arguments that are passed by reference (which happens to be empty in this example) and those passed by value; Functions, in addition, return a single result of arbitrary type. The codes corresponding to these procedures and functions do not contain any reactive statements and are to be written in the host language program. Consequently, their execution is instantaneous.

Tasks are like procedures having reference and value arguments, declared in ESTEREL but the actual code in the host language. The difference between procedures and tasks is that task execution is non-instantaneous. Execution of tasks are initiated by the ESTEREL code by executing `exec` statements; completion of a task is indicated to the ESTEREL module by an input signal called the *return* signal of the task whose type is also included in the task declaration.

The above declarations, in addition to the data object and signals used by the module contains a *relation* that specifies the signals invalid_number and valid_number to be incompatible in the sense that they will never occur together. Such a relation is called *exclusion* relation. The other kind of relations is called *implication* relation, denoted by =>. For example, the relation S=>R specifies that whenever signal S occurs then signal R will also occur. Relations are useful in generating optimized code as using them one can avoid unreachable execution sequences.

5.2 ESTEREL Statements

The statements of ESTEREL are divided into *kernel* statements and *derived* statements. The kernel statements are further classified as data handling statements, signal handling statements and control flow statements. There is a rich set of derived statements and they can be expressed in terms of kernel statements. Table 5.1 lists all the kernel statements of ESTEREL.

Data Handling Statements

`X:=e`
`call P(X,Y)(e1,e2)`
`if b then S1 else S2 fi`

Signal Handling Statements

`emit S`
`present S then stat1 else stat2 end`
`abort stat when S`
`weak abort stat when S`
`suspend stat when S`

Control Statements

`nothing`
`pause`
`halt`
`stat1;stat2`
`loop stat end`
`stat1‖stat2`
`trap T in stat end`
`exit T`
`signal S in stat end`
`exec T(x)(y)`

Table 5.1: ESTEREL Statements

An ESTEREL statement, when becomes active, remain active for zero, one or more instants of time. All data handling statements are instantly executed with no passage of time while the other statements may wait for one or multiple instants of time or wait for certain external events to happen. Upon termination of a statement, the control is transferred to next statement in the program; the control transfer does not consume any time. The statements that wait for time to elapse or for some events to happen, may be terminated abnormally due to the presence of exceptional statements like `Trap` and `abort`. When exited abnormally the control is transferred instantly to the appropriate exception handling statement or to the lexically next statement. The inputs to the ESTEREL program may change only when it is waiting; during the execution it remains the same.

5.2.1 Data Handling Statements

ESTEREL has all the traditional data handling statements, assignment statements, procedure calls and conditional testing.

The expression 'e' on the right hand side of the assignment statement are built as usual by combining basic data values using operators and function calls. Their evaluations is instantaneous. In addition to constants and data variables, expressions may contain terms of the form ?S, where S is a signal/sensor. Such a term evaluates to the value of the signal/sensor at the instant when the assignment is executed. The types of left hand side variable and the right hand side expression should match.

A typical 'procedure call' statement is described in the table. This statement indicates the actual parameters: two call by reference parameters and two call by value parameters. X and Y are variables and are actual reference parameters while e1,e2 are expressions whose values are passed to the procedure. the types of actual and formal parameters should match.

In the `if` statements, the'then' or 'else' case may be missing. The nested 'if' statements are written using 'elseif' keyword.

5.2.2 Reactive Statements

The reactive statements are broadly divided into two classes: *kernel* or primitive statements and *derived* statements. The kernel statements themselves are divided into two categories: temporal or signal handling statements and control statements.

5.2. ESTEREL *Statements* 37

Signal handling statements

Signals are primary means of communication between an ESTEREL program and its environment or between concurrent statements. By default, signals are absent; a signal is present at an instant if and only if it is an input signal that is present in the input event or is emitted as the result of an execution of the `emit` statement. ESTEREL has parallel constructs which allow more than one statement to be active at an instant. When a signal is input or emitted, it is consistently seen as present or absent by all active statements; thus it is as if the signals emitted in one active statement are *broadcast* to all the other active statements in the same instant.

Of the signal handling statements, only one statement is for generating signals while the rest are meant for signal receptions. `emit S` broadcasts the signal S and terminates instantaneously.

Signals can carry values. The values carried by a signal are indicated in the emit statement as follows: `emit S(10)`. The execution of this statement results in the generation of signal S with a value 10. The value of a signal can be accessed in a statement by writing the term ?S. If S is present in an instant, when ?S is executed, then ?S will evaluate to the current value of the present signal; if S is absent then the last value of S is the value of this term. Note that signal status is well defined for both pure signals and value signals while values carried by a signal are defined only for valued signals.

Signal status can be checked by the **present** construct which is similar to `if-then-else` statement found in traditional languages.. When **present S then stat1 else stat2** is executed in an instant, either stat1 or stat2 is executed depending upon whether signal S is present or not at that instant.

`abort stat when S` is the important *preemption* statement of ESTEREL. Execution of this statement starts its body `stat` and behaves like it until the occurrence of signal S. If `stat` terminates or aborts *strictly* before signal S occurs, then the whole 'abort' statement terminates. If signal S occurs when the body is active, then the statement *aborts* instantaneously *killing* `stat` by not activating the latter in that instant. Note that the body is not killed in the first instant in which the 'abort' statement is started even if the signal S is present (note that it is not an immediate abort).

Here, is a simple example that illustrates the typical use of 'abort' statements.

```
emit req_clearance;
abort
   halt
when get_clearance;
run land_proc.
```

This example also illustrates the use of signal handling statements in real-time applications. The above piece of code could be part of an air traffic control software: when a pilot wants to land, this program sends the signal 'req_clearance' and waits (in the body of the 'abort' statement) until the clearance signal comes; 'halt' is a statement in Esterel that never terminates. When the clearance signal comes, the waiting is aborted, the control leaves the 'abort' statement and the landing procedure 'land_proc' is executed.

The above kind of 'abort' statement (whose body is just 'halt') is so common in many applications that there is a derived statement **await**. Using this statement, we can simply write **await get_clearance** in the place of the above 'abort' statement.

The abort statements can be nested as illustrated by the following example. This is an improvement over the previous example from the point of view of air traffic control: in the previous example, the control software waits indefinitely for getting the clearance signal which is undesirable since either the request message or the response message could be lost. To avoid this, typically the waiting program 'times-out' when the required response does not reach within a fixed time, by taking an alternate action.

```
emit req_clearance;
abort
   await get_clearance;
when too_late;
present too_late then run abort_land
              else run land_proc.
```

In the above code fragment, await statement, which is essentially an abort statement is nested inside the other abort statement. 'too_late' is a signal whose presence indicates that the period of waiting for the clearance signal is over and aborts the inner await statement. The statement following the outer abort statement checks the presence of the 'too_late' signal; note that the control could come out of the abort statement even when the body of the 'abort' terminates before the aborting signal appears. In this example, if the body terminates before the time_out signal, then the clearance signal has been obtained in time and hence, the normal landing procedure 'land_proc' is executed. On the other hand, if the too_late signal is present then the landing is aborted by executing the module 'abort_land'.

Note that in the above example, even if 'too_late' and 'get_clearance' signals appear simultaneously, the former signal takes precedence (or has a priority) and the reception of the other signal by the body of the abort statement is preempted with the result that only 'abort_land' procedure

5.2. ESTEREL Statements

is executed. In this sense, the above preemption is too strong: when the preemption takes place, the body of the abort statement is not executed. A weaker preemption primitive is the 'weak abort' statement. In

> weak abort stat when S

"stat" is preempted when signal S appears in the input. But the difference is that stat is not killed instantaneously; the control leaves the whole statement only after the completion of the current action that was being executed when signal S arrived.

Note that in both kinds of 'abort' statements, the first occurrence of the signal at the time the control just enters the 'abort' statement is ignored.

If the 'abort' statement can be compared to the 'Ctrl-C' of Unix, then 'suspend' statements can be compared to 'Ctrl-Z'. When

> suspend stat when S

starts, `stat` is immediately started. From then on, the presence of S is tested in each instant. If S is present then the exception of `stat` at that instant is paused; otherwise, it is executed. If `stat` terminates or exits a trap then so does the whole 'suspend' statement.

Control statements

The control statements affect the flow of control in a program execution. All the statements except the `trap` statements are single-entry and single-exit constructs. The `trap` statement is an exception mechanism which may, in addition to terminating normally, may 'exit' via the trap specified. The general form of trap statement is:

> trap T in stat

defines lexically the scope for the trap T: the statement `stat` may contain statement `exit T`. When the control reaches this point, it leaves the entire trap block and reaches the statement that immediately follows the trap block. In such a case, we say that the control exits via the trap. The exit via the trap, causes the termination of the whole 'trap' statement instantaneously. If the body `stat` terminates without encountering the `exit T`, then the whole trap statement terminates.

Compare and contrast the two exception handling statements `abort` and `trap`. While `abort` is used for modeling external (event-driven) interrupts or exceptions, `trap` describes the exceptions caused by the program.

The simplest control statement is: **nothing**. It does nothing and terminates instantaneously. In contrast, the statement **pause** delays the termination by a single instant. That is, the control leaves the **pause** statement exactly one instance after the control reaches it. As we saw earlier, `halt` never terminates and remains active always.

The current version of ESTEREL, ESTEREL v7, treats `halt` as a derived statement and is equivalent to the following

```
loop pause end
```

Early versions of ESTEREL treated `halt` as a basic statement and expressed `pause` as `await tick`. `tick` is a special signal which is present in every instant. Since `await` ignores the first occurrence of a signal `await tick` results in a delay of one instance.

`stat1;stat2`, upon execution, behaves first like `stat1`. If and when `stat1` terminates, `stat2` is started immediately. If `stat1` exits via a trap then `stat2` is *not* started and the whole statement exits via the same trap.

`loop stat end` involves repeatedly executing its body, `stat` for ever. Thus, the control leaves the statement only when `stat` exits via a trap. When the body terminates, it is restarted instantaneously. To avoid instantaneous execution of infinite repetitions of the body at a single instant, the body is not allowed to terminate instantaneously. Here, is an example that illustrates the use of loop statements in periodic monitoring of external environment:

```
Module monitor;
input ring,alive,restart;
output start_timer,raise_alarm;
loop
   emit start_timer;
   weak abort
       await alive;
   when ring;
   present alive else raise_alarm;await restart
end loop
end Module
```

The above module, named `monitor` monitors the working of a device by doing the following sequence of actions repeatedly: emits the signal `start_timer` that starts a timer; then waits for one of the signals `alive` or `ring`; it is expected that the device being monitored sends the signal `alive` periodically; if this signal does not arrive within a specified interval then it is assumed that the device is faulty; hence the module waits for this signal within the time the timer signal `ring` comes. If `alive` does not arrive before the `ring` signal then the module raises the `alarm` signal; the module starts monitoring after the device is repaired which is indicated by signal `restart`.

5.2. ESTEREL Statements

If more than one device is to be monitored then the above module can be reused by renaming the appropriate signals. For instance, suppose there are two devices to be monitored, then we can get two instances `monitor1` and `monitor2` shown below:

```
monitor1 :: input ring1,alive1,restart1;
           output start_timer1,raise_alarm1;
           run monitor[ring/ring1,alive/alive1,restart/restart1,
                  start_timer/start_timer1, raise_alarm/raise_alarm1]

monitor2 :: input ring2,alive2,restart2;
           output start_timer2,raise_alarm2;
           run monitor[ring/ring2,alive/alive2,restart/restart2,
                  start_timer/start_timer2, raise_alarm/raise_alarm2]
```

Note that all the input and output signals are renamed; in the general case, a subset of signal may be renamed. The above two instances assume two separate instances of the timer modules that accept the 'start_timer' signals and generate the 'ring' signals.

Like signals, variables in a generic module can also be renamed using similar syntax. Note that the generic modules are essentially 'macros' in which signals and variables can be renamed using the parameters.

The meaning of other statements are given below:

`stat1∥stat2` involves simultaneous execution of `stat1` and `stat2`. It terminates instantly if and when both the parallel components are terminated; the two components can terminate at two different instants and the parallel statement terminates at the latest of the two instants. If one or both the components exit via trap(s) then the parallel statement also exits via a trap; the trap via which the latter exits is the *outermost* (in the lexical scope) of the two traps via which the components exit.

`signal S in stat` encapsulates the body `stat` by confining the influence of the signal S to `stat` alone. Any occurrence of the signal S inside `stat` is a fresh signal that is different from any signal with the same name in other components.

5.2.3 Derived Statements

There exists a rich set of useful statements in ESTEREL called derived statements. These statements provide expressive power to ESTEREL and can be rewritten in terms of the kernel statements and hence the name derived statements.

As we have seen earlier that 'await' statement is a useful derived statement. If it is required to wait for a fixed number of occurrences of a signal

S, say, 5 times then one can write `await 5 S`. As can be noted from the definition of `await S`, the first occurrence of `S` is ignored. If it is required to react for the first occurrence then one can write `await immediate S`.

Note that the 'await' statements corresponds to the classical 'delay' construct found in real-time languages, if the signal which is awaited is the time signal. Classical languages either ignores time or gives a special status to time whereas ESTEREL treats time on par with any other input signal.

A useful generalization of the above 'await' statement is the statement that waits for multiple signals, which can be written in ESTEREL as

```
await
  case S1 do stat1
  case S2 do stat2
  case S3 do stat3
end
```

Here one of the statements `stat1,stat2,stat3` is executed depending upon the occurrence of signals. If more than one signal occur then the statement corresponding to the signal that has occurred and that appear first in the above list, i.e., if S2 and S3 occur at the same time, then `stat2` is executed rather than `stat3`. Thus, the syntactic ordering implied in the statement specifies the priority.

Another useful construct for real-time programming is the 'time-out' construct. This can be written using abort statements as follows:

```
abort
  stat1
when S
timeout stat2 end
```

Here, statement `stat2` is executed when the signal S occurs strictly before the statement `stat1` terminates. This is also a derived statement whose *kernel expansion* is

```
trap T in
  abort
    stat1;exit T
  when S;
  stat2
end
```

Another important derived statement is the 'sustain' statement that allows the emission of a signal at each reaction. It is written `sustain S` and is equivalent to

```
loop
  emit S;
```

```
    pause
    end
```

5.3 Illustrations of ESTEREL Program Behaviour

In this section, we shall highlight the subtle behaviour of ESTEREL programs using some code snippets of ESTEREL.

In ESTEREL, no statement except `halt` takes time; any other statement that consumes time has an implicit halt contained in it. In particular, signal emission and signal sensing are simultaneous. Also, emitted signals are instantaneously 'broadcast' to all the parallel components. These facts are illustrated by the following example:

Example 1
```
    emit S
||
    present S then emit T
||
    present S then emit U
||
    present T then emit V
```
The behavior of this code fragment is as follows: In the very instant it is executed, the signal S is emitted by the first parallel component and is broadcast to all the other components. In the same instant, the next two components, sense the presence of S and, in turn, emit instantaneously the signals T and U. The emission of T is sensed in the same instant by the fourth component and it generates V. Thus, execution of this statement in an instant results in the emission of all the signals S,T,U and V in the same instant and the system then terminates.

Emitted signals can go back and forth and cause more signals as illustrated by the following example:

Example 2
```
    emit S;
    present T then emit U
||
    present S then emit T;
    present U then emit V
```
Execution of the above code snippet in an instant results in the generation of all the four signals S,T,U and V. Note that S causes T (in one direction), T causes U (in the reverse direction) which in turn causes V (in the forward

direction). This is something like an *instantaneous dialogue* in which a sequence of multiple signal exchanges between two or more processes.

Note that the above example also illustrates that sequential composition does not take time.

Abort statement is an interesting primitive of ESTEREL. To illustrate this, consider the following code fragment:

Example 3

```
abort
  emit T;
  abort
    halt
  when S1;
  emit U
when S2
```

Execution of the code fragment results in the emission of T in the starting instant. From the next instant onwards, it waits for one of the signals S1,S2. If S1 occurs before S2, then the inner abort statement terminates, U is emitted and the body as well as the outer abort statement terminates all in the same instant. On the other hand, if S2 occurs first then the body of the outer abort statement is preempted. The behavior of this statement is interesting when both S1 and S2 occur for the first time at the same instant. Then outer abort statement preempts instantaneously its body and as a result no U is emitted. Thus, the signal S2 has a higher priority over S1. The occurrence of S1 or S2 in the first instant, however, has no effect as the abort statement ignores the first occurrence.

As we had mentioned earlier, 'weak abort' statements are weaker than 'abort' statements. This is illustrated through the following example:

Example 4

```
weak abort
  pause; emit U
when T
```

Suppose that signal T arrives in the second instant after the control reaches the above statement. Then its body is preempted at the end of this instant after the body emits signal U.

As in the case of 'abort' statements , 'weak abort' statements can also be nested and as before the outer abort has got higher priority over the inner ones.

While abort models preemption due to an external signal, traps are used for preemption caused locally. In the following example:

Example 5

```
Trap T in
  sustain S
  ||
  stat;
  exit T
end
```

This program keeps emitting signal S in each instant until the statement in the concurrent task is exited. When the later happens, **exit T** is executed which triggers the exit of the whole trap statement.

The general form of preempt statements include a time-out clause, as illustrated below

```
Trap T in
  sustain S
  ||
  stat;
  exit T
end
timeout
    stat1
  end
```

When the timeout clause is present, the control enters the body of the timeout clause whenever the preemption occurs.

5.4 Causality Problems

The characteristic feature of instantaneous broadcasting and control flow makes it possible to write syntactically correct ESTEREL programs which are semantically unacceptable. According to ESTEREL, a semantically correct program should be

- *reactive*: it produces a well-defined output(s) for every possible input(s),

- *deterministic*: in every reaction, for a given set of input signal, it produces a unique set of output signals and

- *causal*: an acyclic cause-effect relation should exist between the inputs and the various outputs produced.

One can write syntactically correct ESTEREL programs that are non-reactive, nondeterministic or causal. Consider the flowing classical example of a non reactive program :

```
present O else emit O end
```

This program specifies that the signal O is generated iff it is not present, which is inconsistent. The following program is consistent but nondeterministic:

```
present O then emit O end
```

This program has two possible reactions: one in which it assumes that O is present, takes the then branch emitting O thereby discharging the assumption and the other in which it takes the else branch without emitting O. Here is another program which is reactive and deterministic but non causal.

```
present O then emit O else emit O
```

This program has unique output but it is non causal as this unique behavior can be inferred only using boolean reasoning rather than in operational terms as a sequence of executions.

Of course, an easy way of achieving the three conditions of semantic correctness is to forbid programs that have syntactically cyclic dependency of signals. But this is too restrictive as it disallows many valid and efficient programs. For example, consider the following program:

```
present I then present O2 then emit O1
||
present I then emit O2
||
present O1 then emit O2
```

where I is an input signal. There is an apparent cyclic dependency between the signals O1 and O2. But they have unique and causal solutions: if I is present then the second parallel component can be executed generating O2 which then can trigger the execution of the first component emitting O1. On the other hand, if I is absent then one can conclude that neither O1 nor O2 can be emitted.

While discussing the semantics of ESTEREL 10, a precise definition and a detailed discussion on causality will be given.

5.5 A Historical Perspective

Among the synchronous languages, ESTEREL is the oldest as its design started in 1980 by Gerard Berry and his group in INRIA and ENSMP

5.5. A Historical Perspective

Sophia Antipolis. The first version of ESTEREL compiler came up in the year 1985. It has been evolving since its inception and the result of this has been a series of compilers starting from version 1 to the current version 7 being developed. Of these, ESTEREL version 5 onwards is being developed by ESTEREL Technologies and has strong industrial backing; there is an ongoing attempt to standardize the current version of the language.

Besides addition of a few new constructs and increased efficiency and improved representation, one reason for the evolution of different versions has been to give a more refined solution to the *causality problem* which is a common problem in all synchronous languages. Causality problem is peculiar to synchronous languages arising due to the existence of some cyclic dependency of signals, called the *causal cycles*. Programs having such causal cycles are considered to be erroneous as they are either nondeterministic or inconsistent. One of the major tasks of the compiler is to look for existence of causal cycles in the program and reject ones having such cycles. The detection of causal cycles is, in general, an unsolvable problem and the various solutions that have been proposed in the different compilers has been to take a conservative approach; they reject some correct programs, in addition to the wrong ones. Interestingly, there is no agreement as to what should be considered as causal cycles and different languages adopt different notions. More details on the evolution of ESTEREL can be found in [33].

It may also be noted that the language ESTEREL is being standardized by IEEE. The standardization committee is being chaired by Gerard Berry. The standard ESTEREL while maintaining the rationale discussed above may differ from the classical ESTEREL discussed above structurally.

To expose large users of C to reactive programming, F. Boussinot[30] designed the language Reactive C with a weaker notion of synchrony; the later aspect has been formalized in [1]. Reactive C has lead to other works on enriching languages for design automation purposes such as ECL for design automation purposes. Another interesting work has been the reactive extension of Java referred to as Jester [4] (Java Esterell) designed in the context of reactive embedded system design. Of course, one also needs to address Java memory models for semantic consistency.

As our focus has been on languages founded on the synchrony hypothesis and supporting fully reactivity, we have not discussed another important language SIGNAL that has both under-sampling and over-sampling operators. This is a relational language and is fully compositional. However, not all programs can be synthesized due to over-sampling operators (hence, non reactive behaviours). Thus, in this language one makes a distinction between what can be compiled and specified. For details the reader is referred to [38].

Another very interesting work has the language proposal based 2-adic number representation of circuits [88]. An initial language proposal based on this work by Gerard Berry and Jean Vuillemin is referred to as 2Z.

Open Source ESTEREL **Compiler**: An open-source ESTEREL compiler designed for research both in hardware and software has been lead by Stephen Edwards. It currently supports a subset of ESTEREL V5, and can generate a C program or a Verilog or BLIF circuit description from an ESTEREL program. For details, the reader is referred to (http://www1.cs.columbia.edu/ sedwards/cec/).

Chapter 6

Program Development in ESTEREL

As in the development of programs in traditional high level languages, there is certainly a need to have a good programming environment that supports development of embedded systems. The classical programming cycle involves develop-compile-test-debug steps. In model based development, this cycle is enhanced as follows: Modelling, model execution, referred as *simulation*, model debugging and code generation. Here the additional steps are modeling, simulation and code generation. The programming environments for embedded system hence includes model editors, simulators and code generators for various platforms. A general methodology for the development ESTEREL programs is depicted in Figure 6.1. Note that "time" is not part of the classical ESTEREL. However, in practice after developing the model (verified), one needs to tune the same with respect to time. In other words, the figure depicts the iterative refinements from conception to embedding the ESTEREL code. We shall not discuss these aspects further here; for related discussions the reader is referred to [84]. We now describe in some detail, one of the important components of ESTEREL programming environment, the ESTEREL Simulator.

6.1 A Simulation Environment

ESTEREL tools include a graphical simulation environment called Xes.

Figure 6.2 contains the screen shots of the main panel of the simulation environment. Through this panel, the simulation engine of ESTEREL, Xes, can be invoked. In the simulation panel, there will be four main columns,

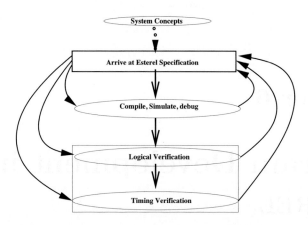

Figure 6.1: ESTEREL Methodology

two of which correspond to pure and valued input signals and the other two for output signals; in the figure, the column corresponding to the valued input signals is absent as the model being simulated does not have valued inputs. The status and value of input signals can be fed through the two columns corresponding to the input signals. There is a button named 'tick' which invokes the reactive kernel. Once a particular combination of status and values of input signals are given, the kernel can be invoked by pressing the 'tick' button. The kernel upon invocation, may generate output signals which can be observed through the two output columns. Through repeated use of input, tick and output columns/buttons, we can observe the behaviour of an ESTEREL program and debug, if necessary. In addition to displaying the external observable behavior, the simulator also displays the position of the control on the various concurrent fragments of code. Using a rich set of colour codes, many additional information like emitted signals, passed control points etc. can be read off from the code.

There is also a recording facility so that an entire sequence of simulation runs can be stored and rerun when necessary. The software for driving the panel are automatically generated and is independent of the program being simulated.

Figure 6.2 shows the snapshot of a simulation run of an ESTEREL model of a DLX processor. In this panel, the first column, corresponding to a pure input signal I (for issuing a new instruction) at every tick causes a new instruction to be inserted into the pipeline. The pure output signal IC indicates that an instruction has completed execution. The restart and stall

6.1. A Simulation Environment

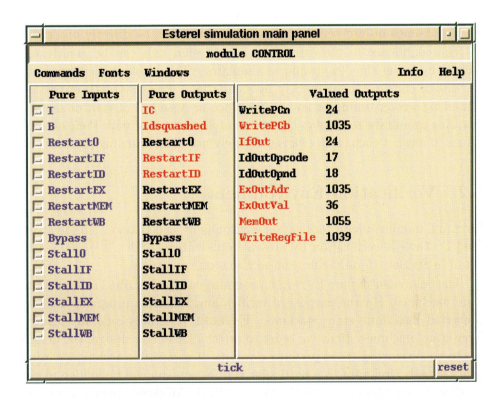

Figure 6.2: Xes Simulator Main Panel

signals can be given as input in any tick and their effect can be observed by noting the transfer of data between the pipe registers, indicated by the valued signals such as `IfOut` and `IdOutOpcode`.

The properties that can be easily checked using the simulator include progress and guarantee properties. For instance, it is easy to test that a `B` signal (for a taken branch) at any tick when the `EX` stage is active is followed by a `RestartID` signal for aborting the next instruction in the pipeline. Similarly, the property that the input signal `I` (issue a new instruction) is followed by the output signal `IC` (instruction completed) after five clock ticks (in the absence of intervening stalls and restarts) can be directly observed.

The confidence in the correctness of a design unit can be greatly enhanced by using the Xes graphical simulator. The most obvious errors in the design can be caught quickly by simulation. Typically such errors are caused by wrong timing or status (presence or absence) of control signals. The Xes capability to display the status of signals along with their current values (if any) at each clock tick is extremely useful for catching these errors.

6.2 Verification Environment

ESTEREL tool includes a verification environment, called `Xeve`. The strategy used by `Xeve` is verification by abstraction strategy, which is explained in detail in Section 15 on verification of ESTEREL programs.

The behaviour of pure ESTEREL programs can be described using a finite state machines. For the purpose of verification, ESTEREL programs are first converted into finite state machines. ESTEREL programs generally lead to large state machines. Hence in order to prove a particular design, the design has to be abstracted. `Xeve` provides a variety of abstraction techniques using which signals irrelevant to a particular verification run can be hidden to get small state machines that can be easily verified. All these operations can be carried out these operations automatically. `Xeve` makes use of a tool called FCtoolset, that can manipulate, minimize and compare finite state machine descriptions.

Another useful feature of `Xeve` is that it can generate different representations of finite state machine models of ESTEREL programs, which can then be displayed visually using the tool `atg`. The tool `atg` enables creating, editing and viewing state diagrams developed either directly or through the `Xeve` generated finite state machines. Such a facility makes itself amenable for using ESTEREL and Xeve to verify protocols. An experiment of using ESTEREL for verifying cache protocols is reported in [60].

6.2. Verification Environment

All these tools are commonly used in developing, debugging and analyzing programs during the development phase. In the next section, we describe a number of moderate-sized examples. These examples will also illustrate the use of these tools.

Chapter 7

Programming Controllers in ESTEREL

In this chapter, we shall look at a number of examples that illustrate the features of ESTEREL language constructs. The examples that we have chosen though hypothetical, highlight the kind of controller applications for which ESTEREL is intended.

7.1 Auto Controllers

Current day automobiles are embedded with powerful controllers which monitor the various parameters of the cars and their motion; depending upon the values of these, they respond to driver's commands like acceleration, starting or stopping and breaking. ESTEREL language is most suitable for describing complex behavior of such controllers. In this section, we shall illustrate this by describing the behaviour of some hypothetical controllers in ESTEREL.

7.1.1 A Very Simple Auto Controller

This controller initially waits for the driver to switch on the engine for start the car. Then it starts the car and waits for further inputs from the driver. The driver may accelerate or decelerate the car, depending upon which the controller increases/decreases the throttle valve position of the engine so that the vehicle moves faster/slower. This behaviour continues until the driver stops the motor by switching off the ignition.

The behavior of this controller can be simply described by the following ESTEREL program:

```
module simple:
input ignition_on,ignition_off,accel;
output control_throttle;
loop
   abort
      await ignition_on;
            every accel do
                emit control_throttle
            end every
   when ignition_off
end
end module
```

This module has three input signals: ignition_on, ignition_off, accel corresponding to the three input commands given by the driver. It has one output signal, control_throttle that controls the throttle valve position. This module first waits for input signal ignition_on to be present. Once ignition_on is present it emits output signal control_throttle for every accel. If at any point input signal ignition_off comes it aborts and restarts the whole process.

7.1.2 A Complex Controller

This controller has an additional safety feature that monitors status of the door (whether it is closed or open) and sends out warning signals when the door is open while the car is in motion. Also while starting the car, it ensures that the car doors are closed.

Here is the description of the ESTEREL program corresponding to this controller:

```
module complex:
 input ignition_on,ignition_off,accel;
 input door_opened, door_locked;
 output alarm,control_throttle,door_lock;
   loop
    abort
       await ignition_on;
       emit door_lock;
       loop
          await door_locked;
          abort
             every accel do
                emit control_throttle
```

7.1. Auto Controllers

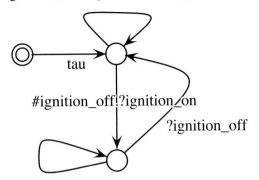

Figure 7.1: Simple Controller

```
            end every
          when door_opened;
          emit alarm;
          emit door_lock;
        end;
      when ignition_off
    end
  end module
```

This program has two additional input signals: door_opened, door_locked, and two output signals:alarm and door_lock. This module after receiving the ignition_on signal checks whether the door is closed, before starting the engine. As before it generates the signal control_throttle for every accel input signal. It has an additional watchdog statement that aborts the above activity when door_opened signal is present. It resumes controlling the throttle valve only when the door is locked.

Automata of Car Controllers

The behavior of the two controllers can also be described using standard finite state machines as given in Figures 7.1 and 7.2.

Compared to the automata descriptions, ESTEREL descriptions are more structured and concise and makes it easy to debug and understand.

The above automata have actually been generated using ESTEREL tools. ESTEREL compiler actually generates automata corresponding to the input

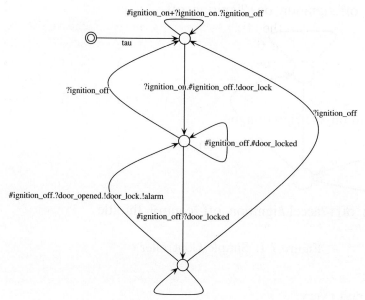

Figure 7.2: Complex Controller

programs in some internal representation which can be converted using the tools Xeve and ATG to a graphical representation of the above forms.

7.1.3 A Cruise Controller

Here we build on the previous examples to describe a more complex auto controller which we call cruise controller. The cruise controller includes the feature of putting a vehicle in the cruise mode of driving found in modern vehicles. It also illustrates many other features of ESTEREL like modules, valued signals and procedure calls.

First we briefly state the required behavior of our hypothetical controller. The controller waits till the ignition is turned on. Then for safety reasons the status of seat belts are checked. If not fastened, it sends an alarm and waits till they are fastened to start the engine. When the engine is started the engine should be in the manual mode. Then while running depending upon the commands from the driver, it can switch the motor to cruise or motor mode. In the cruise mode, the car is kept in the cruise speed while in the manual mode the speed of the vehicle can change as per the wish of the driver. The breaking of the vehicle in the cruise mode brings it to the

7.1. Auto Controllers

manual mode while an explicit set command from the driver in the manual mode switches the vehicle to the cruise mode. The speed of the vehicle is, as before, controlled by setting the position of the throttle valve. All the time while running, a check is continuously made on the status of the belts and whenever they are unfastened an alarm is emitted.

The following ESTEREL program describes the behaviour of the controller:

```
module cruise:
input cruise;
input accel,brake_pressed;
input engine_off;
input accel_released;
input ignition_on,belt_fastened,belt_unfastened;
output chk_belts,start_engine;
output control_throttle:double;
output alarm;
input current_speed:integer;
output cruising;
procedure increase_speed(double)(integer);
procedure compute_throttle(double)(integer,integer);
loop
    await ignition_on;
    emit chk_belts;
    await belt_fastened;
    emit start_engine;
    abort
     [ loop
          abort
       run manual_mode;
       when cruise;
        abort
        run cruise_mode;
       when brake_pressed;
         end loop
       ||
         every belt_unfastened do
     emit alarm
         end
     ]
    when engine_off
  end loop
 end module
module manual_mode:
```

```
    input accel_released,accel;
    output control_throttle:double;
            var th_value:=5.0:double,val:=0:integer in
              loop
                abort
              every accel do
                emit control_throttle(th_value + 2.0);
                  end every
                    when accel_released;
                  end
              end var
    end module
module cruise_mode:
  input current_speed:integer;
  output control_throttle:double, cruising;
  procedure compute_throttle(double)(integer,integer);
    var cruise_speed:=?current_speed:integer,
  th_value:double in
    cruise_speed:=?current_speed;
    [
      every tick do
        call compute_throttle(th_value)(?current_speed,cruise_speed);
        emit control_throttle(th_value);
        emit cruising
      end
    ]
  end var
  end module
```

The main module cruise first waits for ignition to be turned on (ignition_on). When this signal arrives, it emits the chk_belts signal, and then waits till the belts are fastened. After this is done it indicates (emit start_engine) that the engine should be started. After this, it 'loops' forever keeping a constant vigil on the belt status and simultaneously switching modes as and when the driver wants.

Switching between manual mode and cruise mode is enabled by the accel_rreleased/break signals. The abort constructs of ESTEREL comes very handy in describing this.

There is an outermost abort statement which aborts the whole computation when the engine is turned off(engine_off).

The manual module starts with a default throttle value and for every "accel" input signal, increases this value by some arbitrary units (which we have taken to be 2 for the sake of illustration) and emits the output signal to indicate this change in the throttle value (control_throttle). The variable th_val

7.1. Auto Controllers

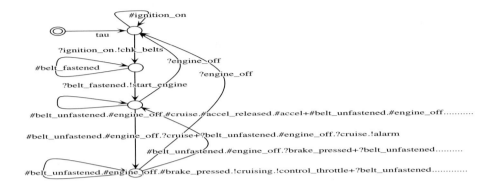

Figure 7.3: Complex Cruise Example

is used to keep track of the throttle value. The signal control_throttle is valued and it carries the value stored in the variable th_val. The loop which contains the above computation is aborted whenever the accelerator is released(accel_released input signal)

The module cruise_mode module) takes the current speed and at regular intervals (which we taken to be every 'tick') computes the throttle value using the current speed at this tick and the cruise speed which is the current speed value at the previous tick. It then emits the output signal to indicate this change in the throttle value(control_throttle). It also emits the cruising output signal to indicate its cruise_mode status.

As in the previous example, the above ESTEREL program can be compiled into a finite state machine which is shown in Figure 7.3. The FSM, in this case, is more complex and difficult to understand compared to the previous cases. Some of the labels of this transitions are too long to display and hence have been truncated in the figure.

7.1.4 A Train Controller

Here, we look at another hypothetical controller that controls the movement of an automatic train that moves back and forth between a set of stations. When there is no request the train remains idle in one of the stations. When there is a request at a station, the train eventually moves to the station, opens its doors allowing the people to board after which it closes the door and moves in the appropriate direction. Appropriate input sensors like buttons are provided at each stations and inside the train for the passengers to indicate their requests.

The controller for this train can be described by the following ESTEREL program:

```
module Train:
input d_closed,d_opened,stn_arrived(integer),request(integer);
output d_close,d_open,t_run,t_stop;
loop
   var X: integer in
      emit d_open;
      await d_opened;
      await request; X:=?request;
      emit d_close;
      await d_closed;
      trap Stop in
         loop
            abort
               sustain t_run
            when stn_arrived;
            if X=?stn_arrived then
               emit t_stop;
               exit Stop;
            end
         end %loop
      end %trap
   end %var
end %outer loop
end module
```

When the train stops in a station, the controller emits the door open output signal and and waits for the door_closed input signal. Then the destination request is accepted. This destination request is stored in the variable X. After that the door close signal is output and the corresponding door_closed input signal is awaited. The train is in a run state at each 'tick' until the station_arrived input signal is present. If the station_arrived value is equal to the actual destination request, then only the train stops.

The outermost loop allows the entire process to be repeated, so that new destinations can be accepted every time a fresh destination request is satisfied.

Figure 7.4 gives the automaton describing the behaviour of this controller.

7.1. Auto Controllers

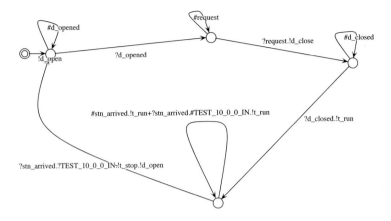

Figure 7.4: A Simple Train Controller

7.1.5 A Mine Pump Controller

A mine pump controller is one of the standard examples discussed in the literature. Here in this section we will examine how ESTEREL could be used for describing a mine controller.

The mine pump controller controls the operation of a pump which is used to drain the excess water in the mines. The controller should start the pump to drain the water as soon as the water level raises above a certain upper limit. Since the pump can not operate when the water level is below some lower limit, it has to be stopped when the water hits this lower limit. The mines might have combustible and dangerous gases like methane and carbon monoxide. Methane when present in high concentration might explode when the pump is operating while carbon monoxide present in high doses is fatal. So the controller has to monitor the concentration of these gases and switch off the pump and give alarm whenever they are high.

The pump can operate in two modes: auto or the manual mode; the default is auto mode. In the auto mode, the pump is operated when the water level goes high and is switched off when the level goes low. Whereas, in the manual mode, the pump is run or shut off under the operator control.

Here is a decryption of the controller in ESTEREL.

```
module pump_controller:
input start,stop,methane,co,hw_level,lw_level,manual;
input auto;
output p_run,p_stop,m_alarm,c_alarm;
[
loop
```

```
        abort
          loop
            await hw_level;
            await immediate [not methane];
            abort
               sustain p_run
            when [methane or lw_level];
            emit p_stop
          end
        when manual;
        abort
          loop
            await start;
            await immediate [not methane];
            abort
               sustain p_run
            when [methane or stop];
             emit p_stop;
          end
        when auto;
      end loop
    ||
      every methane do
         emit m_alarm;
      end every
    ||
      every co do
         emit c_alarm
      end every
    ]
    end module
```

The program consists of a single module `pump_controller`. The inputs `start,stop,manual,auto` are signals from the operator to start,stop the pump and to switch to manual and auto respectively. The signals `methane,co` indicate respectively that the methane and carbon monoxide levels have reached the critical values while the signals `hw_level,lw_level` are input when the water level upper or lower limits. The outputs `p_run, p_stop, m_alarm,c_alarm` are emitted by the controller to start, stop the pump or when the concentration of the gases crosses the danger levels.

The module has three parallel process that run for ever. The first process switches between the manual and auto mode under the control of the signal `manual` or `auto`. This switching between the modes is implemented using the 'abort' construct of ESTEREL.

7.1. Auto Controllers

In the auto mode, the pump remains idle until the input signal hw_level arrives. Then the signal prun is sustained till the signal lw_level or the signal methane. prun is an output signal that triggers the running of the pump is continuously emitted

In the manual mode, continuous emitting of prun is initiated by the start signal and ended by stop, these signals coming directly from the operator. As in the auto mode, the arrival of the signal methane aborts the above activity and the controller returns to the auto mode.

The second and third parallel processes generates the signals m_alarm and c_alarm for every methane and CO signal.

Chapter 8

Asynchronous Interaction in ESTEREL

In ESTEREL, computations that take time are modeled as tasks; that is, there is non zero time between initiation and completion of a task. In the terminology of ESTEREL, this means that there will be at least one instant between initiation and completion. The `exec` constructs of ESTEREL is used to initiate the tasks and thus, form asynchronous gateway. The general form of 'exec' statements is

```
exec T(ref-params)(value-params) return R
```

Like procedure calls, 'exec' can have both actual reference and value parameters. But unlike procedures, it is not instantaneous. Its execution is asynchronous but controlled by the ESTEREL module. it is initiated by execution of the 'exec' statement. When it terminates (not instantaneously), the return signal 'R' is input to the ESTEREL module indicating termination; the return signal is like any other input signal and can be pure or valued. Since the ESTEREL module is executed along with the task, the latter's execution can be suspended or preempted.

Task Declaration

An asynchronous task is declared as follows:

```
task task_id (f_par_lst) return signal_nm (type);
```
where

- `task_id` is the name of the task;
- `f_par_lst` gives the list of *formal* parameters (reference or value);

- the signal returned by the task is given by the **signal_nm** with its type after the keyword **return**; it is possible to have multiple return signals.

Task Instantiation

Instantiation of the task is done through the primitive **exec**. For example, the above task can be instantiated from an ESTEREL program as follows:

```
exec task_id (a_par_lst);
```
where

- **task_id** is the name of the task;

- **a_par_lst** gives the list of *actual* parameters (variables/expressions corresponding to reference/value parameters);

- There is no explicit need to specify the **return** signals as it is the same as in the task declaration.

For example, a typical task declaration appears as

```
task ROBOT_move (ip, fp) return complete;
```
and the call appears as

```
exec ROBOT_move (x,y);
```

The execution of the above statement in some process starts task **ROBOT_move** and awaits for the return signal **complete** for it to proceed further. Of course, the number and type of arguments, and the return signal type should match with the task declared. In other words, **exec** requests the environment to start the task and then waits for the return signal (which also indicates the termination of the task).

Since there can be several occurrences of **exec T** in a module for the same task **T**, several simultaneously active tasks having the same name can coexist. To avoid confusion among them one can assign an explicit label to each **exec** statement; a labeled **exec** statement is of the form **exec L:T**. The label name must be distinct from all other labels and input signal names. An implicit distinct label is given to **exec** statements, if no explicit label is given.

The primitive **exec** provides an interface between ESTEREL and the asynchronous environment. Given an **exec** statement labeled L, the asynchronous task execution is controlled from ESTEREL by three implicit signals **sL** (output signal), **L** (input signal), and **kL** (output signal) corresponding to starting the task, completion and killing the execution of the task respectively. The output signal sL (called the start signal) is sent to the environment when the exec statement starts. It requests the start of an asynchronous incarnation of the task. The input *return signal* L, is sent by the environment when the task incarnation is terminated; it provokes instantaneous termination of the exec statement. The output *kill signal* kL is emitted by ESTEREL if the exec statement is preempted before termination, either by an enclosing watching statement or by concurrent exit from an enclosing trap. Note that L and kL can co-exist; depending upon the abort statements which aborted the exec statement, either the L or the kL signals produces the desired effect. If the abort is a weak abort, then the reactive kernel assumes that the task is completed while a strong abort statement ignores the completion signal. The return signals corresponding to the exec labels are like input signals. Like input signals, two or more return signals can be declared to be incompatible; this prevents the corresponding tasks to terminate at the same instant. Note that this implies that we have constrained the environment, i.e., we assume that both of then can never be observed simultaneously.

Chapter 9

Futurebus Arbitration Protocol: A Case Study

In this chapter, we take a reasonably large program and give a solution in ESTEREL. This would illustrate the power and usage of ESTEREL constructs.

Futurebus+ [29], is a set of tools with which to implement a bus architecture providing performance scalability over both cost and time for multiple generations of single and multiple-bus multiprocessor systems. The specification of arbitration specification plays a crucial role in the performance of the system. In the following, we describe the arbitration process as in [29].

9.1 Arbitration Process

1. When a module needs to send data to, or obtain data from another module, it must first gain access to the bus. Since two or more modules may attempt to gain tenure of the bus at the same time, an arbitration step is used to select one unique at any time. This arbitration step takes place over a separate arbitration bus to which all the nodes are connected.

2. Each module is assigned a unique *arbitration number*, which is used to resolve the *arbitration competition*. When two or more modules compete for the bus, the winner (the one that will have exclusive control of the bus) is the one whose arbitration number is the largest. Parallel contention arbitration is a process whereby modules assert their unique arbitration number on the **arbitration bus** and release

signals according to an algorithm which after a period of time will ensure that only the winner's number remains on the arbitration bus.

3. The value of the arbitration numbers used by modules in a competition determine the sequence of arbitration process. Because of limitations in the number of bus lines used for arbitration, some numbers require two passes (or more – see the step below) of the control cycle. The module with the highest arbitration number at the end of the arbitration competition is referred to as the *Master Elect*. A master elect can take the bus when the module using it releases it. On taking the bus, it is referred to as the *Master* (the competition for the bus can begin after the master elect becomes the master).

4. There may be times when a module has urgent need of the bus after a master elect has been chosen, but before the master elect has become master. If that module has a higher arbitration number than the master elect, it may initiate a new competition to establish a new master elect. This process is referred to as *preemption*. Preemption allows a high priority module to acquire tenure of the bus with minimum latency (although with some sacrifice to the overall performance of the system since it forces a new arbitration competition).

In the following, we describe the abstraction of the protocol with an algorithm for solving contentions for the bus. The abstraction integrates the *preemption* mode described above.

9.2 Abstraction of the Protocol

There are N *modules* running in parallel and sharing a *bus* made of P lines. Each module is connected to the bus by, say P lines. Each module has its own *arbitration binary number of length equal to the number of lines P* (a priori given). The problem is to design a protocol such that each module can get a mutually exclusive access to the bus. The operations that can be performed by the module and the bus are given below.

Each module can perform the following operations:

- Whenever the module wants to get an access to the bus, it places its number on the lines.

- After placing its value, it can read the value on the bus.

9.2. Abstraction of the Protocol

- If its arbitration number is equal to the number on the bus then it gets the bus.

- If its arbitration number is not equal to it then it performs the following operation:

    Let the arbitration number of the module be: $m_1, m_2, \cdots, m_P$ and the number on the bus be $b_1, b_2, \cdots, b_P$. Let k be the first digit from left-to-right such that $b_k > m_k$. Then, the module puts a number corresponding to $m_1, \cdots, m_{k-1}, 0, \cdots, 0$ on the lines and waits indefinitely until the kth bit becomes zero and then reenters the competition.

- Each module can use the bus for a finite amount of time.

The bus performs the following operations:

- The value on the bus is equal to the bitwise "or" of the values put on the lines from all the modules.

Now, the design of the protocol can be described as follows:

Given that the arbitration numbers assigned to the modules are distinct and are composed of just 1's or just 0's, design a protocol such that access to the bus is done in a mutually exclusive way and there is no deadlock.

To fix the ideas, consider the case where N equals 3 and P equals 4. This is shown in Figure 9.1. The 3 modules are named mod0, mod1 and mod2 and their arbitration numbers are respectively 1100, 0010, 1001. The order is the natural order 0010 < 1001 < 1100, so mod1 has the lowest priority and mod0 has the highest.

The behaviour of the protocol is briefed below:

1. Place the arbitration number on the lines.

2. Read bus lines in order and compare them with the arbitration number. Because of the "or" function implemented by the bus, there is no possibility for a module to read a 0 on a line if it has previously put a 1 on it.

    Now, when a module reads a 1 corresponding to a 0 in its arbitration number, it stops to compete in the current round and places 0's on

74   *Chapter 9. Futurebus Arbitration Protocol: A Case Study*

all the successive lines to let others the possibility to win and remains blocked reading the same line until a 0 appears on the line on which it is blocked. This is done to avoid the blocking (or the deadlock).

3. After a module places its number on the last line without getting stuck, it tests whether its number and the number on the bus are the same. If they are the same then the module knows that it is the winner. Otherwise, it is inferred that another module has already won over it and hence, waits on the line corresponding to the position of the most significant digit position which is less than that on the corresponding bus line.

Now we describe a solution in ESTEREL and discuss its properties.

9.3 Solution in ESTEREL

A solution in Esterel with N = 4 and P = 3 is described below; the generalization to any N and P follows naturally. The solution has the following structure: Each module has two phases: reading and checking. In the reading phase, the module places its number on the lines; in the checking phase, it checks whether its number and the number on the bus are the same. If so, it captures the bus and releases it; otherwise, it awaits for the higher priority processes to finish and lets other to win over it by placing 0's from the point it is stuck. The actual solution in ESTEREL is given below:

```
module Cell1:
input   compete;
output next, raise;
     every immediate compete do
           emit next; emit raise;
     end.
module Cell0:
input   compete, raised;
output next;
inputoutput stuck;
every immediate compete do
      abort
        sustain stuck
      when immediate [not raised];
      emit next
```

9.3. Solution in ESTEREL

end.

```
module line:
input   raise;
output  raised;
loop
    present raise then await tick; emit raised
                  else await tick
    end;

end.

module start_result:
input   start, result;
inputoutput stuck;
output go, success;

signal lstuck in

loop
  await start;emit lstuck;
  trap term in
    [sustain go
    || await immediate [result and not lstuck];
       emit success;exit term
    ||every immediate stuck do await tick;emit lstuck end
    ];
  end;
end;
end.

module FUTUREBUS:
input   start1,start2,start3;
output  success1,success2,success3;
inputoutput stuck1,stuck2,stuck3;
output  raise1,raise2,raise3,raise4;

signal raised1,raised2,raised3,raised4,
       result1, result2, result3 in
```

```
signal pass1, pass2, pass3, go in
    run Cell1[signal go/compete,pass1/next,raise1/raise]
  || run Cell0[signal pass1/compete,pass2/next,
                        raised2/raised,stuck1/stuck]
  || run Cell1[signal pass2/compete,pass3/next,
                                            raise3/raise]
  || run Cell1[signal pass3/compete,result1/next,
                                            raise4/raise]
  || run start_result[signal start1/start,
            success1/success,result1/result, stuck1/stuck]
end signal
||
signal pass1, pass2, pass3, go in
    run Cell0[signal go/compete,pass1/next,
                        raised1/raised,stuck2/stuck]
  || run Cell1[signal pass1/compete,pass2/next,raise2/raise]
  || run Cell1[signal pass2/compete,pass3/next,raise3/raise]
  || run Cell0[signal pass3/compete,
                result2/next,raised4/raised,stuck2/stuck]
  || run start_result[signal start2/start,
              success2/success,result2/result,stuck2/stuck]
end signal
||
signal pass1, pass2, pass3, go in
    run Cell1[signal go/compete,pass1/next,raise1/raise]
  || run Cell0[signal pass1/compete,pass2/next,
                        raised2/raised,stuck3/stuck]
  || run Cell0[signal pass2/compete,
                pass3/next,raised3/raised,stuck3/stuck]
  || run Cell0[signal pass3/compete,
                result3/next,raised4/raised,stuck3/stuck]
  || run start_result[signal start3/start,
              success3/success,result3/result,stuck3/stuck]
end signal
|| run line[signal raised1/raised,raise1/raise]
|| run line[signal raised2/raised,raise2/raise]
|| run line[signal raised3/raised,raise3/raise]
|| run line[signal raised4/raised,raise4/raise]
end.
```

9.3. Solution in ESTEREL

An informal description of the program is given follows:

1. Each process is defined as a parallel composition of four cells (modules `cell0` or `cell1` which carry zero and one respectively) and an interface process modelled as a ESTEREL module `start_result`. The module `start_result` maintains the start of modules and the success propagation. The bus is modelled as a parallel composition of four lines.

2. On receiving a `compete` input signal, the process initiates the competition; the first cell triggers the action of placing the numbers from the most significant position onwards till the complete number is put on the arbitration bus; all the processes wanting to take the bus do the same thing. This corresponds to the registering phase as per the specification. The reading is initiated by a `compete` and the next cell is triggered by the `next` signal after placing `raise` on the bus line if it is the cell carrying one. The completion of the registering phase is signaled by the respective `result` signal and the checking phase starts. In the checking phase, the process proceeds as in the registering phase till its value and the bus value are not the same; on each "1" it sustains the `raise`. Once it finds that some other process has put a "1" and its own value is zero then it gets stuck; as the 1's in the subsequent positions are not sustained there is no explicit need for placing 0's. At this time it generates a `stuck` signal.

3. A process that is stuck can reenter registration phase in the next step when the line on which it is waiting becomes zero (i.e., `not (raised)`). Then the reading (for the subsequent bits) and the checking (for the whole number) repeats. If the process completes checking the line twice without getting stuck consecutively then it knows that it is the largest and takes the bus and releases it.

Assuming that the arbitration numbers of processes are distinct and are not composed entirely of only 1's or only 0's. one can show that this solution satisfies many desirable properties: guarantee of mutually exclusive access to the bus and deadlock freedom (at least one registered process will eventually access the bus).

78   Chapter 9. Futurebus Arbitration Protocol: A Case Study

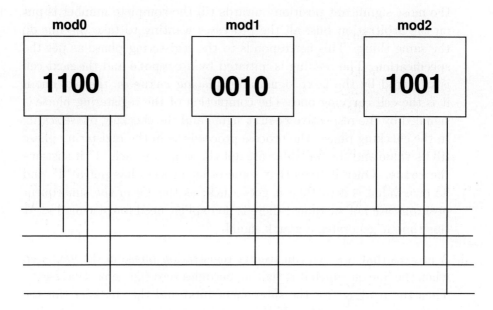

Figure 9.1: The system

Chapter 10

Semantics of ESTEREL

First, we describe the semantics for pure ESTEREL without variables, valued signals and `exec` statements. The semantics is essentially the constructive semantics given in [33]. Later, we illustrate how the semantic definition can be extended to include more complex constructs of ESTEREL, like `exec` constructs and signals with variables.

10.1 Semantic Structure

Given a pure ESTEREL module M and an input event I, the behavioral semantics essentially describes what happens in a single reaction of the module for the given input event. The things that can happen are emission of signals and flow of control from one set of points to another. This is captured by a mathematical relation, called the *transition relation*, denoted by $M \xrightarrow[I]{O} M'$ where O is the set of output signals generated by the module in the reaction and M' is a new module that results as a consequence of reaction. M', called the derivative of the reaction, has the same interface as M and differs only by its body; the flow of control is modeled by M' which is obtained from M by removing all those statements in M that will not be executed any more in the rest of the computations of the program.

The reaction to a sequence of input events is computed by chaining such one-step transitions. The transition relation is defined, by using an auxiliary inductive relation

$$stat \xrightarrow[E]{E',k} stat'$$

over statements where

1. `stat`, `stat'` are the statements before and after the reaction,

2. E is the current event to which stat reacts; E gives information about present as well as absent signals; E consists of elements of the form s^+ and s^-; the former indicates that the signal s is present while the latter denotes that the signal is absent in the event.

3. E' is the event emitted by *stat* in response to E; it contains only positive signals.

4. Since signals are broadcast, *stat* receives the signals it emits and E' will always be contained in E.

5. The integer *termination level* k determines how control is handled. In each reaction, any statement can behave in three ways: it can terminate and release the control, it can retain the control and wait for further events, or it can exit a trap. We set $k = 0$ for proper termination, $k = 1$ for waiting, and $k = \ell + 2$ for an exit T, where ℓ is the number of traps declarations one must traverse from *stat* to reach the declaration of T. In the example given below, the first "exit T" and "exit U" statements has level 2 since they concern the closest trap statement, while the second "exit T" has level 3 since one must traverse the declaration of U to reach that of T:

```
trap T in
   exit T²
||
   trap U in
      exit U²
   ||
      exit T³
   end
end
```

The exit levels can be determined statically; we assume that all exit statements are labeled by their level. With this coding, the synchronization performed by a "||" statement amounts to computing the *max* of the levels returned by its branches: a parallel terminates only when all branches have terminated, an exit preempts waiting, and only the outermost exit matters if several exits are done concurrently.

Given the auxiliary relation, $M \xrightarrow[I]{O} M'$ is defined to be true iff $stat \xrightarrow[I \cup O]{O,k} stat'$ where *stat* and *stat'* are the bodies of M and M' respectively; we assume the harmless restriction that *stat* cannot internally emit input signals.

10.2 Transition Rules

Now we define the auxiliary transition relation. The definition is given as a set of rules based upon the syntactic structure of statements. For brevity, we describe the relation only for the kernel statements. The relation for the derived statements can be directly obtained from the definitions, in terms of kernel statements, of the derived statements.

First we give the rules for basic kernel statements:

$$\texttt{nothing} \xrightarrow[E]{\phi,0} \texttt{nothing} \qquad (\text{nothing})$$

$$\texttt{pause} \xrightarrow[E]{\phi,1} \texttt{nothing} \qquad (\text{pause})$$

$$\texttt{exit } T^k \xrightarrow[E]{\phi,k} \texttt{nothing} \qquad (\text{exit})$$

$$\texttt{emit s} \xrightarrow[E \cup \{s^+\}]{\{s^+\},0} \texttt{nothing} \qquad (\text{emit})$$

In the above, it is assumed that the trap-exit statements are decorated with an integer code $k \geq (i+1)$ where i is the number of trap statements enclosing the exit statement. The above rules clearly reflect the termination status of the various statements: `nothing` and `emit s` terminate instantaneously and hence k is 0, whereas `pause` does not terminate in the current instant and hence has the value 1 for k; `exit T` has the termination status $k \geq 2$ depending upon the number of `trap` statements enclosing it; the reason for such an encoding would be clear from the semantics of `trap` statement given below. Except for `emit` statement all other statements does not generate any signals and hence E' is empty.

The following rules gives the semantics for the kernel signal handling constructs:

The statement `present s then p else q` behaves like p or q depending the presence of signal s. This is reflected by the following two rules:

$$\frac{s^+ \in E, p \xrightarrow{E',k}_E p'}{\text{present } s \text{ then } p \text{ else } q \xrightarrow{E',k}_E p'} \ (present+)$$

$$\frac{s^+ \notin E, q \xrightarrow{F',k}_E q'}{\text{present } s \text{ then } p \text{ else } q \xrightarrow{F',k}_E q'} \ (present-)$$

The following first two rules capture the behaviour when the body of suspend is suspended or activated depending upon the presence of signal s; the third rule describes that it terminates when the body terminates.

$$\frac{p \xrightarrow{E',k}_E p', s \notin E, k \neq 0}{\text{suspend } p \text{ when } s \xrightarrow{E',k}_E \text{suspend } p' \text{ when immediate } s} \ (susp1)$$

$$\frac{s \in E, k \neq 0}{\text{suspend } p \text{ when } s \xrightarrow{E',k}_E \text{suspend } p \text{ when immediate } s} \ (susp2)$$

$$\frac{p \xrightarrow{E',0}_E p'}{\text{suspend } p \text{ when } s \xrightarrow{E',0}_E \text{nothing}} \ (susp3)$$

In the first rule above, the suspend statement rewrites into immediate suspend statement. The immediate version of suspend statement is not a kernel statement! it is equivalent to the following:

```
trap T in
  loop
    present S then pause
    else exit T
    end present
  end loop
end trap;
suspend p when S
```

The semantics for control flow constructs are given by the following rules; note the capture of the termination status and the signal emission behaviours. The use of *max* function in the parallel rule correctly capture the fact that a parallel program terminates normally, if both the concurrent

10.2. Transition Rules

processes terminate parallel statement terminates normally, i.e., termination level is 0. If one of parallel components, say, p terminates by executing an exit statement then the p|q terminates at the same level as the exit level of p (if q terminates normally or via an inner trap) or at the level at which q terminates which correspond to the trap which is outermost.

$$\frac{p \xrightarrow[E]{E',k} p', k \neq 0}{p;q \xrightarrow[E]{E',k} p';q} \ (seq1)$$

$$\frac{p \xrightarrow[E]{E',0} p', q \xrightarrow[E]{F',k} q'}{p;q \xrightarrow[E]{E' \cup F',k} q'} \ (seq2)$$

$$\frac{p \xrightarrow[E]{E',k} p', k \neq 0}{\texttt{loop } p \texttt{ end} \xrightarrow[E]{E',k} p';\texttt{loop } p \texttt{ end}} \ (loop)$$

$$\frac{p \xrightarrow[E]{E',k} p', q \xrightarrow[E]{F',l} q'}{p|q \xrightarrow[E]{E' \cup F',max(k,l)} p'|q'} \ (parallel)$$

The semantics for trap is as follows:

$$\frac{p \xrightarrow[E]{E',k} p', k = 0 \text{ or } k = 2}{\texttt{trap } T \texttt{ in } p \xrightarrow[E]{E',0} \texttt{nothing}} \ (trap1)$$

$$\frac{p \xrightarrow[E]{E',k} p', k = 1 \text{ or } k > 2}{\texttt{trap } T \texttt{ in} p \xrightarrow[E]{E',\downarrow k} \texttt{trap } T \texttt{ in } p'} \ (trap2)$$

The first rule states that a trap statement Trap T terminates normally if the body of the trap terminates normally ($k = 0$) or exits the trap T ($k = 2$).

The second rule encapsulates two cases. The case $k = 1$ arises when the body does not terminate. In this case, the trap statement also does not terminate. The second case is one where the body terminates at an exit that corresponds to to an outer trap. The notation $\downarrow k$ is defined as follows:

$$\downarrow k = \begin{cases} 0 & \text{if } k = 0 \text{ or } k = 2 \\ 1 & \text{if } k = 1 \\ k-1 & \text{if } k > 2 \end{cases}$$

When the trap body terminates with exit statement at an outer level, the termination level of the trap statement decreases by one. The termination level recursively decreases and ensures the normal termination of the right trap statement,

10.2.1 Rules for Signal Statement

The semantics of signal statement is rather complex. As we have seen in Chapter 5.4, local signal declarations give rise to causal relationship among signals that need to be carefully resolved; there should not be any non causal cycles in the flow of control and emissions of signals. Correct programs should assign correct presence or absence status to all signal at every reaction step. To capture this, we need an elaborate set of rules for capturing causally correct programs. Two auxiliary functions, $Must$ and Can are used for this purpose.

Given a program p and an event E, $Must(p, E)$ is the set of all signals that are emitted in the first reaction of p when the status of the various signals are as specified in E. Similarly, $Can(p, E)$ consists of events that can possibly be generated in the first step of p. Formal definition of these predicates are given based upon the syntactic structure of p.

$Must(p, E)$ is an ordered pair of the form (S, K) where S is the set of signals generated when p is executed with event E and K is the set of return codes $0, 1$ or k that indicates the termination status of p after the execution. The two elements of the pair are denoted by $Must_s(p, E)$ and $Must_k(p, E)$ respectively.

$Can(p, E)$ is similarly an ordered pair (S, K), where S is the set of signals that can possibly be generated and K is the termination status of p. The two elements of the pair are denoted by Can_s, Can_k respectively.

The definition of these functions for basic kernel statements are obvious as defined below:

$$\begin{aligned}
Must(\text{nothing}, E) &= Can(\text{nothing}, E) = <\emptyset, \{0\}> \\
Must(\text{pause}, E) &= Can(\text{pause}, E) = <\emptyset, \{1\}> \\
Must(\text{emit s}, E) &= Can(\text{emit s}, E) = <\{s\}, \{0\}> \\
Must(\text{exit } T^k, E) &= Can(\text{exit } T^k, E) = <\emptyset, \{k\}>
\end{aligned}$$

10.2. Transition Rules

The definition for **present** is given below. A signal must (can) be generated by a **present** statement iff it must (can) be generated by one of the branches that will be taken in the given event set; if the event set does not determine the branch to be taken then we can not say that any signal must or can be generated.

$Must((\text{present s then p else q}), E)$ = $Must(p, E)$ if $s^+ \in E$
$Must(q, E)$ if $s^- \in E$
$<\emptyset, \emptyset>$ if $s^\perp \in E$
$Can((\text{present s then p else q}), E)$ = $Can(p, E)$ if $s^+ \in E$
$Can(q, E)$ if $s^- \in E$
$Can(p, E) \cup Can(q, e)$ if $s^\perp \in E$

where $s^\perp \in E$ holds if and only if neither $s^+ \in E$ nor $s^- \in E$ hold. **suspend** and **loop** statements act like their body and hence the following definitions:

$Must(\text{suspend p when s}, E)$ = $Must(p, E)$
$Can(\text{suspend p when s}, E)$ = $Can(p, E)$
$Must(\text{loop p end}, E)$ = $Must(p, E)$
$Can(\text{loop p end}, E)$ = $Can(p, E)$

The behaviour of $p; q$ is like p or both p and q depending upon whether p terminates in the current reaction or not. The behavior of $p|q$ is the combined behaviour of p, q.

$Must(\text{p;q}, E)$ = $Must(p, E)$ if $0 \notin Must_k(p, E)$
$< Must_s(p, E) \cup Must_s(q, E), Must_k(q, E) >$, otherwise
$Can(\text{p;q}, E)$ = $Can(p, E)$ if $0 \notin Can_k(p, E)$
$< Can_s(p, E) \cup Can_s(p, E),$
$Can_k(p, E) \backslash 0 \cup Can_k(q, E) >$, otherwise
$Must(p|q, E)$ = $< Must_s(p, E) \cup Must_s(q, E),$
$Max(Must_k(p, E), Must_k(q, E)) >$
$Can(p|q, E)$ = $< Can_s(p, E) \cup Can_s(q, E),$
$Max(Can_k(p, E), Can_k(q, E)) >$

where $Max(K, L)$ is $\emptyset$ if one of K, L is; otherwise, it is

$$\{max(k, l) | k \in K, l \in L\}$$

Signal generation capability of a **trap** statement is the same as its body; the termination status, however, is different from that of its body. It is given by the following equations.

$$Must(\texttt{trap T in p}, E) = <Must_s(p, E), \downarrow Must_k(p, E)>$$
$$Can(\texttt{trap T in p}, E) = <Can_s(p, E), \downarrow Can_k(p, E)>$$

Recall the semantic rules of Trap statement given elsewhere, where the notation $\downarrow$ was used to decrease the termination status. This definition ensures that the termination status (for both $Must$ and Can, is decreased by one if the termination status for the body is $k > 1$.

For statements involving local declaration of signal s, first it is checked whether s must or can be generated computed assuming an undetermined status for s. Depending upon the outcome, the event set E is enriched appropriately and the new sets of signals that must or can be generated are computed. Formally,

$$Must(\texttt{signal s in p}, E) = \begin{array}{l} Must(p, E * s^+)\backslash s \text{ if } s \in Must_s(p, E * s^\perp) \\ Must(p, E * s^+)\backslash s \text{ if } s \in Can_s(p, E * s^\perp) \\ Must_s(p, E * s^\perp), \text{ otherwise} \end{array}$$
$$Can(\texttt{signal s in p}, E) = Can(p, E * s^\perp)\backslash s$$

This completes the definition of $Must$ and Can functions.

Now we can give the rules for signal statement as follows.

$$\frac{s \in Must_s(p, E * s^\perp), p \xrightarrow[E*s^+]{E'*s^+,k} p', S(E') = S(E)\backslash s}{\texttt{signal s in p} \xrightarrow[E]{E',k} \texttt{signal s in } p'} \ (sig+)$$

$$\frac{s \notin Can_s(p, E * s^\perp), p \xrightarrow[E*s^-]{E'*s^-,k} p', S(E') = S(E)\backslash s}{\texttt{signal s in p} \xrightarrow[E]{E',k} \texttt{signal s in } p'} \ (sig-)$$

where the notation $E * s^x$ is used to denote the event set E' s.t. the signal emission status of s in E' is x, i.e., for example, if $x = +$ then $s^+ \in E'$.

The first rule corresponds to the case, where s is necessarily emitted by the body p of the signal statement. Whereas the second rule models the situation where p can not possibly emit s. In both the cases, any occurrence of s is absent in E'.

In the execution of body p, the signal s is assumed to be present (or present) iff s must (or cannot) be locally generated in p for the given set of events $E * s^\perp$; circular inference of presence status or contradictory statuses are avoided by taking an undetermined status for s in the set of events.

10.3 Illustrative Examples

Let us now illustrate the above rules with a number of classical examples including the problematic ones that were discussed in Chapter 5.5. All the examples considered do not include trap statements and hence the second components of the sets *Must* and *Can* are ignored in the following discussions.

Consider the following three programs, where we have annotated program segments with names for easy reference:

Example 1:
```
q: signal S in
    p: present S then emit S end
   end signal
```
Example 2:
```
q: signal S in
     present S else emit S end
   end signal
```
Example 3:
```
q: signal S in
    p: present S then emit S else emit S end
   end signal
```

In order to compute the reaction of q (in each of the above program), given a total set of events E, we need to compute the sets $Must_s(p, E * S^\perp)$ and $Can_s(p, E * S^\perp)$. From the definition of *Must* and *Can* and the fact that $E * S^\perp$ does not contain S, it is obvious that S is not in the first, while it is there in the second set. As a result, neither of the rules of the signal statement is applicable. Hence all the three programs do not have any reaction and are causally incorrect.

Example 4:

In the following example, I is an input signal while O is an output signal.
```
u: signal S1,S2 in
   [ v: present I then present S2 then emit S1
   ||
     w: present I then emit S2 end
   ||
     x: present S1 then emit S2;emit O end
   ]
   end signal
```

For computing a reaction of u, we need to compute $Must_s(u, E * S_1^\perp * S_2^\perp)$ and $Can_s(u, E * S_1^\perp * S_2^\perp)$. These sets are unions of the corresponding sets with respect to v, w, x.

Let us assume that $I \in E$. Then repeatedly applying the definition of *Must* and *Can* for 'present' statement we can conclude that S1,S2 are in E. As a result, the rule (sig+) is applicable to u. By applying this rule, we get $u \xrightarrow[E]{(O,0)} nothing$. In a similar way, we can infer that $u \xrightarrow[E]{(\phi,0)} nothing$, when $I \notin E$.

Example 5:

In this example, O is an inputoutput signal which is treated as a local signal.

```
u: signal S in
      v: emit S;
      w: present O then
             present S then pause end;
             emit O
         end
      end
   end signal
```

To compute the reactions of u, we examine the sets $Must(v;w,E')$ and $Can(v;w,E')$, where $E' = E*S^{\perp}*O^{\perp}$. Since v instantaneously terminates, i.e., $0 \in Must_k(u,E')$ and $0 \in Can_k(u,E')$, we have
$Must_s(v;w,E') = Must_s(v,E') \cup Must_s(w,E')$
$Can_s(v;w,E') = Can_s(v,E') \cup Can_s(w,E')$
Since v is a emit statement, S is in $Must_s(v;w,E')$ as well as in $Can_s(v;w,E')$. As a result, we compute the reaction of $v;w$ under $E*S^+*O^{\perp}$. This reaction terminates the execution of u.

Example 6:

The difference between the previous example and this is that emit S occurs inside the inner present statement.

```
signal S in
   present O then
      emit S;
      present S then pause end;
      emit O
   end
end signal
```

Since the status of O is unknown, the status of S is $\perp$. As a result, neither S belongs to the Must set nor to the Can set. Hence no reaction is possible in u.

10.4 Discussions

We have discussed classical semantic rules as well as constructive semantic rules in the previous sections. One of the important aspects to be noted from the original semantics of ESTEREL by G. Berry and G. Gonthier is that it does not make constraints of discreteness of the underlying semantic structure. This makes it possible to provide dense semantics; one attempt has been explored using the Durational Calculus approach in [59].

Another interesting question is: the orthogonality of the various preemption and suspension operators. Gerard Berry in [35] has provided a nice basis for notions of completeness of various preemption and suspension operators including *immediate* operators in an algebraic setting. A taxonomy of preemptive and suspension operators have been studied in [75]. The power of preemptions and synchrony hypothesis can also be seen in the application to define semantics of web scripting languages [93].

10.5 Semantics of Esterel with `exec`

In order to define the semantics of `exec`, an additional component is required in the label of the transition relation. This component is the set of labels of `exec` statements at which currently control resides. For this purpose, the structure of rewrite rules needs to be changed. For clarity, we define below the transition relation completely in this case.

Given a module M and an input event I, the behavioral semantics determines a transition $M \xrightarrow[I]{O} M'$ where O is the generated output event and M' is another module suited to perform further reactions. The derivative M' has the same interface as M and differs only by its body. The reaction to a sequence of input events is computed by chaining such elementary transitions. The transition relation is defined by using an auxiliary inductive relation

$$<stat, \rho> \xrightarrow[E]{E',L,k} <stat', \rho'>$$

on statements where

1. The old and the new signal environments are defined by,

    - E is the current event to which *stat* reacts; the return signal (input signal) of `exec` appears in E.

    - E' is the event emitted by *stat* in response to E; the start and kill signals (output signals) of `exec`'s appear in E'.

    - L is the set of labels of the `exec` statements currently active in *stat*;

    - The integer *termination level* k (cf. [12]) determines how control is handled. In each reaction, any statement can behave in three ways: it can terminate and release the control, it can retain the control and wait for further events, or it can exit a trap. We set $k = 0$ for proper termination, and $k = 1$ for waiting; other values correspond to trap-statements.

    - Since signals are broadcast, *stat* receives the signals it emits and E' will always be contained in E.

2. The old and the new states are defined by,

    - ρ is the memory environment at the beginning of the transition.
    - ρ' is the memory environment at the end of the transition.

10.5. Semantics of Esterel with exec

$$\text{exec } L : P \xrightarrow[E]{sL,\{L\},1} \text{exec\_wait } L : P \qquad (exec\_start)$$

$$\frac{L \in E,\ P \in TASK}{\text{exec\_wait } L : P \xrightarrow[E]{\emptyset,\emptyset,0} \text{nothing}} \qquad (exec\_comp)$$

$$\frac{L \notin E,\ P \in TASK}{\text{exec\_wait } L : P \xrightarrow[E]{\emptyset,\{L\},1} \text{exec\_wait } L : P} \qquad (exec\_wait)$$

Table 10.1: **Transitions for EXEC**

The relation between the two transition systems is given by $M \xrightarrow[I]{O} M'$ iff $< stat, \rho > \xrightarrow[I \cup O]{O,L,k} < stat', \rho' >$ where $stat$ and $stat'$ are the bodies and ρ and ρ' are the states of M and M' respectively; we assume the harmless restriction that $stat$ cannot internally emit input signals.

With respect to the set $\mathcal{L}$ of active exec labels, we use the notation,

$$E \# L = E \cup \{kL | L \in \mathcal{L} \text{ and } sL \notin E\}$$
$$\quad - \{sL | L \in \mathcal{L} \text{ and } sL \in E\}$$

to denote the set obtained from E by killing exec's started before the current instant and ignoring the one's started at the current instant.

Using the above notation, the rules for exec are shown in Table 10.5. The rule (*exec_start*) is used to start an exec statement. A distinct label is used for keeping track of several instances and the statement is rewritten into an auxiliary exec_wait statement which has been introduced for the sake of convenience. The rule (*exec_comp*) expresses the termination of the asynchronous task with the receipt of the return signal from the task. The (*exec_wait*) rule reflects the waiting for the arrival of the return signal from the task.

With respect to the set $\mathcal{L}$ of active exec labels, we use the notation,

$$E \# L = E \cup \{kL | L \in \mathcal{L} \text{ and } sL \notin E\}$$
$$\quad - \{sL | L \in \mathcal{L} \text{ and } sL \in E\}$$

(present1) $$\frac{S \in E, \quad stat_1 \xrightarrow[E]{E'_1, L_1, k_1} stat'_1}{\texttt{present}_L \ S \ stat_1 \ \texttt{else} \ stat_2 \ \texttt{end} \xrightarrow[E]{E'_1 \# L, L_1, k_1} stat'_1}$$
(present2) $$\frac{S \notin E, \quad stat_2 \xrightarrow[E]{E'_2, L_2, k_2} stat'_2}{\texttt{present}_L \ S \ stat_1 \ \texttt{else} \ stat_2 \ \texttt{end} \xrightarrow[E]{E'_2, L_2, k_2} stat'_2}$$
(abort) $$\frac{stat \xrightarrow[E]{E', L, k} stat'}{\texttt{abort} \ stat \ \texttt{when} \ S \xrightarrow[E]{E', L, k} \texttt{present}_L \ S \ \texttt{else} \ \texttt{abort} \ stat' \ \texttt{when} \ S}$$

Table 10.2: **Transitions for present and abort**

to denote the set obtained from E by killing exec's started before the current instant and ignoring the one's started at the current instant.

The semantics of all other statements, except present statements, are the same with the only difference that the additional component of exec labels. The semantics for present is given in Table 10.5. A more general form of present statement which is decorated with the set of currently active exec-labels L, is used. This set is used in rule *present1* to generate the appropriate kill signals when the then-branch is taken (that is at preemption time). This general form of present statement would be required for defining the semantics of abort statements, which is also given below for the sake of completeness.

Let us illustrate this rule-set using a simple example. Conside the following program, denoted by P:

    exec L:p; emit T

This program has the following sequence of transitiions:

- $P \xrightarrow[\{sL\}]{\{sL\},\{L\},1} exec\_wait L : p; emit T$

- $exec\_wait \ L : p; emit \ T \xrightarrow[\emptyset]{\emptyset, \{L\}, 1} exec\_wait \ L : p; emit \ T$

10.5. Semantics of Esterel with exec

- $exec\_wait\ L:p; emit\ T \xrightarrow[\emptyset]{\emptyset,\emptyset,0} nothing$

Note that the left hand side and right hand side of the second derivation is the same and hence can be repeated for many steps. This models the computation of tasks spanning across multiple reaction instances. Also the rewriting of exec L:P to exec_wait L:p models the fact that the at least one instance should elapse between the start and end of a task instance. Note the termination code correctly illustrates the termination status of the statement. The final derivation includes emisson of signal T as the emit statement is executed in the same reaction at which the the task terminates.

Part III. Other Synchronous Languages

Summary

In the the next two chapters, we shall provide an overview of Lustre- a dataflow synchronous programming language (based the dataflow language Lucid) and Argos derived from the Statechart graphical formalism .

Chapter 11

Synchronous Language LUSTRE

11.1 An Overview of LUSTRE

The language LUSTRE is a synchronous dataflow programming language[20], designed for programming reactive control systems [39]. LUSTRE borrows many ideas from the way control engineers describe and develop controllers. Controller behaviors are often expressed in declarative style as a set of data flow equations. For example, the following equation is a typical example of a data flow equation:

$$x_n = p * y_n + q * x_{n-1}$$

This equation defines the value of variable x at the nth instance as a weighted sum of the variable y at the same instant and x at the previous instant.

LUSTRE provides a rich set of constructs for writing equations in such declarative style. It includes a powerful programming environment that enables compilation, simulation, and verification of Lustre programs. The industrial version is supported bo a power graphical environment called `Scade` and it supports validated code generation.

In this section, we provide an overview of the language.

11.2 Flows and Streams

In LUSTRE , a program is a system of equations defining a set of variables in terms of input variables. Each variable is a (finite or infinite) stream of values of the same type that are associated with different indices, called time instances. As the example suggests LUSTRE programs often have cyclic behaviours and hence can describe feedback loops found in control systems.

A program or a subprogram is referred to as a **node** which is essentially a function of input and output flows (streams). A program is made up of the following component structures:

1. Flows or Streams,

2. Equations, Variables and Expressions, and

3. Data Types and Operators

Flows or Streams:

In LUSTRE, any variable and expression denotes a *flow*, i.e., a pair made of

- A possibly infinite sequences of values of a given type.

- A *clock*, representing a sequence of times.

A flow takes the n-th value of its sequence of values at the n-th time of its clock. Any program, or piece of program has a cyclic behaviour, and that cycle defines a sequence of times which is called the *basic clock* of the program: a flow whose clock is the basic clock takes its n-th value at the n-th execution cycle of the program. Other, slower clocks can be defined. The clock concept is not necessarily bound to physical time. As a matter of fact, the basic clock should be considered as setting the minimal "grain" of time within which a program cannot discriminate external events, corresponding to its response time.

11.3 Equations, Variables and Expressions

In the LUSTRE, variables should be declared with their types, and variables which do not correspond to inputs should be given one and only one definition, in the form of equations. The equation X = E; defines variable X as being identical to expression E. Both have the same sequence of values and clocks. Equations can be written in any order, and variables used to denote subexpressions etc.

Data types and Operators in Lustre LUSTRE has only few elementary basic types: boolean, integer, real and one type constructor: *tuple*. The complex types can be imported from a host language and handled as abstract types. Constants are those of the basic types and those imported from the host language(for instance constants of imported types). Corresponding flows have constant sequences of values and their clock is the basic one. Usual operators over basic types are available (arithmetic: +, -, *, /, div, mod; boolean: and, or, not; relational: =, <, <=, >, >=,; conditional: if then else) and functions can be imported from the host language. These are called *data operators* and only operate on operands sharing the same clock; they operate point wise on the sequences of values of their operands [20].

There are four temporal operators in Lustre that are defined below:

- *pre* (*previous*): Let $(e_1, \cdots, e_n, \cdots)$ be the sequence of values of expression E. Then $pre(E) = (nil, e_1, \cdots, e_n, \cdots)$ and has the same clock as E. Note that *nil* denotes an undefined value denoting uninitialized memory. It may observed that *pre* acts as a memory.

- − > (*followed by*): Let E and F be expressions with the same clock with respect to sequences $(a_1, a_2, \cdots)$ and $(b_1, b_2, \cdots)$ respectively. Then $E-> F = (a_1, b_1, b_2, \cdots)$ and has the same clock as E and F. That is, $E-> F$ is always equal to F except at the first instant of its clock.

- *when* (*under-sampling*): This operator samples to a slower clock.

- *current* (*interpolate*): This operator interpolates on the clock immediately faster than its own. Let E be an expression whose clock is not the basic one and let B be the boolean expression defining its clock. Then *current E* has the same clock as that B, say C, and its value at any time of this clock C, is the value of E at the last time when B was true. Thus, it preserves the value between points.

Figure 11.1 illustrates the main operators described above.

11.4 Program Structure

A LUSTRE system of equations can be represented graphically as a network of operators. This means that some notion of subroutine: a subnetwork can be encapsulated as a new reusable operator which is called a *node*. A node declaration consists of an interface specification - providing input and output parameters with their types and possibly their clocks - optional internal variables declarations, and a body made of equations and assertions

A	true	false	true	false	true	false
B	true	true	true	false	false	true
C = A when B	true	false	true			false
D = not B	false	false	false	true	true	false
E = pre A	nil	true	false	true	false	true
F = A and B	true	false	true	false	false	false
X	x1	x2	x3	x4	x5	x6
Z = X when A	x1		x3		x5	
K = current Z	x1	x1	x3	x3	x5	x5

Figure 11.1: Operators and Expressions

11.4. Program Structure

defining outputs and internal variables as a function of inputs. A node can be functionally instantiated in any expression. Concerning clocks, the basic clock of a node is defined by its inputs, so as to be consistent with the dataflow point of view. A node may admit input parameters with distinct clocks. Then the faster one is the basic clock of the node, and all other clocks must be in the input declaration list. Outputs of a node may have clocks different from its basic clock. These clocks must be visible from outside the node and these are certainly slower than the basic one.

11.4.1 Illustrative Example

In this section, we shall illustrate writing of simple programs.

Let us define a counter of natural numbers: That is, we should define the flow starting from 0 to all successive integers. This is represented by the following equation:

```
NAT = 0 -> (pre(NAT)+1)
```

Here, the sequence will be (0,1, 2, ...). This follows from the definitions of $->$ and *pre*.

Let us augment the above specification as follows:

- The flow is to be set to 0 whenever the variable RESET is true.

The equation then takes the form:

```
NATR = 0 -> (if RESET =0 then 0 else (pre(NATR)+1))
```

It is easy to see that the above can be represented as a logical diagrams and thus it enables engineers to write programs in a graphical formalism. This is one of the features used in the SCADE environment. We shall not be going into these aspects.

The above equation can be cast a program or a subprogram through the definition of node. The structure for the above equations is given below:

```
node natcounter(RESET:integer) returns (NATR:integer)
let
NATR = 0 -> (if RESET =0 then 0 else (pre(NATR)+1))
tel
```

It can be seen that node essentially specifies a function from input flows into output flows. It can also interpreted to mean the definition of user defined operators.

Let us consider the following problem: There are three inputs A, B, and C that are of type boolean. We should write a function Threshold that gives true if any two of the inputs are true. Initially the value is false.

```
node Threshold (A,B,C: boolean) returns (value: boolean)
let value = false -> if A and B then true
                     elseif B and C then true
                     elseif C and E then true
                     else false
tel
```

11.5 Arrays in LUSTRE

In recent versions (Lustre -V4), the data type array LUSTRE !arrays which is extremely useful has been introduced. In a sense, array can be naturally interpreted to define a flow or a stream. These data types have been introduced avoiding unpredictable runtime errors such as index out of bounds.

Typical Array declarations are:

```
vector:int^100;
const bound = 50
type stack = int^bound
X: stack;
register:bool^32
```

Array Access: Elements of array are given by A[0], A[1], ..., A[n] where n is defined at compile time. The expression A[i] is legal if i in the range of the array.

Array Expressions:

Expressions [z,x-1,m*4], true^10 (denotes [true ... true] – 10 times) are referred to as constructors.

A[3..6] denotes [A[3],A[4],A[5],A[6]]

A[6..3] denotes [A[6],A[5],A[4],A[3]]

Arrays Expressions:

$A|B$ denotes [A[0], ..., A[n], B[0], ... B[m]] where n and m are compile time bounds of the arrays A and B respectively.

A or B = [A[0] or B[0], ..., A[n-1] or B[n-1] where n is the size of the arrays.

Further, operators "if then else", "pre", "$\rightarrow$" are polymorphic in nature and can be applied to arrays. Arrays provide a good expressive power to the programmer. For further details, the reader is referred to [55].

In the next section, we shall illustrate little more complex controller programs.

11.6 Further Examples

In this section, we will look at some examples used earlier while discussing ESTEREL (cf. section 7)to illustrate the features of dataflow in LUSTRE . Purposely, we have kept some repetitions so that it can also be read independently.

11.6.1 A Very Simple Auto Controller

The following LUSTRE program models the auto controller discussed in Section 7.

```
include "boolmisc.lus"
include "boolarray.lus"
include "math.lus"
include "kalyanmisc.lus"
node SIMPLE(ignition_on,ignition_off,accel:bool)
                         returns (control_throttle:bool);
let
   control_throttle = false ⟶
     if Once_Since(ignition_on,ignition_off) and accel then true
        else if (ignition_off or once(ignition_off)) then false
            else false;
   assert not(ignition_on and ignition_off);
tel
```

The LUSTRE model has a single node that responds to three input signals: ignition_on, ignition_off, accel corresponding to the three input commands given by the driver. It has one output signal, control_throttle that controls the throttle valve position. This node first waits for input signal ignition_on to be present. Once ignition_on is present it emits output signal control_throttle for every accel. If at any point input signal ignition_off comes it aborts and restarts the whole process.

11.6.2 A Complex Controller

Recall that this controller is required to have the additional safety feature to monitor the door status and to send out warning signals when the door is open while the car is in motion.

The LUSTRE program corresponding to this controller is given below.

```
include "boolarray.lus"
include "boolmisc.lus"
include "kalyanmisc.lus"
include "math.lus"
```

```
node COMPLEX(ignition_on,ignition_off,accel,door_opened:bool)
        returns (alarm,control_throttle,door_lock:bool);
let
  control_throttle = false ⟶
          if Once_Since(ignition_on,ignition_off) and accel
             and (not(door_opened)) then true
          else if (ignition_off or once(ignition_off)) and accel
                   and (not(door_opened))
          then false
          else if door_opened then false
             else false;
  alarm = false ⟶
          if door_opened and Once_Since(ignition_on,ignition_off)
          then true
          else if door_opened and (control_throttle or accel) then true
          else false;
  door_lock = false ⟶
              if Once_Since(ignition_on,ignition_off)
                 and door_opened
              then true
              else if (control_throttle or accel) and
                       door_opened then true
                    else false;
  assert not(ignition_on and door_opened);
  assert not(ignition_on and ignition_off);
tel
```

Like the ESTEREL model, this program has an additional input signal: door_opened, and two output signals: alarm and door_lock. The equations defining the two output signals set the values of these signals appropriately to raise the alarm signal and lock the door when the door is opened as indicated by the door_opened signal.

11.6.3 A Cruise Controller

Recall the complex cruise controller model described in Section 7. The following LUSTRE program models this controller:

```
include "math.lus"
include "boolarray.lus"
include "boolmisc.lus"
include "kalyanmisc.lus"
node CRUISE(cruise,accel,brake_pressed,engine_off,accel_released,
            ignition_on,belt_fastened:bool;current_speed:real)
       returns (chk_belts,start_engine,alarm,cruising:bool;
```

11.6. Further Examples

```
                        control_throttle:real);
let
chk_belts = false ⟶
              if xedge(ignition_on) or belt_fastened then false
              else if (not belt_fastened) or (not once(ignition_on))
                  then true
                  else false;
start_engine = false ⟶
              if Once_Since(belt_fastened,chk_belts) and
                  not(ignition_on)
              then true
              else if ignition_on then false
                  else false;
(control_throttle,cruising) = (0.0,false) ⟶
          if belt_fastened and once(ignition_on) and not(engine_off)
              and accel and not(cruise)
          then (MANUAL_MODE(true,false),false)
          else if belt_fastened and once(ignition_on) and
                  not(engine_off) and accel_released and not(cruise)
              then (MANUAL_MODE(false,true),false)
              else if belt_fastened and once(ignition_on) and
                      not(engine_off) and cruise and not(brake_pressed)
                  then CRUISE_MODE(current_speed)
                  else (0.0,false);
alarm = if once(ignition_on) and not belt_fastened then true
        else false;
tel
node MANUAL_MODE(accel,accel_released:bool) returns (control_throttle:real);
var th_value:real;
let
  th_value = 5.0;
  controlxi_throttle = th_value ⟶
        if accel and not accel_released then pre control_throttle + 2.0
        else if accel_released and (pre control_throttle >= 6.0)
        then pre control_throttle - 1.0
        else if (pre control_throttle = 5.0) then th_value
              else pre control_throttle;
  assert not(accel and accel_released);
tel
node CRUISE_MODE(current_speed:real)
      returns (control_throttle:real;cruising:bool);
var cruise_speed,th_value:real;
let
   th_value = 5.0;
   cruise_speed = current_speed;
```

```
            control_throttle = cruise_speed;
            cruising = true;
        tel
```

The node **CRUISE** corresponds to the Esterel main module while the nodes **MANUAL_MODE** and **CRUISE_MODE** correspond to the other two Esterel modules.

% first waits for ignition to be turned on (ignition_on).

When this signal arrives, it emits the chk_belts signal, and then waits till the belts are fastened. After this is done it indicates (`emit start_engine`) that the engine should be started. After this, it 'loops' forever keeping a constant vigil on the belt status and simultaneously switching modes as and when the driver wants.

Switching between `manual mode` and `cruise mode` is enabled by the accel_rreleased/break signals.

The **MANUAL_MODE** starts with a default throttle value and for every "accel" input signal, increases this value by some arbitrary units (which we have taken to be 2 for the sake of illustration) and emits the output signal to indicate this change in the throttle value (control_throttle). The variable `th_val` is used to keep track of the throttle value. The signal `control_throttle` is valued and it carries the value stored in the variable `th_val`.

Th node **CRUISE_MODE** takes the current speed and at regular intervals (which we taken to be every 'tick') computes the throttle value using the current speed at this tick and the cruise speed which is the current speed value at the previous tick. It then emits the output signal to indicate this change in the throttle value(control_throttle). It also emits the cruising output signal to indicate its cruise_mode status.

11.6.4 A Train Controller

Another controller that was considered in Section 7 is the train controller. Recall that this controller controls the movement of an automatic train that moves back and forth between a set of stations. When there is no request the train remains idle in one of the stations. When there is a request at a station, the train eventually moves to the station, opens its doors allowing the people to board after which it closes the door and moves in the appropriate direction.

A LUSTRE model of the controller is given below:

```
include "boolarray.lus"
include "boolmisc.lus"
include "kalyanmisc.lus"
```

11.6. Further Examples

```
include "math.lus"
node tcontrol1(d_closed,d_opened:bool;stn_arrived,request:int)
                returns (d_close,d_open,t_run,t_stop:bool);
let
 t_run = false -> if Once_Since(d_closed,d_close) and Once_Since(d_close,t_stop)
                     and not(stn_arrived = request)
                  then true
                  else if (stn_arrived = request) then false
                  else pre t_run;
 t_stop = true -> if not(stn_arrived = request) or t_run then false
                  else if (stn_arrived = request) then true
                  else pre t_stop;
 d_open = true -> if (xedge(d_opened)) or Once_Since(d_opened,t_stop)
                  then false
                  else if ((stn_arrived = request) or
                           t_stop and xedge(not t_stop))
                     then true
                     else false;
 d_close = false -> if (Once_Since(d_closed,not(stn_arrived = request)))
                      or Once_Since(d_closed,t_stop)
                   then false
                   else if not(t_stop) or not(stn_arrived = request) then true
                   else if Once_Since(not(stn_arrived = request),t_stop)
                           or (not(t_stop) or not(stn_arrived = request))
                     then true
                     else false;
tel
```

11.6.5 A Mine Pump Controller

Here in this section we will examine how LUSTRE could be used for describing the mine controller considered earlier.

The mine pump controller controls the operation of a pump which is used to drain the excess water in the mines. The controller should start the pump to drain the water as soon as the water level raises above a certain upper limit. Since the pump can not operate when the water level is below some lower limit, it has to be stopped when the water hits this lower limit. The mines might have combustible and dangerous gases like methane and carbon monoxide. Methane when present in high concentration might explode when the pump is operating while carbon monoxide present in high doses is fatal. So the controller has to monitor the concentration of these gases and switch off the pump and give alarm whenever they are high. Here is a description of the controller in LUSTRE.

```
include "math.lus"
include "boolarray.lus"
include "boolmisc.lus"
include "kalyanmisc.lus"
include "manual_cpy.lus"
node mpump(start,stop,methane,co,hw_level,lw_level,manual,auto:bool)
     returns (p_run,p_stop,m_alarm,c_alarm:bool);
let
   m_alarm = false -> if methane then true
                            else false;
   c_alarm = false -> if co then true
                            else false;
   (p_run,p_stop) = (false,true) ->
             if manual or Once_Since(manual,auto)
             then MAN(start,stop,methane)
             else if auto or Once_Since(auto,manual)
                  then AUTO(hw_level,lw_level,methane)
                  else (pre(p_run),pre(p_stop));
tel
node MAN(start,stop,methane:bool) returns (p_run,p_stop:bool);
let
  (p_run,p_stop) = (false,true) ->
  if start or (once(start) or xedge(start)) and Once_Since(start,stop)
     and not(methane) and not(stop)
  then (true,false)
  else if stop or Once_Since(stop,start) or methane
       then (false,true)
       else if methane then (false,true) -> AUTO(true,false,true)
            else if start then (true,false)
                 else (pre(p_run),pre(p_stop));
tel
node AUTO(hw_level,lw_level,methane:bool) returns (p_run,p_stop:bool);
let
(p_run,p_stop) = (false,true) ->
       if hw_level or (once(hw_level) or xedge(hw_level)) and
          Once_Since(hw_level,lw_level) and not(methane) and not(lw_level)
       then (true,false)
       else if lw_level or Once_Since(lw_level,hw_level) or methane
            then (false,true)
            else if hw_level
                 then (true,false)
                 else (pre(p_run),pre(p_stop));
tel
```

11.6. Further Examples

The program consists of three nodes mpump, MAN and AUTO. Like the ESTEREL model considered earlier, the inputs start,stop,manual,auto are the signals to start,stop the pump and to switch to manual and auto respectively. The signals methane,co indicate respectively that the methane and carbon monoxide levels have reached the critical values while the signals hw_level,lw_level are input when the water level upper or lower limits. The outputs
p_run,p_stop,m_alarm,c_alarm are emitted by the controller to start, stop the pump or when the concentration of the gases crosses the danger levels.

Chapter 12

Modelling Time-Triggered Protocol (TTP) in LUSTRE

Time-triggered architectures are being widely deployed in safety-critical systems such as automotive systems. TTP [43, 48, 78] is a widely used protocol for these applications. These protocols have much in common and are based on *a priori* fixed schedule of interaction of processes at known intervals of time and thus depend heavily on the correctness and tightness of clock synchronization of the underlying processes. In this section, we shall model TTP in LUSTRE .

12.1 Time-Triggered Protocol

Time-triggered systems consist of a number of autonomous subsystems ("processes" or "nodes"), communicating with each other through a broadcast bus, as shown in Figure 12.1. As the name suggests, the system activities are triggered by the progress of time as measured by a local clock in each node. Each node in the system is allotted time-slots to send messages over the bus. These time-slots are determined by a Time Division Multiple Access (TDMA) scheme, which is pre-compiled into each node in the cluster. In each node, the TDMA schedule is embedded in a structure called *MEssage Descriptor List (MEDL)*, which has global information pertaining to all the nodes in the cluster. Thus, the system behaviour is known to all the nodes in the cluster.

Each time-slot determined by TDMA can be visualized to consist of two phases - the *communication phase* during which a node sends message over the bus, and the *computation phase* during which each node changes its

Chapter 12. Modelling Time-Triggered Protocol (TTP) in LUSTRE

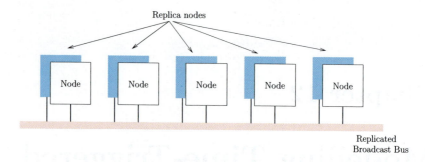

Figure 12.1: TTA - Nodes and the Broadcast Bus

internal state (i.e., updates the values of the state variables); the duration of these phases are denoted by *comm_phase* and *comp_phase* respectively, as shown in Figure 12.2. These phases roughly correspond to the "receive window", during which a node awaits a message, and the "inter-frame gap" during which there is silence on the bus, respectively.

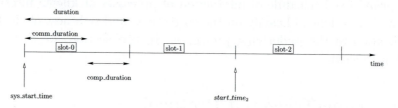

Figure 12.2: Communication Slots in a TTA

The Time-Triggered Protocol (TTP) is the heart of the communication mechanism in time-triggered systems. Each node sends a message over the bus during its allotted time-slot, while the remaining nodes listen to the bus waiting for the message, for a specified period of time, the *receive window*. Since the system behaviour is known to all the nodes (through MEDL), there are no special acknowledgment messages sent on successful receipt of a message, and the arrival of the message during the corresponding "receive window" of a node itself suffices to consider the sending node as active. A complete round during which every node has had access to the bus once is called a *TDMA round*. After a TDMA round is completed, the same communication pattern is repeated over and over again. TTP uses clock synchronization, and *Bus Guardian* to achieve a robust fault-tolerant system. We shall delve into these aspects below.

12.1. Time-Triggered Protocol

12.1.1 Clock Synchronization

Each node in TTP initiates activities according to its own physical clock, implemented by a crystal oscillator and a discrete counter. As no two crystal oscillators resonate with exactly the same frequency, the clocks of the nodes drift apart. Since the system activities crucially depend on time, it is important that the clocks of the nodes are synchronized enough so that the nodes agree on the given time-slot and access the bus at appropriate times to send messages. TTP uses an averaging algorithm for clock correction and it is different from other synchronization algorithms in the sense that there are no special synchronization messages involved. The drift of a particular node's clock is measured by the delay in the arrival of the message from the expected arrival time. Further, such time deviations for computing the average are collected from only four *a priori* determined nodes in the cluster, (in a sense, these four are the most accurate clocks) even if the cluster consists of more than four nodes.

Clock synchronization is the key issue of reliability in any time-triggered architecture. It is the task of the clock synchronization algorithms to compute the adjustments for the clocks and keep them in agreement with other nodes' clocks, in order to guarantee reliable communication, even in the presence of faulty nodes in the cluster. Since there are no explicit acknowledgment messages sent on receipt of a message by a node, it is very likely that the fault propagates in the cluster during message transfer.

TTP uses Fault-Tolerant Average (FTA) algorithm, an *averaging algorithm* [1], for clock correction. Averaging algorithms typically operate by collecting clock deviations from the nodes and computing their average to be the correction for the individual clocks. In TTP the clock deviations are collected only from an ensemble of four *a priori* known clocks of high quality resonators. So, in the minimal configuration, it requires at least four nodes in order to tolerate a single Byzantine fault $((3m + 1); m = 1)$. The timing deviations of the messages from the expected arrival time are stored only if the *SYF* Flag (for *SYnchronization Frame*) is set in the MEDL for the particular slot. These flags are set when the sending node is one among the four nodes whose clock readings are used for correction. If the *CS* Flag (for *Clock Synchronization*) is set for a particular slot, then the clock correction is computed by applying FTA on the time deviations collected. In short,

---

[1] *Non-averaging* algorithms operate by applying a fixed adjustment to clock values and *averaging algorithms* apply varying adjustments at fixed intervals. TTP uses FTA and FlexRay uses FTM (Fault-Tolerant Midpoint) algorithm which are averaging algorithms.

114 Chapter 12. Modelling Time-Triggered Protocol (TTP) in LUSTRE

the clock synchronization operates as follows:

1. If *SYF* flag is set for the current slot, the time difference value is stored in the node.

2. If *CS* flag is set for the current slot, the FTA is applied, correction factor computed and the clock is corrected.

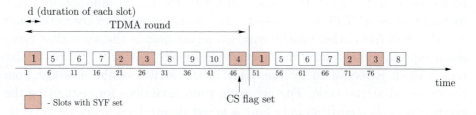

Figure 12.3: TDMA round

Consider a TTP cluster with ten nodes and communication pattern shown in Figure 12.3. Here, there are four slots per TDMA round with *SYF* flag set. In TTP, the clocks are corrected only when four time difference values are obtained, i.e., when there are at least four slots with the *SYF* flag set. In this case, the clock will be corrected during the tenth slot, when the *CS* flag is set.

12.1.2 Bus Guardian

Due to cost considerations, clocks with low quality resonators are also used in time-triggered systems . Due to the presence of such non-accurate clocks, the clock readings of the nodes in the system are not uniform. Since the nodes access the bus at particular time as read by their individual clocks, the varying clock drifts may lead to a disturbance in the schedule. To prevent a node from sending messages out of its turn, the bus interface is guarded by a *Bus Guardian*, that has independent information about the system and gives access to the nodes only at appropriate times. It plays an important role in maintaining the correct schedule for communication in the system. The TTP, besides fault-tolerant clock synchronization, also offers other tightly integrated services like group membership, redundancy management, etc. The main characteristics of TTP are summarized below:

1. The communication is through TDMA scheme which is pre-compiled into every node in the cluster.

12.2. Modelling TTP in LUSTRE

2. The system behaviour is known to all the nodes in the cluster and hence there are no special acknowledgment messages.

3. The clock synchronization provided by TTP (using Fault-Tolerant Average or FTA algorithm) differs from other synchronization algorithms, as there are no separate synchronization messages involved.

4. The time deviations from only four clocks in the cluster is considered for computing clock correction. These deviations are collected during slots where the SYF flag is set.

5. The FTA algorithm is used to compute the correction factor for the clocks during slots where the CS flag is set.

6. TTP guarantees reliable operation in the presence of at most one faulty node in the cluster.

12.2 Modelling TTP in LUSTRE

We consider a TTP cluster with a fixed set of nodes, say ten [2] for the sake of simplicity. Let the communication pattern in the TDMA cycle be as shown in Figure 12.3. The shaded slots indicate the slots where the SYF flag is set and the numbers inside the boxes indicate the node that is participating in the particular slot. In this model, during each slot, a node k sends a message, while the remaining $(10 - k)$ nodes (all assumed to be active), listen to the bus waiting for the message. The slots are equally divided, and when every node has had access to the bus once, the communication pattern is repeated again, as shown in Figure 12.3. As highlighted already, clock synchronization is the crux of TTP; our modelling of TTP in LUSTRE will also confine to this aspect.

Each TTP node will have a structure shown in Figure 12.4. The items inside the dotted box in Figure 12.4 are derived during the communication process. We shall use the following data structure for a TTP Node:

- Two counters $(node\_clock)_k$ and $(local\_clock)_k$, which denote the physical clock, and the corresponding adjusted physical clock of node k.

- A counter $(slot\_count)_k$ that maintains the number of the current slot.

- An array $(timedevn)_k$ of size four for storing the time difference values.

---

[2] We have experimented using a cluster of 25 nodes. In automotive applications, which this is intended for, the number of ECUs is roughly around this value.

Chapter 12. Modelling Time-Triggered Protocol (TTP) in LUSTRE

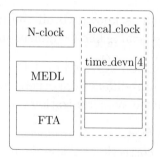

Figure 12.4: Structure of a TTP Node

- A variable $(clock\_correction)_k$ for storing the correction value of the current slot or the most recent slot.

and the following functions:

1. N-clock - It is a simple counter that takes the increment rate for the clock as input and generates clock with the increment rate as drift rate. By using different increment values, clocks of varying drift rates can be generated.

2. FTA - this implements the Fault-Tolerant Average algorithm, which is used for clock correction. It takes four time deviation values, and computes their average, after ignoring the maximum and minimum deviations.

3. MEDL - this maintains the TDMA schedule for each node. By fixing the duration of each slot, duration of a TDMA round, and the number of nodes, it simulates the repeating behaviour of the TDMA. It takes the drift rate of the corresponding node as input and generates the schedule for the node.

Each of the above functions is described in detail below.

N-clock

In order to simulate TTP nodes, we need to generate clocks with different drift rates. The module `N-clock` is an initialized counter with an increment value and a "reset" parameter, which is set to "false". The increment value can be changed to obtain clocks with different rates. The corresponding LUSTRE code is given in Table 12.1.

12.2. Modelling TTP in LUSTRE

```
const init=1.0;   -- initial value of the clock
const incr= x;    -- increment rate for the counter
node N-clock(in: real) returns (lc: real);
let
        lc = COUNTER(init,incr,false);
tel
```

Table 12.1: N-clock module

Fault-Tolerant Average (FTA) Algorithm

TTP uses FTA, an averaging algorithm for computing clock correction. It operates by computing the average of four time deviation values collected during a TDMA round. The algorithm makes periodic adjustments to the physical clocks of the nodes to keep them sufficiently close to each other. Let $(local\_clock)_k$ denote the adjusted physical clock of node k, $LC_k(t)$, its reading at time t and adj_i, the clock correction made during slot i of TDMA round, we have

$$LC_k(t) = PC_k(t) + adj_i \qquad (12.1)$$

In a TDMA round of n slots, for each node k with a local clock reading LC_k, and for slots i ($1 \le i \le n$):

$$(timedevn)_k[1..4] = \begin{cases} (LC_k - LC_p^i) & if\ SYF_i = true \\ pre((LC_k - LC_p^i)) & if\ SYF_i = false \end{cases}$$

where LC_p^i is the clock reading of sending node p that is active during slot i when SYF flag is set, and $pre(x)$ denotes the previous value of x. Now, if the CS flag is set for a particular slot i, for a node k, the clock correction in the current TDMA round denoted $clock\_correction_k$ is given by:

$$clock\_correction_k = ((\sum_{i=1}^{4} timedevn)_k[i])$$
$$-max(timedevn)_k - min(timedevn)_k\ /\ 2)$$
$$if\ CS_i = true \qquad (12.2)$$

where $max(timedevn)_k$ and $min(timedevn)_k$ denote the maximum and minimum values of the array $(timedevn)_k$ of time deviation values. These new values of the local clocks will be used by the nodes for further communication. The corresponding LUSTRE code given in Table 12.2 shows the averaging algorithm for tolerating 'f' faults. TTP can be considered as a

```
const k=4;     -- Number of time difference values
const f=1;     -- Number of faults to be tolerated
node FTA (time_diff : real^k) returns (avg_devn: real);
var NF,NFMIN: real^f;
let
   NF[0..(f-1)]=MAXFINDER(time_diff);
   NFMIN[0..(f-1)]=MINFINDER(time_diff);
   avg_devn = (TOTAL(k,time_diff)
- (with f > 1 then   TOTALNEW(fi,NF[0..(f-1)])
-            else NF[0])
- (with f > 1 then   TOTALNEW(fi,NFMIN[0..(f-1)])
-            else NFMIN[0]))/(k-2*f);
tel
```

Table 12.2: The FTA module

special case where f equals '1', since it can tolerate at most one Byzantine fault.

where TOTAL returns the sum of k time deviation values, and MINFINDER and MAXFINDER are functions that return the minimum and maximum values of the arguments.

MEssage Descriptor List (MEDL)

MEDL contains the TDMA schedule information of all the nodes in the cluster, like sending times of the node, the identity of the sending node and the slots where SYF flags are set. The corresponding LUSTRE module is given in Table 12.3.

S(a,b) is true when a and b do not differ by more than a particular value, that characterizes the drift. R_STABLE(n,x) is a function that sustains the true value of n for x time units. This x may be considered as the "receive window" of the node.

The modules defined above can be used to model a TTP Node. The corresponding LUSTRE module for a TTP node is given in Table 12.4.

The module NODE can be instantiated using different values for inc (drift rate) to simulate nodes in a cluster. For example,

($Node\_One$, avg_1) = NODE(1.00);
($Node\_Two$, avg_2) = NODE(1.02);

Simulations of TTP: A snapshot of the simulation of TTP consisting of ten nodes using SIM2CHRO is shown in Figure 12.5. In the Figure, $l\_1, \cdots, l\_9$ indicate the local clock readings of the ten nodes. Here, the ten nodes were

12.2. Modelling TTP in LUSTRE

```
--        sc       - counter maintaining slot number
--        tx_time  - sending time of the nodes in the cluster
--        dc       - counter maintaining the duration of each TDMA slot
--        i1,i2,i3,i4 - slots where SYF flag is set
const init=1.0;   - initial value of the counters used
const no=4;       - number of nodes with good clocks
const tn=10.0;    - total number of nodes
const t=5.0;      - duration of each slot
const mx=tn*t;    - duration of TDMA round
const i1=1.0; const i2=5.0; const i3=6.0; const i4=10.0;
node MEDL(incr: real) returns (syf: bool;count: int);
var   bs, sc, dc, j, tx_time, ock, nc: real;
      reset, reset_1, reset_2: bool;
let
   nc = 0.0 -> COUNTER(init,incr,pre nc >= mx);
   j = 1.0 -> if pre ock >= mx then  pre j + 1.0
              else pre j;
```
tx_time = mx*(j-1.0) + [t*(sc-1.0)] + 2.0;
```
   dc   = COUNTER(init,1.0,pre(dc=t));
   sc   = NEWCOUNTER(init,incr,false -> pre(dc)=t,
```
$reset_1$);
```
   ock  = COUNTER(init,incr,pre(ock>=mx));
   bs   = NEWCOUNTER(init,incr,false -> pre(ock)=mx,reset);
   syf  =
```
$R_S TABLE$((S(sc,i1) or S(sc,i2) or S(sc,i3) or
            S(sc,i4)) and dc=1.0,1.0);
```
   count =
```
$INT_N EW COUNTER$(0,1,xedge(not syf),$reset_2$);
```
   reset = pre(bs) >=tn and pre(ock)>=mx;
```
$reset_1$ = pre(sc) >= tn and pre(dc)=t;
$reset_2$ = false -> pre ock>=mx;
```
tel
```

Table 12.3: MEDL module

```
--      nc              -- node_clock
--      sc              -- slot counter
const no = 4;           -- Number of accurate clocks
const tn = 10.0;        -- Total number of nodes
const t  = 5.0;         -- Duration of a TDMA slot
const mx = n*t;         -- Duration of a TDMA round
const init = 1.0;
const inc1 = 1.0;       --
const inc2 = 1.0004;    -- inc1..inc4 are the drift rates of the four
const inc3 = 1.002;     -- accurate clocks in the cluster
const inc4 = 1.00001;   --
node NODE(inc: real) returns (local_clk: real; avg: real);
var     d:real$^n o$; k: int;
        nc, x, j, y, sc, dc: real;
        syf, cs, $reset_1$: bool;
let
        nc = COUNTER(init,inc,pre nc >= mx);
        y  = COUNTER(init,1.0,pre y = mx);
        dc = COUNTER(init,1.0,pre(dc=t));
        sc = NEWCOUNTER(init,inc,false -> pre(dc)=t,$reset_1$);
        j  = 1.0 -> if pre nc >= mx then pre j + 1.0
                    else pre j;
        x = mx*(j-1.0) + [t*(sc-1.0)] + 2.0;
        (syf,k) = MEDL(inc);
        cs = (k=4);
        d[0] = 0.0 -> if (syf and k=1) then  (nc - N-clock(inc1))
                      else pre d[0];
        d[1] = 0.0 -> if (syf and k=2) then  (nc - N-clock(inc2))
                      else pre d[1];
        d[2] = 0.0 -> if (syf and k=3) then  (nc - N-clock(inc3))
                      else pre d[2];
        d[3] = 0.0 -> if (syf and k=4) then  (nc - N-clock(inc4))
                      else pre d[3];
        $reset_1$ = pre(sc) >= tn and pre(dc)=t;
        avg = 0.0 -> if k=4 then  FTA(d)  else pre avg;
        local_clk = nc -> if cs then  nc + a  else nc;
tel
```

Table 12.4: LUSTRE module for a TTP Node

12.2. Modelling TTP in LUSTRE

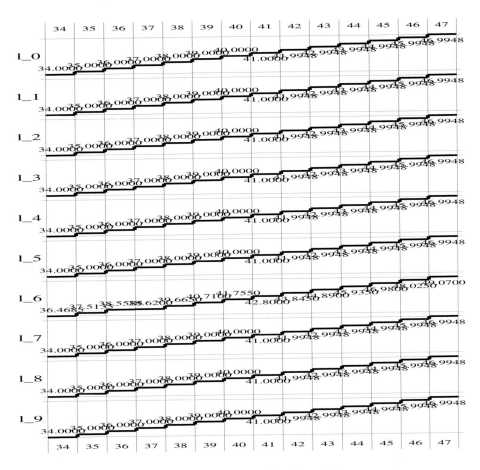

Figure 12.5: Screen shot of a Simulation run

simulated assuming a drift rate of 1.0 for the non-faulty nodes (nine of them) and a drift rate of 1.04 for the faulty node (node 6 with clock reading l_6). We can see that at the end of the TDMA round, the clock l_6 deviates from the rest by a factor of around 2.0 units.

The above model has been further used in the verification of clock-synchronization algorithms, the interested reader is referred to [94].

Chapter 13

Synchronous Language ARGOS

Argos is a graphical synchronous programming language. It is based on statecharts [52] but has a simpler syntax, minimal features and cleaner synchronous semantics. We shall briefly overview the main features and illustrate the same through examples.

13.1 ARGOS Constructs

The basic components of Argos are automata, which are simple edge labeled finite state Mealy machines. It has an initial state but no final state. An Argos automaton or machine describes an unending computation of reactive controllers.

A transition connecting a pair of states has a label of the form b/S where b is a boolean expression involving only input signals while S is a set of output signals generated as a result of taking the transition. Input signals are boolean variables which take appropriate values (true or false) indicating the presence or absence of certain external real signals generated by the sensors; the output signals trigger appropriate actions on the actuators. The input expression describes a combination of signal presence/absence status which when true, triggers the transition. The future behavior of the machine is decided by the resultant state. Thus using such a machine, the complete behavior of a controller for any possible input situations starting from the initial state can be described.

Such finite state machines suffice for the description of small controllers but large such descriptions can be hard to understand, due to their flat nature. Three constructs *hierarchy, concurrency and signal hiding* are defined to structure large descriptions:

Hierarchical composition:
A hierarchical structure can be introduced in flat state machine descriptions using this construct. Given a machine A with a state, say, q, another machine, say, B can be placed inside q. The behavior of the resulting machine is decided by A except in the state q; in this state the behavior is decided both by q and B. The state q expresses the important operation *preemption* that is found useful in controllers: in state q, computation proceeds as specified in B so long as none of the transition out of q can be taken; when an outgoing transition from q can be taken, the 'inside' computation is preempted and the system transits to the target state of the transition and then on behaves like A.

Synchronous Parallel Composition:
Given two machines A, B, a *parallel* machine that runs both A and B concurrently can be written using this construct. Such a description specifies that the system (being described) behaves simultaneously both like A and B: given a set of input signals representing the state of the environment, appropriate transitions in *both* the automata are taken and the result is the union of the sets of signals generated by both the automata. In general, one can have concurrent compositions of more than two automata. Further that, the concurrent components can interact: signals generated by one component can trigger transitions in the other components; such a triggering is instantaneous with no delay between the firing of the transitions in different components.

Signal Hiding:
The hiding construct is defined to limit the scope of interaction between concurrent subcomponents. Using this construct, a signal can be declared local to a subset of components so that the generation of signal will not trigger any transition in other components. This construct can also be viewed as an abstraction primitive that enable hiding of internal details like the signals that have no effect on the environment.

These three constructs form the basis of the language Argos. It has been shown that large descriptions can be concisely written using these three constructs.

We will now illustrate the features of Argos through a simple example. Figure 13.1 shows an Argos program that models a 3-bit counter [52]. The counter counts from 0 up to 7. It can be initialized to 0 and can be reset during counting.

The Argos description is, at the top level, a two state machine (`counting`

13.2. Illustrative Example

and not_counting) in which the signal end is made local. not_counting is the initial state, denoted by the 'half-arrow'. The transition to counting takes place when the signal init is given.

The state counting is refined to contain concurrent composition of three machines, each representing one of the three bits. Each of these machines has two states corresponding to the two values that a bit can take. Initially all the three bit values are zero indicated by the initial states A0, B0, C0. External signal tick changes the state of the right most machine (representing the least significant bit). When this machine is in state A1, the external signal tick results in the generation of the local signal lt1 which simultaneously triggers the state transition of the next machine from B0 to B1; the first machine changes its state to A0. The next tick signal results in the transition to A1 of the first machine. In this state, the next tick will generate lt1, triggering the transition from B1 to B0. This will generate another local signal lt2 which will trigger the transition from C0 to C1 on the left most machine.

When all the 'bits are set to 1', the end signal is generated which triggers the transition from counting to not_counting. At any stage of counting, the stop signal can effect the transition to not_counting state. The signals lt1,lt2,end are local as indicated by the decoration of states in the diagram.

As this example illustrates, the operators of Argos allow hierarchical and concurrent description of complex state machines. It has been shown in [26, 69] that Statecharts can be translated to efficient synchronous hardware circuits.

13.2 Illustrative Example

In Chapter 6, we considered a number of simple reactive controllers for illustrating ESTEREL features. Here we take up some of these and describe their behaviours using Argos.

Figures 13.3 describes the belt controller. This has one super state S1 that contains S2, S3 and S4 as substates. The belt controller is always in state S1 but in one of S2, S3 and S4. S1 is a super state and hence whenever the signal reset appears on the input then the control leaves the S1 (momentarily) weakly preempting computations inside S1 and returning back to S1 and the default initial state S2. In state S2, it is monitoring the signal key_on while in S3 it is waiting for end_5 signal which indicates

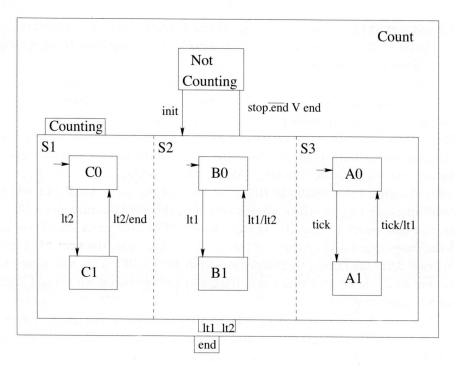

Figure 13.1: An example in Argos

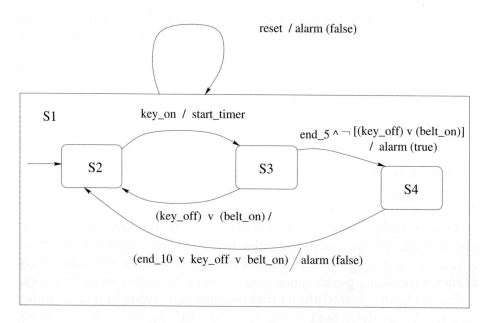

Figure 13.2: Belt Controller

13.2. Illustrative Example

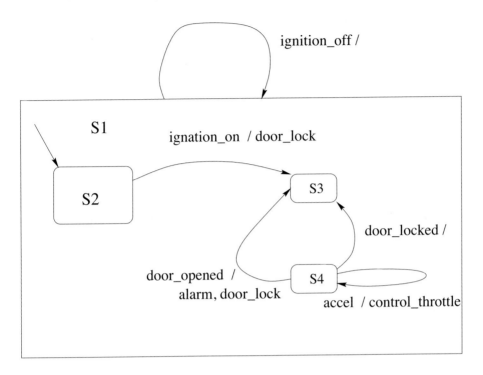

Figure 13.3: Auto Controller

5 seconds have elapsed for checking belt fastening etc. Similarly S4 waits for 10 seconds to elapse (through the signal end_10).

It is a simple exercise to compare Argos solution with ESTEREL and Lustre solution, given earlier, for the same problem.

Figure 13.3 describes the auto controller described earlier. Like the belt controller, it is a single super state machine having three inner states.

The train controller description in Argos is given in Figure 13.4. It is slightly more complex than the previous two controllers: one of the inner state, S5, is a super state. S5 is entered after a request for a destination comes from the user and the door is closed. Control remains in S5 as long as the destination is not reached. When the train reaches the destination, transition from S6 and S7 takes place which generate the signal **Stop**. This signal triggers the transition from S5 to S1. Recall that super states model weak preemption and this example illustrates one powerful feature of Argos that enables exiting a superstate once the computation inside the state has been completed.

Finally, the pump controller behaviour is given in Figure 13.5. As in the case of ESTEREL model, Argos model has also concurrent state machines.

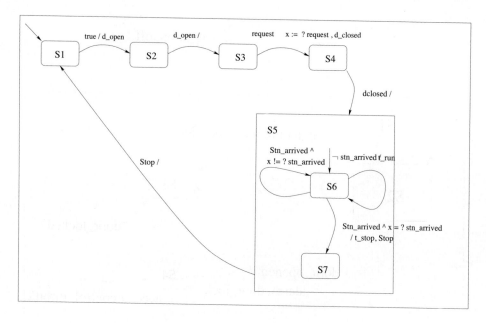

Figure 13.4: Train Controller

The top two machines essentially monitor the CO and Methane gas level and emits appropriate alarms when the limits are exceeded. The bottom concurrent component models operation of the pump: it has two super states S9 and S10 which model automatic and manual modes. Recall that in the manual mode starting and stopping of motor are triggered by the external user while in the auto mode they are triggered by external physical events.

13.3 Discussions

The original ESTEREL is based on textual syntax and Statecharts was based on graphical (visual) formalism. The textual form enabled ESTEREL to succinctly define concepts like priority etc. in syntactic manner easily (as in textual form one need not get constrained by 2- or 3-dimensions). However, the graphical formalism is an attractive formalism for the designers. Thus, in a sense, Argos could be considered as nice subset of Statecharts which could go along with ESTEREL in a consistent manner. In other words, this laid the foundations for a visual formalism for ESTEREL. Later, [3] defined SyncCharts which is in a sense forms the visual formalism for ESTEREL. On another front, due to the wide usage of Statecharts, a translation of State-

13.3. Discussions

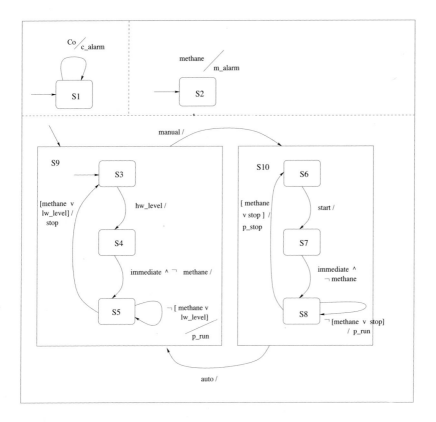

Figure 13.5: Pump Controller

charts (satisfying properties like deterministic response) was explored in [79] and a complete environment for real-time systems that uses the translation can be found in [15].

Part IV: Verification of Synchronous Programs

Summary

In this part, we will describe important approaches that are used for the verification of programs in synchronous languages like ESTEREL, and Lustre. First we will discuss in detail the verification approaches used for verification of ESTEREL programs. This will be followed by an illustration of verification techniques for LUSTRE programs.

Chapter 14

Verification of ESTEREL Programs

There are two broad approaches for verification of ESTEREL programs: transition system based approaches and logic based ones.

In the transition system based approach, programs as well their specification are modeled as transition systems and verification involves comparing the two transition systems using the standard transition system relations like bisimulation [53].

In the logic based approaches, specification of a program is a list of desired properties of the program written in some logical language, like many-sorted first order logic or temporal logic. The verification process involves checking whether the program (to be verified) satisfies the given specification. The verification is carried out using deductive or model-theoretic techniques.

14.1 Transition System Based Verification of ESTEREL Programs

This approach is useful for proving pure ESTEREL programs. The basic idea behind this approach is as follows: The specification is a collection of small properties each one specifying certain aspect of the program being verified. The automaton corresponding to the program being verified is analyzed to see whether these properties are satisfied. But this automaton would be quite large even for a moderate sized programs, involving a large number of signals and signal combinations and many internal states. Hence, special reduction techniques have been suggested using which transition systems can be reduced to smaller transition systems that then can be easily analyzed. Certain *observation* and *reduction* criteria have been proposed for this purpose. system . An observation criterion states which of the signals are observable. In the reduction based upon this criterion, transitions labeled with other signals would be replaced by null transitions and identifying states that were different in the original automaton because of their different behavior on the hidden signals. A reduction criterion on the other hand would replace certain sequence of edges in the original automaton by a single edge thereby hiding certain states and bringing in a reduction.

This approach is the basis for a tool called fctools [50] developed at INRIA, Sophia Antipolis. Now we will discuss this approach in detail now.

14.1.1 Detailed Discussion

This approach suggests the following steps for the verification of a given simple property:

- Translate the given ESTEREL program into a finite labeled transition system.

- Abstract and reduce the ESTEREL transition system based upon the property to be verified and

- check the reduced system by simple inspection whether it satisfies the given property.

Arbitrary properties of general ESTEREL programs can not be checked simply by inspection. A property should be sufficiently 'small' in order to do this. Thus this approach suggests that for the purpose of verification, one should have the property of a program as a number of small properties each of which can be checked by inspection. For many real applications, this is indeed possible.

The transition system corresponding to the ESTEREL program being verified consists of all possible states of the program and in each state there are outgoing edges which are labeled with all possible events each event being a logical combinations of presence/absence of input signals. Hence the transition system will be quite large even for moderate programs having tens of signals; real systems would have hundreds of signals. For this reason special reduction techniques have been developed [16, 2] that reduce the size of transition systems. There are three such techniques suggested in the literature:

- **Hiding:** A property may involve a fewer signals than what the entire program would have; or in other words one should decompose the property being verified into a number of properties each of which refers to few signals. For verification of a property, it may be sufficient to keep only the corresponding set of signals and hide other signals. The transition system corresponding to the program then can be reduced by *hiding* all signals other than those required.

- **Equivalence Quotient:** Many times, in the transition system of a program, many states though equivalent in behavior might have been distinguished. Significant reduction would be achieved by 'quotienting out' equivalent states.

- **Context Filtering:** Typically a program is designed to work in only certain restricted environments and a property of the program would hold only when the program runs in this restricted environments. But the transition system constructed out of a program would include behaviors that correspond to arbitrary environments. Hence for verification, one has to filter out those parts of the transition system and work on the relevant part to verify the property. This is referred to as context filtering.

14.2 ESTEREL Transition System

The behavior of a pure ESTEREL program is describable by a labeled transition system. The states in this transition system are the possible states that the program can enter into during its execution; a pure ESTEREL program has only finite number of states. Each edge from a state represents an execution step from the state. The label describes the exact condition under which such a transition takes place and the effect of the transition. More precisely, the transition for a pure ESTEREL program is an ordered tuple (Q, q_0, I, O, T), where Q is a set of *states*, $q_0 \in Q$ is the *initial* state, I is a set of input signals, O is the set of output signals, and T is the transition relation given by $T \subseteq Q \times \mathcal{B}(I) \times 2^C \times 2^O \times Q$; $\mathcal{B}(I)$ is the set of all boolean combinations of the signals in I. Any edge in this transition system is of the form (q, b, o, q') where q, q' are the source and target states, b is a boolean expression that describes the condition on the presence and absence of various input signals under which this edge is taken; o is the set of output signals generated as a result of taking this transition.

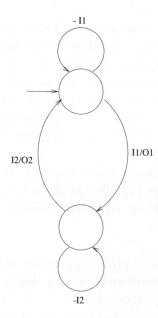

Figure 14.1: A Simple Transition System

To illustrate, the behavior of the following program is described by the transition system given in Figure 14.1.

```
input I1,I2;
emit O1;O2;
loop
await I1;emit O1;
await I2;emit O2;
end loop
```

Such a transition system for a given pure ESTEREL program can be automatically derived using the compositional semantics rules given in Chapter 2.

It may be easily seen that the transition system for even a moderate sized programs would be quite large due to the fact that in each state there would be an exponential (on the size of the input signal-set) number of edges corresponding to all possible input status.

14.2.1 Abstraction and Hiding

Abstraction and hiding are some simple operations on transition systems developed for reducing the size [53, 16].

Given a transition system, a new transition system can be obtained by hiding one or more signals occurring in the original system. The new system

14.2. ESTEREL Transition System

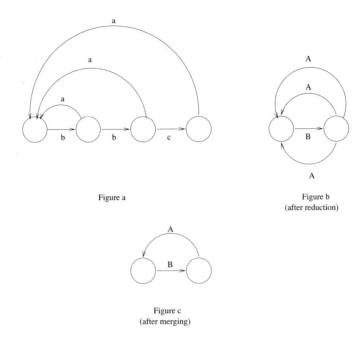

Figure 14.2: **Abstraction and Hiding**

will not contain occurrence of the hidden signal(s). In certain restricted case, the new system will have edges (from the same state) labeled identically and their target states being either identical or equivalent in the sense that the subsequent input-output behaviors are the same, i.e., the subgraphs 'starting' with these target states are identical. In such cases, all these edges and the subgraphs can be merged into one in the sense that all but one of the edges and the corresponding target subgraphs can be removed thereby bringing about a reduction.

Hiding is a special case of abstraction which is a very powerful operation for reducing the size of transition system. In a general abstraction, signals and signal combinations can be renamed and paths of edges can be replaced by a single edge removing all the intermediate states. As an example, consider the system given in Figure 14.2-a. Using an abstraction, this can be reduced to the system given in Figure 14.2-b. The latter has been obtained from the former by renaming the signal combinations b^*a by A and $b.b.c$ by B and replacing the paths by single edges. The system resulting out of an abstraction may contain states with identical 'subgraphs' of states and edges which can be merged to get a smaller system as shown in Figure c.

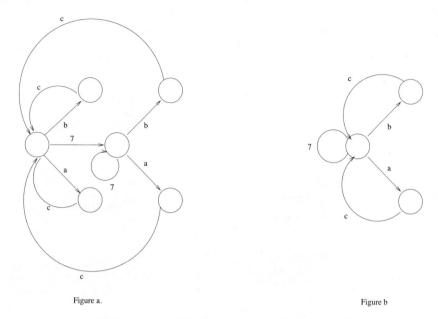

Figure a. Figure b

Figure 14.3: **Observation equivalence**

14.2.2 Observation Equivalence Reduction

In the earlier section we saw that reduction can be achieved by merging distinct occurrences of identical subgraphs. But the criteria used here for reduction is too restrictive as it requires that the subgraphs are identical. There are subgraphs that are not identical but the programs with these behaviors can not be distinguished by any external observer. For instance, consider the two distinct labeled graphs given in Figure 14.3. Suppose that the labels on the edges a, b are communication alphabet that require synchronization with the environment and τ represents internal action. Then no environment can distinguish between the two programs. Milner [53] has defined an equivalence relation, called *observational equivalence relation* that is coarser than the simple identity relation, which we shall define now for ESTEREL transition systems.

Suppose that $A_i = (Q_i, q0_i, I_i, O_i, T_i)$, $i = 1, 2$ are two ESTEREL transition systems. Then

Definition 1 A_1 *is observational equivalent to* A_2, *denoted by* $A_1 \equiv A_2$, *provided if there exists a relation* $\mathcal{R} \subseteq Q_1 \times Q_2$, *such that* $q0_1 \mathcal{R} q0_2$ *and for any pair of states* q_1, q_2, $q_1 \mathcal{R} q_2$ *implies that*

- *If* $q_1 \xrightarrow{b/o} q_1'$ *then there exists* $b_1, \cdots, b_m, r_1, \cdots, r_m$ *such that:*

14.2. ESTEREL Transition System

1. $q_2 \xrightarrow{b_i/o} r_i$ for each $i = 1, \cdots, m$ and
2. $b \to \bigvee_{i=1}^{m} b_i$

- and vice versa.

This definition is essentially the bisimulation relations defined in [31, 2], which is an adaptation of the original definition [53] to ESTEREL transition systems.

Based upon the definition, one can define a reduction called *observational equivalence reduction* that simplifies a transition system by merging subgraphs that are observational equivalent. This transformation is, in general, useful in the beginning when one constructs the transition system from the ESTEREL program and after any reduction transformation based upon abstraction.

14.2.3 Context Filtering

Typically programs are designed making some assumptions about the environment in which they will work; they are not expected to behave as required when they run in other environments. But the definition of transition systems described earlier does not take into account this environmental assumptions. They contain behaviors which are not expected to be real behaviors in the sense that these behaviors will not be exhibited by the programs when run in intended environments. The idea of context-filtering reduction is to take into account the environmental assumptions and removing those execution paths that do not reflect the right environments. In order to carry out this reduction, the intended environment is specified as a transition system. Then a new transition system is developed that is a parallel composition of the environmental transition system and the transition system corresponding to the program being analyzed. This new transition system will have only those behaviors of the program, that are expected in the given environment. This system will be smaller in size for analysis. This system may further be subjected to observational equivalence reduction to obtain a smaller system that may be easily analyzable than the original one.

As an example consider the following program schema where S1 and S2 are some arbitrary ESTEREL program fragments:

```
present a then stat1 else stat2
||
present b then stat3 else stat4
```

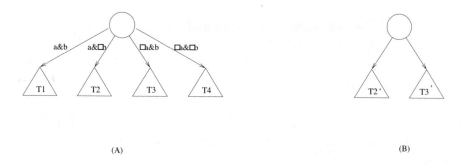

Figure 14.4: **Context Filtering**

This program is expected to work in an environment in which the environment produces the signal a if and only if it also produces the signal b. If we ignore this context constraint and generates the transition system then it will be of the form given in Figure 14.4 a, where $T1, T2, T3, T4$ are subgraphs of transition systems that describe behavior of the system corresponding to the statements `stat1`, `stat2`, `stat3` and `stat4` respectively.

On the other hand if the constraint is taken into account, then the transition system reduces to the one shown in Figure 14.4 b, where $T2', T3'$ are also reduced versions of $T2, T3$ respectively by pruning the edges that correspond to exactly one one of the signals being present. It can be easily seen that such a reduction based upon context constraints decreases the size of the transition systems significantly.

14.3 Temporal Logic Based Verification

In this approach programs are verified against specifications that are temporal logic formulae. Depending upon the program to be verified one can use either fully automatic model-theoretic approach or semi-automatic theorem proving technique for verification.

If the program to be verified is pure then fully automatic methods are available for verification. The verification, then involves converting the program into an automaton and checking whether the automaton satisfies the given temporal logic formula. Standard techniques and tools are available for carrying out this checking. The approach is automatic in the sense once the program and the specification are given, one can algorithmically determine whether the program satisfies the specification or not. Another advantage is that if the program does not satisfy the specification then the method can produce the execution sequences that violate the property which will be useful in debugging the program.

If the program involve data variables of unbounded types like integers, then in general verification can not be carried out automatically. Theorem proving techniques can be used for verification in this case. The idea behind this technique is as follows: correctness of a program with respect to a temporal logic specification is posed as a theorem in some some formal axiomatic system. which typically consists of a number of axioms and inference rules. If the program is correct with respect to the given specification then it should be possible to derive the statement of correctness as a theorem in this axiomatic system.

14.4 Observer-based Verification

In this section, we will present in detail an automatic method for verifying the class of *safety* properties of ESTEREL programs. This method is based upon the foundational work on the automata theoretic approach [87] and is inspired by the synchronous observers approach designed for the verification of Lustre programs [39]. Based upon this method the tool *Tempest* [19] has been developed for verification of ESTEREL programs.

This method takes as input, the ESTEREL program and the temporal property to be verified; the property is expressed in a restricted class of temporal logic, the class of *canonical* safety formulae [51]. The input formula is first translated into an ESTEREL program, called the observer which is then composed with the input ESTEREL program to get a new ESTEREL program. The observer program essentially observes the behavior of the input ESTEREL program at every instant and checks whether it violates the property being verified; if the property is violated then the observer generates a special signal 'violation'. Whether 'violation' signal is emitted by the combined program can be easily checked by compiling (using the standard ESTEREL tools) the latter into an automaton and inspecting the automaton for the presence of the signal 'violation'. The automaton enumerates all possible execution paths of the program being verified, presence of the violation signal implies that there is an input sequence for which the program violates the safety property. As a side product of this inspection one can get the input combination that causes the property to be verified. This can be useful in debugging the program.

An important advantage of this approach is that the verification is carried out on the program itself rather than on a model of the program;

typically in other verification approaches, verification is carried out on an abstraction or a model of the program being verified. This method is restricted to safety properties. However, for real-time systems it is sufficient to deal with safety properties as one is not interested in unbounded liveness properties; bounded liveness properties can always be expressed as safety properties.

A Brief Overview of Temporal Formulae

The class of formulae used for specification are subclasses of linear propositional temporal logic formulae. We confine here to a very brief and informal discussion of this logic; for more details refer to [51]. This temporal logic is built on top of standard propositional logic by adding a number of temporal operators. The propositional symbols of the propositional logic are, in addition to the constant symbols $TRUE, FALSE$, the names of signals used in the program being verified. The temporal operators are: the future 'always' operator, $\square$, and all the past operators: Previous, $\ominus$, eversince, $\boxminus$ and since $\mathcal{S}$. Temporal formulae are interpreted over state sequences. The intuitive meaning of any temporal formula is as follows:

- The simplest propositional formula is of the form S, where S is a signal name. This formula is true in a state provided the S is present in the state; $\neg S$ is true provided S is absent in the state. The truth value of any arbitrary propositional formula is computed from the truth values of the constituent propositional symbols and the standard truth tables of boolean connectives.

- The formula $\square A$ holds in a particular state of a state sequence provided A holds in that state as well in all successive states in the sequence.

- $\ominus A$ holds in a state (of a sequence) provided the latter has its immediate predecessor state in which A holds; in particular, it is false in the initial state which does not have an immediate predecessor.

- $\boxminus A$ holds in a state provided A hold in all states 'Eventually' operator.

- $A\mathcal{S}B$ holds in a state if A holds in this state and in all states in the past since a state where B holds.

Now we can define *canonical safety formulae*. Intuitively safety formulae state that nothing bad happens.

Definition 2 *A safety formula in canonical form is a temporal property of the form* $\square A$, *where A is an arbitrary formula involving only past-time temporal operators.*

A canonical safety formula can be automatically translated into an ESTEREL program that observes the preservation/violation of the formula; let E_ϕ be the program corresponding to the formula ϕ. Table 1 gives a recursive definition of E_ϕ using which the translation can be carried out. Note that $VIOLATED$ is the output signal of E_ϕ.

Suppose P is the ESTEREL program to be verified with respect to the safety property ϕ then the following ESTEREL program Verif is constructed:

```
module Verif
  input I_P;
  inputoutput O_P;
  output VIOLATION;
  [run P || run E_φ]
end module
```

where I_P, O_P are the input and output signals of P and the input signal of E_ϕ is included in $I_P \cup O_P$. Verif runs both P and E_ϕ in parallel and may emit the signal VIOLATION. It can be easily shown from the construction of E_ϕ that Verif emits the signal VIOLATION iff it has an execution sequence that violates ϕ.

14.5 First Order Logic Based Verification

The idea behind this approach is similar to the deductive technique for temporal logic discussed in the previous section. The main difference is that the specification language is expressed in some versions of first order logic. Typically it is a many-sorted logic with as many sorts as there are found in the program being verified; in particular it includes arithmetic.

Chapter 15

Observer Based Verification of Simple LUSTRE Programs

In this chapter, we shall see how the examples presented in the previous section can be effectively verified for some of the safety-critical properties using the notion of observers. An *Observer* is a simple LUSTRE program which will take as inputs, the inputs and outputs of the main program, and test it for one or more specified properties. In this section, the example programs of the previous section are analyzed to pick out certain common safety properties, and the verification of the programs is presented with the help of LUSTRE nodes(Observers).

15.1 A Simple Auto Controller

Some of the easily observable properties of such a simple auto controller are listed below:

- Once the `ignition_off` is turned on, the `accel` should not have any effect until the `ignition_on` is turned on.

- The assertion that `ignition_on` and `ignition_off` cannot be true simultaneously.

The LUSTRE observer for one of the properties is given below[1]:

```
node observer_simple(ignition_on,ignition_off,accel,control_throttle:bool)
                    returns (relevant:bool);
```

---
[1] Note that as the language is conjunctive, we can add observers as needed.

```
let
    relevant = SIMPLE(ignition_on,ignition_off,accel) ->
               if not(Once_Since(ignition_on,ignition_off)) and accel
                   then false
                   else if ignition_on and ignition_off then false
                       else true;
tel
```

15.2 A Complex Controller

Some simple safety properties in a complex auto controller would be like:

- Once the `ignition_off` is turned on, the `accel` should not have any effect until the `ignition_on` is turned on.

- The `accel` should not have any effect until the door is closed.

- If the door is open and if the `accel` is pressed, the `alarm` should go high.

The LUSTRE observer for one of the safety properties is given below:

```
node observer_auto(ignition_on,ignition_off,accel,
                   door_opened,alarm,control_throttle,door_lock:bool)
                                            returns (relevant : bool);
let
    relevant = true ->
        if accel and not(Once_Since(ignition_on,ignition_off)) then false
        else if (door_opened and accel) then false
            else if (door_opened and accel and not(alarm)) then false
                else true;
tel
```

15.3 A Cruise Controller

In the case of a cruise controller, there may be many safety properties. For the purpose of illustration, the most relevant safety properties have been considered and they are verified using observers. Some of the properties are:

- If the engine is `off` or the `brake` is pressed, the `cruise` mode cannot be in "on" state.

- The belt should be fastened while trying to accelerate.

15.4. A Train Controller

- When the accelerator is released, the `control_throttle` value should no longer increase, until the accelerator is pressed again.

- If the accelerator is pressed without the belt being fastened, the `alarm` should be emitted.

Apart from the above mentioned properties, the observer given below includes some assertions also:

```
node observer_cruise(cruise,accel,brake_pressed,engine_off,accel_released,
                    ignition_on,belt_fastened,chk_belts,start_engine,alarm
                         ,cruising:bool;control_throttle:real)
                                          returns (relevant : bool);
let
relevant = true ->
    if (engine_off or brake_pressed) and cruising then false
    else if accel and not belt_fastened then false
         else if accel_released and (control_throttle > pre control_throttle)
              then false
              else if accel and not(Once_Since(ignition_on,engine_off))
                   then false
                   else if not(belt_fastened) and accel and not(alarm)
                        then false
                        else if Once_Since(ignition_on,engine_off) and
                                accel and belt_fastened and alarm
                             then false
                             else if Once_Since(ignition_on,engine_off) and
                                     accel and belt_fastened
                                  then true
                                  else true;
assert not(accel and accel_released);
assert not(ignition_on and engine_off);
assert not(brake_pressed and accel);
tel
```

15.4 A Train Controller

A simple train controller would have a couple of properties like:

- The door can not be opened when the train is running.

- The train should stop when the requested station has arrived.

The observer would look something like:

```
node observer_train(d_closed,d_opened,d_close,d_open,t_run,t_stop:bool;
                                                stn_arrived,request:int)
                                                returns (relevant :bool);
let
relevant = true ->
            if d_opened and t_run then false
            else if (stn_arrived = request) and not(t_stop) then false
            else true;
assert not(t_run and t_stop);
assert not(d_closed and d_opened);
tel
```

15.5 A Mine Pump Controller

The Mine pump controller's safety properties are generally related to the functioning of the various alarms, on detection of certain abnormal deviation of the parameters of the chemicals in the mine. Two simple properties would be:

- The m_alarm should be emitted when the methane level goes high.

- The c_alarm should be emitted when the carbon monoxide level exceeds the desirable limit.

The observer would look like:

```
node observer_pump(start,stop,methane,co,hw_level,lw_level,manual,auto,
                        p_run,p_stop,m_alarm,c_alarm:bool)
                                        returns (relevant : bool);
let
   relevant = true -> if methane and not(m_alarm) then false
                     else if co and not(c_alarm) then false
                     else true;
   assert not(p_run and p_stop);
   assert not(start and stop);
   assert not(hw_level and lw_level);
   assert not(auto and manual);
tel
```

Part V: Integration of Synchrony and Asynchrony

Summary

Programming languages that have been used for real-time programming can be broadly categorized into:

1. *Asynchronous Languages*: Here, a program is treated as a set of loosely coupled independent execution units or processes, each process evolving at its own pace. Interprocess communication is done by mechanisms such as message passing. Communication as a whole is *asynchronous* in the sense that *an arbitrary amount of time can pass between the desire of communication and its actual completion*. This class includes languages such as Ada, Occam, CSP etc.

2. *Perfectly Synchronous Languages*: In this class, programs react instantaneously to its inputs by producing the required outputs. Statements evolve in a tightly coupled input-driven way deterministically and communication is done by instantaneous broadcast where the receiver receives a message exactly at the time it is sent. That is, a perfectly synchronous program produces its outputs from its input with *no observable time delay*. Languages such as Esterel [12], Lustre, Signal, Statecharts belong to this category. These languages are often referred to as *reactive* languages. These languages use the multiform notion of time rather than clock time.

Programming languages based on the *perfect synchrony paradigm* have proven useful for programming reactive systems where determinism is a must and logical concurrency is required for good programming style. One of the main reasons for its success is due to the fact that it permits the programmer to focus on the logic of reactions and makes it possible to use several automata-based verification systems for correctness proofs. Further, the correctness proofs of programs follow their implementation very closely and hence, are more robust and reliable. On the other hand, asynchronous languages have proven useful in distributed processing and implementing algorithms on a network of computer systems where nondeterminism is an appropriate abstraction at the logical and physical levels. Presently, each class of languages is unable to handle problems to which the other class is tailored. Asynchronous languages are inappropriate for truly reactive systems that require deterministic synchronous (perfect) communication. On the other hand, existing synchronous languages lack support for asynchronous distributed algorithms. However, complex systems do require the abilities of both the languages. For instance, a robot driver must use a specific reactive program to control each articulation, but the global robot control may be necessarily asynchronous because of limitations of networking capabilities.

The chapter introduces the paradigm that combines the capabilities of both synchronous and asynchronous languages to describe such complex applications. One of the first models proposed in this paradigm is *Communicating Reactive Processes* (CRP) [13]. CRP is based upon ESTEREL and CSP. Subsequent to this formalism similar integrations have been proposed in the literature. Very recently another model called *Communicating Reactive State Machines* (CRSM) [71] have been developed. CRSM is pictorial and has intuitive appeal and is based upon State machine descriptions like Statecharts and Argos; asynchronous capabilities of CRSM is based upon CSP.

One of the issues of the CRP experiment is that it distinguishes the Esterel and network parallelism. This leads to issues in specifying hierarchical designs. This drawback has been overcome through an unified approach referred to as *Multiclock Esterel*[7, 67, 65, 66, 80]. Multiclock Esterel in a sense provides a unified approach for synchronous and asynchronous systems with multiple clocks. A similar formalism under the same name was reported in [14].

In this part, we shall be discussing about CRP[13], CRSM [71] and Multiclock Esterel as in [7].

Chapter 16

Communicating Reactive Processes

In this chapter, we present a programming paradigm called Communicating Reactive Processes (CRP) that was one of the first attempts to unify the capabilities of asynchronous and synchronous programming languages. Asynchronous languages such as CSP, OCCAM, or ADA are well-suited for distributed algorithms; their processes are loosely coupled and communication takes no time. ESTEREL synchronous language is dedicated to reactive systems; its processes are tightly coupled and deterministic, communication being realized by instantaneous broadcasting. Complex applications such as process or robot control require coupling of both forms of concurrency. This is the main objective of CRP. A CRP program consists of independent locally reactive ESTEREL nodes that communicate with each other by the CSP rendezvous/handshake communication mechanism. CRP faithfully extends both ESTEREL and CSP and adds new possibilities such as precise local watchdogs on rendezvous. In this paper, we present the design of CRP, its semantics, a translation into classical process calculi for program verification, an application example, and an outline of implementation.

16.1 An Overview of CRP

Programming languages that have been used for real-time programming can be broadly categorized into:

1. *Asynchronous Languages*: Here, a program is treated as a set of loosely coupled independent execution units or processes, each process evolv-

ing at its own pace. Interprocess communication is done by mechanisms such as message passing. Communication as a whole is *asynchronous* in the sense that *an arbitrary amount of time can pass between the desire of communication and its actual completion.* This class includes languages such as Ada, Occam, CSP etc.

2. *Perfectly Synchronous Languages*: In this class, programs react instantaneously to its inputs by producing the required outputs. Statements evolve in a tightly coupled input-driven way deterministically and communication is done by instantaneous broadcast where the receiver receives a message exactly at the time it is sent. That is, a perfectly synchronous program produces its outputs from its input with *no observable time delay*. Languages such as ESTEREL [12], Lustre, Signal, Statecharts belong to this category. These languages are often referred to as *reactive* languages. These languages use the multiform notion of time rather than clock time.

Programming languages based on the *perfect synchrony paradigm* have proven useful for programming reactive systems where determinism is a must and logical concurrency is required for good programming style. One of the main reasons for its success is due to the fact that it permits the programmer to focus on the logic of reactions and makes it possible to use several automata-based verification systems for correctness proofs. Further, the correctness proofs of programs follow their implementation very closely and hence, are more robust and reliable. On the other hand, asynchronous languages have proven useful in distributed processing and implementing algorithms on a network of computer systems where nondeterminism is an appropriate abstraction at the logical and physical levels. Presently, each class of languages is unable to handle problems to which the other class is tailored. Asynchronous languages are inappropriate for truly reactive systems that require deterministic synchronous (perfect) communication. On the other hand, existing synchronous languages lack support for asynchronous distributed algorithms. However, complex systems do require the abilities of both the languages. For instance, a robot driver must use a specific reactive program to control each articulation, but the global robot control may be necessarily asynchronous because of limitations of networking capabilities.

The chapter develops a new paradigm called *Communicating Reactive Processes* (CRP), where a set of individual reactive processes is linked by asynchronous communication channels. In other words, we unify languages ESTEREL and CSP. The unification preserves the spirit and semantics of both ESTEREL and CSP. Further, it also provides a rigorous semantics and implementation for constructs such as precise local watchdogs on asynchronous communications that are indispensable in practice bur are not properly supported by existing languages.

16.2 Communicating Reactive Processes: Structure

A programming paradigm called Communicating Reactive Processes or CRP that unifies the capabilities of asynchronous and synchronous concurrent programming languages is proposed with a view to specify complex reactive systems which usually have both synchronous and asynchronous features. A CRP program consists of independent locally reactive
Esterel nodes that communicate with each other by rendezvous communication as in Hoare's Communicating Reactive Processes. CRP faithfully extends both ESTEREL and CSP and adds new possibilities such as precise local watchdogs on rendezvous.

A CRP program consists of a network $M_1 \; // \; M_2 \; // \; M_n$ of ESTEREL reactive programs or *nodes*, each having its own input/output reactive signals and its own notion of an instant. The network is asynchronous (in the sense discussed earlier) and the nodes M_i is locally reactively driving a part of a complex network that is handled globally by the network. The central idea of establishing asynchronous communication between nodes lies in extending the basic `exec` primitive into a communication primitive. The usual `send` and `receive` asynchronous operations can be represented by particular tasks that handle the communication. Several `send` /`receive` interactions are possible according to various types of asynchronous communication. For instance, `send` can be non-blocking for full asynchrony, or `send` and `receive` can synchronize for CSP-like rendezvous communication. All choices can be implemented through ESTEREL.

Basic Rendezvous Statements

CRP nodes are linked by *channels*. We start by describing the pure synchronization case, where channels are symmetric. Pure channels are declared in CRP nodes by the declaration

    channel C;

A channel must be shared by exactly two nodes. Communication over the channels is handled by the statement

    rendezvous L:C

The label L is optional, an implicit distinct label being created if it is absent. The `rendezvous` statement is a particular instance of `exec` statement; as such, it defines three implicit reactive signals at a node: sL, L, and kL. the output signal sL requests for a rendezvous on C. Rendezvous completion is signaled to the node by the signal L. The signal kL signals abandoning the rendezvous request. A given channel can only perform one rendezvous at a time. Hence, in each node, the return signals of all the **rendezvous** statements on the same channel are implicitly assumed to be incompatible. Values can be passed through unidirectional channels.

16.2.1 Syntax of CRP

In the following, we describe the abstract syntax of CRP programs. We will not describe the syntax of ESTEREL statements for the sake of brevity; we will give the structure of kernel statements only.

```
< crp_prog >    ::=    < stat >   |  P // P
                       (* The usual ESTEREL  kernel statements *)
< stat >    ::=   nothing
                | halt
                | emit S
                | stat1; stat2
                | loop stat end
                | present S then stat1 else stat2 end
                | do stat watching S
                | stat1 || stat2
                | trap T in stat end
                | exit T
                | signal S in stat end

                | task task_id (par_lst)  return signal_nm (type)
                | exec task_id (par_lst)  return signal_name

                  (* Additional Statements in CRP *)
                  (* channel declaration *)
                | channel ch_name (type)
                          (* sending a value on the channel *)
                | rendezvous_send channel_id channel_name
                     (expression) return signal_name (some_type)

                          (* sending a value on the channel *)
                | rendezvous_receive channel_id channel_name
                     (variable) return signal_name (some_type)
```

The additional statements of CRP are the channel declarations and the rendezvous executions which are described below.

16.2. Communicating Reactive Processes: Structure

Channel Declaration

Channels are declared in CRP nodes by the declaration:

```
channel C (type)
```

A Channel is shared exactly by two nodes and the declarations should type-match.

Rendezvous Instantiation

The rendezvous in the sender is initiated through the command:

```
rendezvous_send channel_name (value_expression) return (some_type)
```

The rendezvous in the receiver is initiated through the command:

```
rendezvous_receive channel_name (variable) return (some_type)
```

The other explanations follow on the same lines as that of the task instantiation given above.

We use a construct for nondeterministic guard selection (note that nondeterministic guard selection can be done without introducing additional operator – this will be shown in the sequel) for convenience as shown below:

```
rend_case
    case  L1: rendezvous_receive channel1 (x) do stat_1
    case  L2: rendezvous_send channel2 (exp) do stat_2
end
```

The code corresponds to selecting a *receive* on channel1 followed by the execution of the statement-sequence *stat1* or *send* on channel2 followed by the execution of the statement-sequence *stat2*.

In CRP, the following discipline is enforced on the tasks with reference to sharing of signals and variables, in different processes of CRP:

- Processes on different nodes do not share variables.

- Processes on different nodes can share only pure input signals.

- Any two processes denoting nodes can share common channel signals.

16.2.2 Realizing Watchdog Timers in CRP

One of the advantages of integrating perfect synchrony and asynchrony is that one can provide precise watchdogs. This is illustrated below.

Watchdogs can be imposed on asynchronous communication, which cannot be done properly in the usual CSP-like languages. For instance, if S is an input reactive signal of a node M_i (say "second" or a "cancel" key), we can require a rendezvous request of M_i to be satisfied before S occurs, or else to be aborted. This is written

```
do
    rendezvous C
watching S
```

If S and the rendezvous return signal are simultaneous for the node, the rendezvous is considered to be completed by both parties, but its local effect is canceled by the watching statement. To avoid such tricky situations, it is often convenient to serialize rendezvous and reactive events, through the declaration of the input relations

```
    relation   S # L
```

Thus, using the above features one gets a precise semantics for constructs similar to the delayed/timed select-statements of Ada.

16.3 Behavioural Semantics of CRP

In this section, we extend the semantics of ESTEREL to CRP. Recall that the semantics of an ESTEREL was defined using the two relations: the primary module single step transition relation, $M \xrightarrow[I]{O} M'$ and the auxiliary statement single step relation $stat \xrightarrow[E]{E',L,k} stat'$ where I is an input event, O is the generated output event, M' is the resulting module; and stat, stat' are the statements of M, M' respectively, E is the current event to which $stat$ reacts, E' is the event emitted by $stat$ in response to E, L is the set of labels of the exec statements currently active in $stat$, and k is the termination level. We use the same relations to define the semantics of CRP. The label set now includes labels of rendezvous statements also. Further, the start and kill signals of rendezvous's may appear in E' and the return signals in E.

The semantics of ESTEREL is then extended by adding the following rules for the additional rendezvous statements:

Rules:

16.4. An Illustrative Example: Banker Teller Machine

rend_start

$$\text{rendezvous } L : P \xrightarrow[E]{sL,\{L\},1} rend\_wait\ L : P$$

rend_wait1

$$\frac{L \in E}{rend\_wait\ L : P \xrightarrow[E]{\emptyset,\emptyset,0} nothing}$$

rend_wait2

$$\frac{L \notin E}{rend\_wait\ L : P \xrightarrow[E]{\emptyset,L,1} rend\_wait\ L : P}$$

All other rules remain the same as in the case of ESTEREL with `exec` statements.

16.4 An Illustrative Example: Banker Teller Machine

To illustrate the CRP programming style, and in particular the respective use of local reactivity and asynchronous rendezvous, we present the example of a (simple-minded) banker teller machine in Figure 1. The machine is a CRP node assumed to be connected to another node, the bank. The machine reads a card, checks the code locally, and communicate by rendezvous with the bank to perform the actual transaction. During the whole process, the user can cancel the transaction by pressing a `Cancel` key.

The reactive interface is self-explanatory. The rendezvous interface consists of three valued channels. The output channels `CardToBank` and `AmountToBank` are used to send the card information and transaction amount. The input channel `Authorization` is used to receive a boolean telling whether the transaction is authorized. No rendezvous label is necessary here since there is exactly one `rendezvous` statement per channel.

The body repeatedly waits for a card and performs the transaction. The client- code checking section is purely local and reactive. When the valid code is read, one does two things in parallel; waiting locally for the amount typed by the client, and sending the card information to the bank using a rendezvous. When both these independent operations are completed, one sends the amount to the bank and waits for the authorization. If the return boolean is true, one instantaneously delivers the money and returns the card exactly when the authorization rendezvous is completed, to ensure transaction atomicity. During the full transaction, the user can press the `Cancel` key, in which case the transaction is gracefully abandoned, including the various rendezvous, and the card is returned. Since the bank considers the transaction to be performed when the Authorization rendezvous is completed, one must declare an exclusion relation between Authorization and Cancel to prevent these two events to happen simultaneously. The outer trap handles the abnormal cases of the transaction: the card is kept if the code is typed in incorrectly three times or if the transaction is not authorized. We use a full Esterel extension of the trap statement, in which one can write a trap handler to be activated when the trap is exited. This extension is easily derivable from kernel statements.

16.4. An Illustrative Example: Banker Teller Machine

```
module BankerTeller :
type CardInfo;  function CheckCode (CardInfo, integer): boolean;
input Card : CardInfo;
input Code : integer, Amount : integer;
input Cancel;
output GiveCode, EnterAmount;
output DeliverMoney : integer;
output KeepCard, ReturnCard;
output channel CardToBank : Cardinfo;
output channel AmountToBank : integer;
input channel Authorization : boolean;
relation Cancel # Authorization;
loop
   trap KeepCard in
      await Card; (* read and check code, at most three times*)
         do (* watching Cancel *)
            trap CodeOk in
               repeat 3 times
                  emit GiveCode;
                  await Codep;
                  if CorrectCode(?Card, ?Code) then exit CodeOk end
               end repeat;
            exit KeepCard    (*   failed 3 times !*)
            end trap;
            [
             rendezvous CardToBank(?Card); (* send card to bank*)
                ||
             emit EnterAmount;           (* local dialogue*)
             await Amount;
            ];
            rendezvous AmountToBank(?Amount);(* send amount to bank*)
            rendezvous Authorization;(* receive authorization:boolean *)
               if ?Authorization then
                   emit DeliverMoney (?Amount)
               else
                   exit KeepCard
               end if
         watching Cancel    (* user explicit cancel at any time *)
         emit ReturnCard
      handle KeepCard do
         emit KeepCard
   end trap
end loop
```

Figure 1: The Banker Teller Program

16.5 Implementation of CRP

A series of compilers have been developed at ENSMP-INRIA for ESTEREL with and without the 'exec' primitive; the most recent one is the 'v4' compiler which handles 'exec' as well as some new constructs like 'sustain' and 'suspend'. All these compiler translate ESTEREL programs into deterministic automata. Using one of these compilers, ESTEREL nodes of CRP can be compiled to get a set of automata that communicate with each other using the CSP rendezvous mechanism. It is well-known in the literature of CSP implementation that when output guards are allowed the implementation is quite non trivial [18]. There have been many attempts to obtain efficient implementation for CSP with output guards [18, 68, 5]. We have shown in an earlier section that CRP can simulate output nondeterminism, and hence implementation of CRP also is difficult. However, implementation of CRP is not any more difficult and existing CSP implementations can be directly adapted to CRP. Here we sketch an implementation of CRP which is based on the CSP implementation described in [68].

The implementation of CRP involves a network of nodes each of which runs a ESTEREL process of the CRP program. The execution of a rendezvous requires synchronization of the involved programs in the sense that if one program wants to execute the send statement then the other should be ready to execute *at the same time* the receive statement. This would require exchange of a number of control messages between ESTEREL nodes before the actual communication can take place. The implementation essentially consists of arriving at what types of control messages are required and how and in what sequence they should be exchanged. To a greater extent, exchange of control messages can go on in parallel with the local ESTEREL computations. Hence, we assume that each node, in addition to the ESTEREL program, has a control process which handles the control messages. The control processes would be running all the time in parallel with the local ESTEREL programs and know their states (as to whether they require rendezvous or not).

We make the following assumptions about the the network:

- The nodes are connected to each other via point-to-point communication links.

- The point-to-point links are bidirectional and any control process can communicate with other control processes in other nodes via these links , either directly or through one or more processes.

- A (control) process wishing to send (or receive) a message to (from)

16.5. Implementation of CRP

another would execute a non blocking send command (blocking receive) whose effect would be to transfer the message to (from) the network queues. For the sake of simplicity,we assume that the queues are unbounded so that sends are never blocked while receive would be blocked when the queue is empty.

- The communication network neither corrupt, lose nor change the order in which the messages are exchanged between a pair of nodes.

- The nodes are numbered with distinct natural numbers.

The assumption that the communication network does not change the order of messages is made only for the ease of description of the implementation and not necessary for the working of the implementation. The assumption that the nodes are numbered with distinct numbers is very crucial as it helps in avoiding deadlocks; a more general condition would be to assume that the nodes are labelled with identifiers that are partially ordered.

At any stage of computation, a control process need to know the state of the corresponding ESTEREL process; for instance, a control process should make an attempt to select a rendezvous provided the corresponding ESTEREL process is ready for it. We assume that such exchange of information is done by means of shared variables: i.e., a control process and the corresponding ESTEREL process may have certain variables which are read/written by both the processes.

Now we describe the behavior of the control processes.

Let $M_1//M_2//\cdots//M_n$ be the CRP programs and P_i be the control process corresponding to M_i. All P_is run autonomously and by means of control messages determine which rendezvous can be executed and enable the ESTEREL processes to select the right rendezvous. There should be an agreement over the selection because when a 'send' action of a rendezvous is selected by one process, the corresponding 'receive' action should be selected by the other process. We would like to have a good distributed solution to the problem in which all the control processes are symmetric with no single controller having complete knowledge about the states of the various nodes. More specifically, we provide a solution that has the following properties:

1. The processes involved in establishing a communication between two processes are just the two processes concerned.

2. The amount of system information that any process knows is minimal; a process knows the states of only those processes that may involve in a rendezvous with it.

3. The number of messages exchanged for making a communication is bounded.

4. When two processes are ready to enter into a rendezvous, then at least one of them establishes a rendezvous (not necessarily with the other one) in a finite time.

Now we proceed to describe the solution. In this solution, each control process P_i, is in one of the following states: E-state, W-state and two intermediate states called Q1- and Q2- states. Initially P_i is in E-state. In this state, it is constantly inspecting the state of M_i. When M_i wishes to make one or more rendezvous,

P_i *tentatively selects* one of these rendezvous commands to see whether it can be realized. Suppose that this rendezvous requires the participation of the process M_j. Then P_i transits to Q1-state and proceeds to get the consent for selecting the command, from P_j and itself!. It should be noted that the fact that P_i tentatively makes a selection does not mean that it has agreed to the selection. This is because when it is waiting to get the consent of P_j, it may agree with another process for selecting another command. This happens because the process of reaching agreement is highly asynchronous and follows the discipline given below.

We shall say that P_j is captured by P_i, whenever the former agrees with the latter to select a rendezvous. Note that this involves first a request message by P_i to P_j followed by a 'yes' message by P_j to P_i. In order to select a rendezvous, P_i should first capture itself and P_j. The following discipline is followed for capturing processes:

1. A process can capture itself, only if it is free(i.e. not captured by any one).

2. A process can capture another process, only if the latter is free and is ready to engage in the rendezvous.

3. The capturing of the two processes is done in steps and in the strict ordering of process indices, i.e., if P_j and P_k are the two processes(one of which is P_i itself) to be captured by P_i, where $j < k$, then P_i captures first P_j and then P_k; P_i does not even attempt to capture P_k until it captures P_j .

P_i may be delayed when trying to capture a process P_j(which may be itself) that is already captured by some other process.P_i will eventually get a response from P_j saying that its attempt is successful or not depending

16.5. Implementation of CRP

upon whether P_j is freed by its captor or P_j makes the transition to the E-state. If P_i's attempt fails then it frees the already captured process, if any, and makes a fresh attempt to select another rendezvous, if any. If all the rendezvous have been tried, in vain for selection, P_i transits to W-state. In this state, it remains ready to select any of the enabled commands but does not make any attempt on its own to select a command.

It may be noted that, since only the capturing conditions (1),(2) and (3) given above are to be satisfied to capture a process, P_i may be captured by another process when it is attempting to capture a process. An important point to be noted is that any request to capture a process is *definitely answered eventually*. The definite answer is got thanks to the capturing condition (3), which states that capturing is done in strict sequencing. This avoids the formation of circular chain of delayed processes waiting for each others' response.

When P_i succeeds in capturing both the concerned processes, it is clear that both the captured processes are willing to involve in a rendezvous and have not agreed to some other rendezvous. Now the job of P_i would be to signal the concerned processes to go ahead with the rendezvous. However, one complication arises: the ESTEREL nodes are executing independently of control processes and as part of their computations they could kill the rendezvous actions. Hence P_i has to get the confirmation before it signals the 'go-ahead' signal. The confirmation is got in the state Q2, in the same way as the initial agreement (and hence the behavior of P_i in Q2 state is similar to that in Q1 state): P_i sends the confirmation requests first to the lower-index process and then to the higher-index process. The concerned processes, in turn, respond to these confirmation requests, either positively or otherwise depending upon their states. To avoid infinite regress, a process after confirming should not kill the rendezvous. So, when a process confirms a rendezvous the ESTEREL computation is 'frozen'. When P_i receives a confirm message from both the processes it goes over to the E-state directing the other captured process to go to the E-state. This also releases the frozen ESTEREL computation. However, if one of the processes does not confirm the rendezvous then P_i sends the failure message to the other process and quits to state Q1. The two captured processes are then released as well as the frozen ESTEREL computation.

The proof of correctness of this solution and the fact that this solution satisfies the desired properties follow along the lines of that of the implementation of CSP [68]; complete details are given in [70].

A socket level implementation which constrains the pre-emption as required for consistency across asynchronous networks is discussed in [64, 8].

It describes protocols that would ensure consistency of the distributed implementation in the context of pre-emptions.

Chapter 17

Semantics of Communicating Reactive Processes

In this chapter, we shall describe the trace theory based semantics of CRP. First, we shall provide an overview and semantics of CSP

17.1 A Brief Overview of CSP

We assume the knowledge of CSP [45]. For the sake of simplicity, we do not consider boolean guards, hiding and distributed termination convention in this paper.
Notation:

1. Channels are unidirectional and connect at most two processes. The channels are usually denoted by lower case letters such as d,h etc. possibly subscripted.

2. There are no shared variables among the processes.

The syntax of the language is given below:

P ::= S | P // P
S ::= x:=e | g | $S_1; S_2$ | $[\![_{i=1}^n g_i \rightarrow S_i]\!]$ | $*[\![_{i=1}^n g_i \rightarrow S_i]\!]$
g ::= h!e | h?x

17.2 Translation of CSP to CRP

In this section, we give a translation of CSP into CRP.

1. **Assignment**
   T(x:=e) = x:=e

2. **Send Command**
   T(h!e) = rend_send h($[\![e]\!]$)
   where L is the label given to the rendezvous on channel h (declaration is included in the module definitions of the process).

3. **Receive Command**
   T(h?x) = rend_receive L: h($[\![x]\!]$)
   where L is the label given to this rendezvous on channel h (declaration is included in the module definitions of the process). In fact, we could even avoid an explicit variable as the implicit variable of ESTEREL "?h" would have the value received provided this is used before the next rendezvous on h.

4. **Sequencing**
   $T(S_1; S_2) = [\![S_1]\!]; [\![S_2]\!]$

5. **Guarded Selection Command**
   For the sake of simplicity, we show the translation of the guarded command having only two guards shown below; we assume L1 and L2 as the labels given to the rendezvous on channels h1 and h2.

   T ([h_1?X → S_1 ❘ h_2!e → S_2]) =

```
            trap T0 in
              trap T1 in
                trap T2 in
                    rend_receive L1: h1;
                    exit T1
                ||
                    rend_send L2: h2([ e ]);
                    exit T2
                end;
                [ S₂ ]];
                exit T0
              end;
              X:= ?L1;
              [ S₁ ]
            end;
```

17.2. Translation of CSP to CRP

where $[\![S]\!]$ is the translation of S.

The two communications are requested simultaneously when the `rendezvous` statements are started. Assume that `h1` is completed first. Rendezvous provokes instantaneous termination of "`rend_receive L1: h1`" and hence, it exits trap T1 immediately; the immediate exit of T1 provokes abortion of the other pending request "`rend_send L2: h2(...)`" (effected by sending the kill signal $kL2$ as can be seen from the earlier explanation as well as the rules given later. Again from the trap-constructs, it can be seen that the appropriate continuation of $[\![S_1]\!]$ is taken after assigning the value received to the variable X. Conversely, if `h2` is done first, then T2 is exited, signal $kL1$ is emitted leading to the abortion of the other rendezvous. The statement "exit T0" is necessary to avoid executing $[\![S_1]\!]$.

It may be easily seen from the translation that there is no explicit need of an explicit nondeterministic operator. However, for the convenience of programming, it is preferable to have a construct in which one can express the possibility of a choice at a point. Such a concrete syntax follows on the lines of the syntax of the await-case-statement of ESTEREL. For instance, the choice corresponding to the CSP program given above is expressed in CRP as follows:

```
rendezvous
    case L1: rend_receive h1(X) do  S₁
    case L2: rend_send h2(e) do  S₂
end
```

In fact, it possible to do away with the variable X if need be as the ?h1 can be used in place of X.

6. Iterative Statement

As we are ignoring the distributed termination convention, the translation follows from the guarded-statement; essentially one introduces a loop-statement inside a trap containing the translation of the underlying guarded statement. The outermost trap-statement handles the termination of the guarded statement taking into account the boolean part of the guards.

7. Programs

Let $P = P_1 \| \cdots \| P_n$. Then,

$T(P)$ = module Main
            channel ... declarations ...
            exclusion .... relation ...
            $T(P_1)$ || $T(P_2)$ $\cdots$ $T(P_n)$
          end main.

17.3 Cooperation of CRP Nodes

Given the set C of channels declared in a node, the projection I/C of an input event I on C is defined as the set of channels in C having a return signal in I (notice that there is at most one return signal for a given channel in I because of the implicit label exclusions.

The projection on C of an history $I_0 \cdot .O_0, \cdots, I_n \cdot .O_n, \cdots$ is the sequence on nonempty I_i/C that represents the communication history over C; formally, using "$\bullet$" to add an element at the head of a list:

$$(I.O \bullet H)/C = I/C \bullet H/C \text{ if } I/C \neq \emptyset$$
$$= H/C \text{ otherwise}$$

An *execution* of a set of nodes $\{M_i | i \in I\}$ is a set of ESTEREL histories H_i, one for each node M_i, events must match for each channel between any two nodes.

Formally, for any distinct i and j, if C_{ij} is the set of all common channels between M_i and M_j, then one must have $H/_i/C_{ij} = H_j/C_{ij}$.

In the following, we show that the ready-trace semantics is embedded in the CRP semantics described above.

17.4 Ready-Trace Semantics of CRP

In this section, we shall first briefly describe the classical ready-trace semantics due to [OlHo83] and define the ready-trace semantics of CRP by showing how the semantics can be extracted from the behavioural semantics of CRP.

17.5 Ready-Trace Semantics of CSP

The ready-trace semantics [45] is compositional and associates with any component of a CSP program (be it a sequential process or a parallel composition of sequential processes), a set of computation histories. A computation history records details like the values exchanged via different channels and the channels at which a process is ready to send/receive values. More precisely, a history is a finite sequence of sets of elements (communication assumption records) of the form:

1. **Communication Assumptions:** These assumptions can be interpreted as the possible communication actions in some environment. For each

17.5. Ready-Trace Semantics of CSP

channel $c \in CHAN$, for every value v in the value space, $<c,v>$ denotes the fact the value v has been sent/received via c.

2. **Ready_actions**: This assumption can be interpreted as the possible set of actions that a process is ready to perform (but not yet performed – can also denote waiting for the progress of the communication). This is indicated by R_A where A is subset of channel names. As the channels are unidirectional, there is no need to distinguish the sending or the receiving end of channels. Note that, R_ϕ denotes a deadlock as the process is not ready to do any action including local action.

3. **Local actions**: Local actions could result in state change; however, they do not affect the history.

Let us denote the set of histories by $\mathcal{H}$. Then $\mathcal{H}$ is given by

$$\mathcal{H} = (\mathcal{P}_{fin}(\{R_A | A \subseteq_{fin} CHAN\} \cup \{<c,v> | c \in CHAN, v \in Val\}))^*$$

where $\subseteq_{fin}$ is a finite subset relation, $\mathcal{P}_{fin}$ denotes finite subset operator and Val is the set of values that can be exchanged via channels.

Notations:

1. Typical elements in $\mathcal{H}$ are denoted by h with possible subscripts and superscripts.

2. $|h|$ denotes the length (the number of elements) in history h.

3. *epsilon* denotes the empty history.

The semantic mapping $\mathcal{S}em$ is given by

$$\mathcal{S}em : Prog \times State \rightarrow \mathcal{P}(\mathcal{H} \times State \cup \{\bot\})$$

where $State : (Var \rightarrow Val)$ with Var being the set of variables. Given a program p and a state s, $\mathcal{S}em(p,s)$ is the prefix-closed set of all pairs (h,s') where h is the history of all finite computations of p starting in the initial state s. s' is $\bot$ if h denotes a partial computation; otherwise, it is the final state of the computation corresponding to h. $\mathcal{S}em(p,s)$ is prefix-closed in the sense that whenever it has a pair (h,s) then it has also the pair $(h',\bot)$ where $|h'| < |h|$, and for each $j \leq |h'|$, $h'(j) = h(j)$. We use the usual prefix-closure function PFC which given any arbitrary subset $A \in \mathcal{P}(\mathcal{H} \times State \cup \{\bot\})$, yields the least prefix-closed set containing A. In the sequel, PFC denotes the least prefix-closed operator on sets.

17.5.1 Semantic Definition

Now, we give the semantics of the important constructs of the language.

For the sake of brevity, we use an auxiliary semantics function $\mathcal{M}$ to define the semantic equations such that,

$$Sem(p)s = PFC(\mathcal{M}(p)s).$$

We shall proceed to give the definition of $\mathcal{M}$ for each p.

Notation:

1. h with possible subscripts is used for denoting histories in $\mathcal{H}$.

2. $|h|$ denotes the length of the history h.

3. $h \uparrow S$ denotes the projection of h onto the elements in the set S.

4. We use *comm* to denote the communications over channels and *ready* to denote the waiting actions of the form R_A for some $A \subset CHAN$.

17.5.2 Semantics of Parallel Composition

Let $chan_1$ and $chan_2$ denote the set of channels in S_1 and S_2 respectively and let $chan$ be the set of channels in $S_1 || S_2$. Let *Channel* be a function from histories to set of channels ; $channel(h)$ yields the set of channels referred in the history, h. Then,

$$\begin{aligned}
\mathcal{M}(S_1||S_2)s = \{(h, s_1 \cup s_2)| \; & h_1 = h \uparrow chan_1, \; h_2 = h \uparrow chan_2, \\
& chan \subseteq chan_1 \cup chan_2, \; channel(h) \subseteq chan, \\
& (h_1, s_1) \in \mathcal{M}(S_1)s, (h_1, s_2) \in \mathcal{M}(S_2)s, \\
& h_1 \uparrow cset = h_2 \uparrow cset, \\
& (s_1 = s_2 = \bot) \Rightarrow |h_1| = |h_2|\}
\end{aligned}$$

where *cset* is the set of channel names common to S_1, S_2, and s_1, s_2 are state functions defined over disjoint sets of variables to value domains and $s_1 \cup s_2$ denotes the *strict* function that combines these two state functions in the usual way.

17.5.3 Semantics of 'send' Action

$$\begin{aligned}
\mathcal{M}(c!e)s = \{&(h, \bot)| \; h =< \{R_{c!}\} >\} \\
\cup \{&(h, s)| h =< \{R_{c!}\} >< \{c!s[e]\} >\}
\end{aligned}$$

17.5. Ready-Trace Semantics of CSP

17.5.4 Semantics of 'receive' Action

$\mathcal{M}(c?x)s = \{(h, \perp)|\ h =< \{R_{c?}\} >\}$
$\cup \{(h, s')|\ h =< \{R_{c?}\} >< \{c?v\} >, s' = s[x/v], v \in Val\}$

17.5.5 Semantics of Assignment Statement

$$\mathcal{M}(x := e)s = \{(\epsilon, s')|\ s' = s[x/e]\}$$

17.5.6 Semantics of Sequential Composition

$\mathcal{M}(S_1; S_2)s = \{(h, \perp)|(h, \perp) \in \mathcal{M}(S_1)s\}$
$\cup \{(h_1; h_2, s')|\exists s'' : (h_1, s'') \in \mathcal{M}(S_1)s, s'' \neq \perp, (h_2, s') \in \mathcal{M}(S_2)s''\}$

where $h_1; h_2$ is defined as follows:

$$\begin{aligned} h_1; h_2(i) &= h_1(i), \text{ for } i = 1, \cdots, |h_1| \\ &= h_2(k), \text{ for } i = |h_1| + k, k \geq 1 \end{aligned}$$

17.5.7 Semantics of Guarded Selection

A compositional semantics for guarded selection can be obtained by defining semantics of the guard in the context of other guards. We illustrate the semantics of guarded selection by an example:

```
S ::     [d!e  → S_1
         ⫾
          c?x  → S_2
         ]
```
Then,

$\mathcal{M}(S)s = \{(h, \perp)|\ h = \{< R_{\{c,d\}} >\}\}$
$\cup \{(h; h', s')|h = \{< R_{\{c,d\}} >\}\{< d, \mathcal{V}[e] >\}, (h', s') \in \mathcal{M}(S_1)s\}$
$\cup \{(h; h', s'')|h = \{< R_{\{c,d\}} >\}\{< c, v >\}, (h', s'') \in \mathcal{M}(S_2)s',$
$s' = s[x/v], v \in Val\}$

The semantics of iteration can be obtained by essentially using the least fix point operator in the semantics of guarded selection.

17.6 Extracting CSP Ready-trace Semantics from CRP Semantics

First, we define the behavioral traces of CRP programs.

17.6.1 Behavioural Traces of CRP Programs

Definition 3 *An event $E = S_1(v_1) \cdot S_2(v_2) \cdots S_n(v_n)$, $n \geq 0$, is a set of signals that are simultaneously emitted with the corresponding values. If S appears in E with value v, we write $S \in E$, $S(v) \in E$, and $E(S) = v$. Otherwise, we write $S \notin E$. The empty event is denoted ϵ and it contains no signal.*

Note: Events only contain positive information about emitted signals. For details about modelling complete events, the reader is referred to [12].

Definition 4 *An execution sequence $H = <E_0, s_0>, <E_1, s_1>, \cdots, <E_n, s_n> \cdots$ is a possible infinite sequence of event-state pairs satisfying the declared exclusion relations. If the sequence is infinite, then all the s_i's are nothing but $\bot$. $H[n]$ denotes the finite history $<E_0, s_0>, <E_1, s_1>, \cdots, <E_n, s_n>$.*

Definition 5 *The behaviour, $\mathcal{B}$, of a program P starting from state s is given by all the finite prefixes of the set of all execution sequences of P denoted by $\mathcal{H}$.*

First we abstract a ready-trace behaviour of the CSP program from the CRP program by ignoring some of the *input signals* and substituting the *ready* and *communication* alphabets in the traces appropriately.
Notation:

1. Let $M[\![P]\!]$ be the ready-trace semantics of P.

2. Let $\mathcal{B}[\![P_{crp}]\!]s$ where s is the starting state of P_{crp} be the behavioral semantics of P_{crp}. If H is an execution sequence in $\mathcal{B}[\![P_{crp}]\!]s$, then $H(i)$ denotes the behaviour at the ith instant.

3. Let $events(P_j)$ be the set of all input events of process j.

4. Let $\mathcal{B} \uparrow events(P_j)$ denote the projection of $\mathcal{B}$ onto the input events of $events(P_j)$.

17.6. Extracting CSP Ready-trace Semantics from CRP Semantics

5. Let H^1 and H^2 denote the sequences obtained from H with reference to the first and the second components respectively.

6. Let *Last* be the function which yields the last element of the sequence if nonempty and yields

Any behavior of a CRP node is structurally different from a ready trace; a behavior contains information about the presence and absence of signals whereas a ready trace contains information specific to communication across channels; However, the information contained in both of them are equivalent and one can get a ready trace corresponding to a behavior trace and vice versa. The information that there is a communication via a channel C is represented in the ready trace by including this action in the communication assumption component of the corresponding record; whereas this information is captured in the behavioral trace by having the corresponding input signal C in the record. In contrast, the ready-sets are represented indirectly in behavioral traces: if a process is ready to communicate but yet to do so because of its partner being not ready then the signal sC must have been initiated some times before but so far neither the signal kC nor C signal has been received.

Definition 6 *We shall define a function rtrace that takes a behavior trace and gives the corresponding ready trace. $rtrace(H)$ is defined to be a ready trace, H', of the same length as that of H such that for each $i \leq |H|$,*

$$H'[i]^1 = H[i]^1 \cup \\ \{C | C/inCHAN, \exists j \leq i : (sC \in H[j]^1 \wedge \forall j < n \leq i : kC \notin H[n]^1)\} \\ \cup \{C | C \in CHAN, C \in H[i]^1\}$$

$$H'[i]^2 = H[i]^2$$

Now we can define a ready-trace semantics for each node as a 'point-wise' extension of *rtrace* on sets of behavior traces.

Definition 7 *Let us denote this mapping by $\mathcal{M}$. For any CRP node P,*

$$\mathcal{M}(P) = rtrace(H) | H \in \{\mathcal{B}(P)\}$$

Now we are ready for defining the ready-trace semantics of the entire CRP program. This semantics, also denoted by $\mathcal{M}$ is given for two nodes as follows:

Let $chan_1, chan_2$ denote the set of channels in two CRP nodes P_1, P_2 respectively. Let *Channel* be a function from histories to set of channels such that $channel(h)$ is the set of channels referred in h. Then,

$$\mathcal{M}(P_1//P_2) = \{(h,s) | h_1 = h \uparrow chan_1, h_2 = h \uparrow chan_2,$$
$$channel(h) \subseteq chan_1 \cup chan_2$$
$$(h_1, s_1) \in \mathcal{M}(P_1)s, (h_2, s_2) \in \mathcal{M}(P_2)s,$$
$$h_1 \uparrow cset = h_2 \uparrow cset$$
$$(s_1 = s_2 = \perp) \Rightarrow |h_1| = |h_2|\}$$

where $cset$ is the set of channel names common to P_1 and P_2 and s_1, s_2 are state functions defined over disjoint sets of variables to value domains and $s_1 \cup s_2$ denotes the *strict* function that combines the two state functions in the usual way.

The extension of the above definition to the general case of n-node CRP program is straightforward.

The extension of the above definition to the general case of n-node CRP program is straightforward.

17.7 Correctness of the Translation

Let P be an arbitrary CSP program and P' its translation into CRP. Further let $\mathcal{M}, \mathcal{M}'$ be the ready-trace semantic function of CSP and CRP programs respectively, as defined in the previous sections.

The aim of this section is to show the equivalence of P and P'. Consider the ready traces of P and P'. They are not exactly identical for a minor reason that the ready traces of P are over CSP communication events while that of P' are over ESTEREL input/output events. Also, CRP semantics contains rendezvous initiation signals which are abstracted out of CSP semantics; the latter contains only rendezvous completion events. So first we abstract out the CRP ready traces so that they are over the same alphabet as that of CSP traces.

Let τ' be a ready trace of P'. Then, $Abs(\tau)$ is a CSP ready trace obtained from τ by removing any occurrence of rendezvous signals, replacing completion signals by the corresponding channel names and finally removing any empty records. To define this formally, first let us define Abs on individual record. Given a record r of a CRP trace, let $Abs(r)$ is the record obtained from r by removing all occurrences of rendezvous initiation signals and kill signals and replacing all occurrences of rendezvous completion signals by the corresponding channel names. Note that, $Abs(r)$ could be empty. Now we define Abs on traces as follows.

Definition 8

$$Abs(\epsilon) = \epsilon$$

17.7. Correctness of the Translation

$$Abs(r \bullet \tau) = Abs(tau), \quad \text{if} \quad Abs(r) = \emptyset$$
$$Abs(r \bullet \tau) = Abs(r) \bullet Abs(tau), \quad \text{if} \quad Abs(r) \neq \emptyset$$

Abs can be extended 'pointwise' to sets of CRP traces and we denote this extension by *Abs* itself.

Now we can state the main result of this section.

Theorem 1 *Suppose P, P' are a CSP program and its translation into CRP respectively. Then*

$$\mathcal{M}(P) = Abs(\mathcal{M}'(P'))$$

The proof of this result requires a few lemmata.

Lemma 1 *(Merging Lemma for CSP) Take any ready trace, τ, in $\mathcal{M}(P)$, where P is the CSP program given by $P1//\cdots//Pn$. Then there exists ready-traces τ_i in $\mathcal{M}(P_i)$, for each $i = 1, \cdots n$ respectively such that $\tau|_{Pi} = \tau_i$. That is, informally, any ready-trace of P is obtainable by merging ready-traces of the component terms $P1, \cdots Pn$.*

The proof is by induction on the length of the history.

It is not necessary that the lengths of the histories (τ_i) need not be the same. But we will assume without any loss of generality that the lengths are the same by adding null actions at suitable places in the traces.

Lemma 2 *(Merging Lemma for CRP) Take any ready-trace, τ, of a CRP program $\mathcal{M}'(P')$, where P' is a CRP program given by $P'1//\cdots//P'n$. Then there exists ready-traces τ_i in $\mathcal{M}'(P'_i)$, for each $i = 1, \cdots n$ respectively such that $\tau|_{P'i} = \tau_i$.*

The proof is by again induction on the length of the history.

As before, we shall assume that the local histories are of equal length.

The ready traces of the processes in CSP and CRP related by the following lemma:

Lemma 3 *For any CSP process P_i in P, we have that*

$$\mathcal{M}(P_i) = Abs(\mathcal{M}'(P'_i))$$

Proof: *The proof of this lemma is by induction on the process structure of P_i.*

It is easy to see that the proof of the main theorem follows directly from the above lemmata.

17.8 Translation into MEIJE Process Calculus

The cooperation semantics is not really constructive, in the sense that it does not tell how to execute programs. We now give an implementation of Pure CRP into Boudol's process calculus MEIJE [22, 17]. We choose this calculus because it is able to handle synchrony and asynchrony, which is not possible in less powerful calculi such as CCS. In addition to an implementation of CRP in a classical process calculus, the MEIJE translation provides us with an automatic program verification environment since MEIJE is accepted as input by verification systems such as AUTO [77]. For full CRP programs dealing with values, an approximate translation into MEIJE is feasible by ignoring value handling and only retaining the synchronization skeleton. This can still be useful for proving synchronization properties.

In the sequel, we assume that the reader is familiar with the definition of automata in process calculi using tail- recursive processes.

The actions in MEIJE consist of the free commutative group over a set of elementary signals s. Its elements are products of positive or negative elementary actions $s!$ and $s?$ with $s!.s? = 1$ (these notations point out the ESTEREL reactive input/output directionality better than the more usual s and $\bar{s}$). Prefixing in MEIJE is written ':', the symbol '.' being reserved for instantaneous action product. The only other things one should know about MEIJE is the behavior of the parallel and restriction operators.

MEIJE **Operators:**

MEIJE actions consist of a free commutative group over a set of elementary signals s. Its elements are products of positive or negative elementary actions s and $\bar{s}$ with $s \cdot \bar{s} = 1$. Prefixing in MEIJE is written ':', and the symbol '.' is used usually for instantaneous product. It may be pointed out that ':' is the operator used for *prefixing* in synchronous calculi such as SCCS[54] and MEIJE[22] and '.' is the operator for *prefixing* in asynchronous calculi such as CCS[54]; the distinction is made explicit so that there is no confusion as to whether one wants the capability to wait between its actions or not.

We say the set of actions, α is in *reduced form* if there are no pairs of the form s, $\bar{s}$ in α. In other words, we can get a reduced form of α by equating every pair of the form $s \cdot \bar{s}$ by the identity denoted, 1. Note that, $\alpha \cdot s \cdot \bar{s} = \alpha$ (as it is a commutative structure, the other combinations follow).

The most important aspects from the behavioral aspects are the parallel, ticking and restriction operators. If $P \xrightarrow{a} P'$ and $Q \xrightarrow{b} Q'$ then $P\|Q \xrightarrow{a} P'\|Q$, $P\|Q \xrightarrow{b} P\|Q'$, and $P\|Q \xrightarrow{a \cdot b} P'\|Q'$. Further, if $P \xrightarrow{a} P'$, then $P\backslash s \xrightarrow{a} P'\backslash s$

17.8. Translation into MEIJE Process Calculus

provided neither s nor $\bar{s}$ appear in the *reduced form* of a. The *ticking* is an operator that allows to synchronize on each behavioral step of an agent, without prejudging on the nature of its behaviour. The *ticking*, denoted, $s * P$ is defined by:

$$\frac{P \xrightarrow{\alpha} P'}{s * P \xrightarrow{s \cdot \alpha} s * P'}$$

(17.1)

Operationally the *ticking* operator can be interpreted as: all the actions of P are linked to action s. Hence, it could be treated as the clock of P or could be treated as the synchronizer for P from an external observation.

MEIJE Automaton

We start by translating each node M_i. Since ESTEREL programs are finite-state, the ESTEREL code at M_i can be readily translated into a MEIJE automaton A_i. This is actually done by the standard ESTEREL compiler. All exclusion relations are taken care of in the following way: only input events that satisfy the relations appear in the automaton. Since all rendezvous return signals for a given channel are exclusive, any MEIJE action appearing in A_i contains at most one return signal for each channel, even if there may be several simultaneously active rendezvous on this channel in the source code.

Computing Ready-Sets:

To compute the ready sets at P_i, we use an auxiliary automaton for each rendezvous label lab of channel C. Assume that C links node P_i with another node P_j and call $L(lab, i)$ the automaton defined as a copy of the automaton L of Figure 17.8 as defined by the following renaming:

$$L(lab, i) = L[slab/s, klab/k, lab/l, c!/c] \text{ if } i < j$$

$$L(lab, i) = L[slab/s, klab/k, c?/c] \text{ if } i > j$$

Node Translation:

To complete the node translation, we put all the L_i automata of channel labels used by M_i in parallel with the A_i automaton and hide all the sL, kL, and L signals. Let $[\![M_i]\!]$ denote the translation of the node M_i. The sort of $[\![M_i]\!]$ contains the ESTEREL reactive input/output signals of M_i and the

Chapter 17. Semantics of Communicating Reactive Processes

channels. If a channel C links M_i and M_j, $i < j$, then the MEIJE signal C appears positively in $[\![M_i]\!]$ and negatively in $[\![M_i]\!]$.

To translate the full CRP network we put all the CRP nodes translations in parallel and hide all the channels. In the final translation, the nodes evolve asynchronously of each other except on rendezvous where they share an instant, in the sense that perform a single compound MEIJE transition.

As an example, consider a rendezvous between M_1 and M_2 on a channel C, with labels $L1$ for M_1 and $L2$ for M_2. The node automaton A_1 performs a compound action of the form $a_1.L1?$, where a_1 may itself be some compound action of M_1 involving its reactive signals or other rendezvous; the label automaton L_1 performs the action $L1!C!$; hence the node automaton $[\![M_1]\!]$ must perform $a_1.C! = a_1.L1?.L1!.C!$ since $L1$ is hidden. Symmetrically, at node M_2, A_2 performs an action $a_2.L2?$, L_2 performs $L2!.c!$, and $[\![M_2]\!]$ performs $a_2.C?$ Since C is hidden in the global network, M_1 and M_2 must perform their actions synchronously and the resulting action is the synchronous product $a_1.a_2 = a_1.C!.a_2.C?$ of the local actions of M_1 and M_2.

Of course, such a rendezvous can occur only when both M_1 and M_2 are ready for it. This is just what is computed by the auxiliary label automata. In general CRP, several rendezvous can happen at the same time in the network, and even between the same two nodes on different channels; this is correctly modeled in MEIJE by instantaneous action products.

Now let us formalize the above idea. First a few definitions and notations: Let P be the CRP program with $P_i, i = 1, \cdots, n$ being the constituent ESTEREL nodes. Let L_i be the set of all rendezvous labels in P_i and $L = \cup_i L_i$. Suppose that t_i is the meije term corresponding to P_i. Further, let t'_i be the meije term consisting of parallel composition of label automata corresponding to the labels in L_i. That is,

$$t'_i = //_{l \in L_i} L(l, i)$$

Now let $[\![P_i]\!]$ denote the translation of the CRP process P_i. Then

$$[\![P_i]\!] = [t_i//t'_i] \backslash L_i$$

In order to prove the main result of this section, we need the following two lemmata:

Lemma 4 Merging Lemma for Meije: *Take any history, τ, of a meije term $t = t1// \cdots //tn$. Then there exists histories τ_i of $t_i, i = 1, \cdots n$ respectively such that $\tau|_{ti} = \tau_i$. That is, informally, any history of t is obtainable by merging histories of the component terms $t1, \cdots tn$.*

17.8. Translation into MEIJE Process Calculus

The proof is by induction on the length of the history.

It is not necessary that the lengths of the histories (τ_i) need not be the same. But we will assume without any loss of generality that the lengths are the same by adding null actions at suitable places in the traces.

Lemma 5 Merging Lemma for CRP: *Take any history, τ, of a CRP program $p = p1//\cdots//pn$. Then there exists histories τ_i of $p_i, i = 1, \cdots n$ respectively such that $\tau|_{pi} = \tau_i$.*

The proof is by induction on the length of the history. As before, we shall assume that the local histories are of equal length.

Now we can state the main result.

Theorem 2 *Given is the CRP program P with its constituent processes P_i equivalent to the meije terms $[\![P_i]\!]$. Then P is equivalent to the meije term T,*

$$T = [\![P_1]\!]\cdots//[\![P_n]\!]\backslash C$$

where C is the set of all channel names appearing in P.

Proof *Consider any arbitrary history, τ of T. Then by merging lemma for meije terms, there is a corresponding history τ_i of $[\![P_i]\!]$. Since $[\![P_i]\!]$ is equivalent to P_i, corresponding to the history τ_i of $[\![P_i]\!]$ there is a history, say, σ_i of P_i. Now we can construct a history σ such that $\sigma|_{Pi} = \sigma_i$. It is not difficult to show that σ is a history of P. The proof is complete once we show that τ is equivalent to σ. This is done by proving that for any i less than the length of τ, $\tau[i]$ is same as $\sigma[i]$. The interesting case in this proof is when the step i involves some rendezvous actions among processes. For example, consider the case of two processes P_i and P_j having a rendezvous on a channel c in this step; let l_i, l_j be the labels of the corresponding rendezvous actions. Then t_i performs a compound action of the form $a_i.l_i?$, where a_i itself may be some compound action involving reactive signals and/or rendezvous signals; t'_i performs the action $l_i!.C!$. Hence t_i, t'_i together perform $a_i.C!$ as they are in parallel and the label actions are hidden. Symmetrically, t_j and t'_j perform $a_j.l_j?$ and $l_j!.C?$ respectively and hence together perform $a_j.C?$ with l_j action being hidden. Since C is hidden in T, $\tau[i] = a_i.a_j$. It follows from the equivalence of P_i and t_i and the semantics of CRP processes that, $\sigma[i] = a_i.a_j$. Hence the result.*

Chapter 18

Communicating Reactive State Machines

CRSM is a state machine based language developed along the lines of CRP and is used for describing behaviour of distributed control systems that consist of one of more independent local synchronous controllers that communicate using CSP like message passing primitives. First we illustrate the language constructs of CRSM using a simple example. Infophone[1], a speech enabled Java application for information retrieval. It uses an ARM processor to control the user interface, a DSP to process speech commands, and a wireless web interface.

Figure 18.1 shows an abstract model of a very simplified version of computations that is carried out in the three processors ARM, DSP and WEB. The rectangles and circles represent normal and communication states respectively. Communication states are annotated with the name of the channel with which they are associated. ! and ? are the standard CSP-style notations for sender and receiver communication states. The dashed arrows from communication states are called non-preempting transitions. These transitions are taken when communication succeeds. The solid arrows are called preempting transitions and are taken when their guards are true; guards describe the status of signals in the environment.

When activated by the signal usrMenu, ARM node receives the user's request, say fltReq and forwards it to DSP on the relevant channel, in this case Flight. DSP is then ready to receive speech commands from the user directly, invokes data intensive speech processing and recoginition

---

[1]Infophone was developed on the Open Multimedia Application Platform(OMAP), a trademark of Texas Instruments.

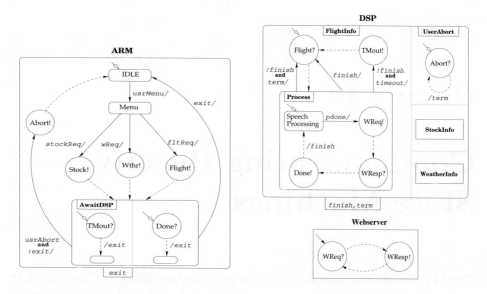

Figure 18.1: *ARM* and *DSP* components of Infophone

computations and sends appropriate requests to the *WEB* node via the channel WReq; DSP notifies *ARM* when a response is received on WResp. A session can end in three ways: successfully, when *ARM* receives a message on the channel Done from *DSP*; times out, when a timeout is issued by *DSP* if *WEB* is not responding, and aborts, when the user issues usrAbort.

The state AwaitDSP in *ARM* has hierarchy and contains two automata. The transitions leaving AwaitDSP allow these automata to complete their ongoing reaction before passivating them, a policy of *weak pre-emption*. The automata FlightInfo, StockInfo, WeatherInfo and UserAbort in *DSP* execute in synchronous parallelism, written FlightInfo‖..‖UserAbort and interact using local signals such as exit, term and finish.

18.1 CRSM Constructs

As illustrated in this example, CRSM language has constructs for expressing hierarchy and two parallel composition operators. It supports two different types of communication primitives: synchronous signal based broadcast communication among synchronous concurrent components (called processes) along the lines of ESTEREL and Argos; and channel based two-process handshake communication between asynchronous components (called nodes) a la CSP. For instance, ARM, DSP and WEB are three top-level nodes that communicate via handshake signals; whereas concurrent components in each node interact using signals. The signals in different nodes are disjoint. The pictorial syntax of each node is inspired by Statecharts and Argos.

A more precise description of CRSM in textual syntax is as follows:

$CRSM \quad ::= \quad CRSM // CRSM \mid RSM$
$RSM \quad ::= \quad HAut \mid RSM \parallel RSM \mid RSM \backslash s$
$HAut \quad ::= \quad Aut \mid HAut[q \rightarrow RSM]$

A CRSM program is a set of nodes or Reactive State Machines (RSMs) composed using $//$, the operator for asynchronous parallel composition. RSMs are built from communicating Mealy-style automata Aut, composed using the synchronous operators for parallel composition, hierarchy, and signal localization. $\parallel$ is the operator for synchronous parallel composition. $q \rightarrow RSM$ denotes that the RSM is in the hierarchy of the state q. $RSM \backslash s$ denotes that the signal s is localized.

The basic building block is an automaton which is defined as a tuple $(Q, q_0, \mathcal{I}, \mathcal{O}, \mathcal{C}, T)$ where
$Q = Q_N \cup Q_C$ - is a set of normal and communication states.
$q_0 \in Q$ is the initial state.
$\mathcal{I}, \mathcal{O}$ - are sets of input and output signals
$\mathcal{C}$ - is a set of communication actions.
$T = T_E \cup T_I \cup T_{NP}$ is a set of preempting, idling and non-preempting transitions.

- $T_E \subseteq Q \times B(\mathcal{I}) \times 2^{\mathcal{O}} \times Q$. $B(\mathcal{I})$ is a boolean expression over inputs.

- $T_I \subseteq Q \times B(\mathcal{I}) \times Q$.

- $T_{NP} \subseteq Q_C \times 2^{\mathcal{O}} \times \mathcal{C} \times Q$.

18.2 Semantics of CRSM

The semantics of CRSM has two parts: node semantics and network semantics. The node semantics is along the lines of ESTEREL semantics, given earlier while the network semantics is similar to CSP semantics. The semantics is defined in terms of Labelled Transition Systems (LTSs) defined on *executing* CRSMs (*eCRSM*) which are CRSMs augmented with information regarding the current state. The executing automaton is a tuple $Aut \times (Q \cup \{\bot\})$ denoted $(Q, q_0, \mathcal{I}, \mathcal{O}, \mathcal{C}, T, q_c)$ or (A, q_c) for conciseness, where q_c is the current state of the automaton.

The semantics of CRSM are formalized as a transition of the form

$$M \xrightarrow[E]{O,C} M'$$

where M and M' are executing RSMs associated with the RSM $\mathcal{M}$. E, O, and C are the set of events, output signals, and communication actions respectively. Each RSM executes in a local environment which is described by a set of signals E. $E = E^+ \cup E^-$ describes the status of all input and output signals of the node as present(E^+) or absent(E^-) at a given reaction instant. In a reaction a node may emit some signals $O \subseteq E$ and communicate on the channels C.

M evolves into M' when an internal state q transitions to a new state q' on being enabled by an input event.

$$\frac{q \xrightarrow{i/o,c} q'}{M \xrightarrow[E]{\{o\},\{c\}} M'}$$

The semantic rules for the asynchronous composition operator are shown in Table 18.1. The rule in the first row describes a reaction when two nodes communicate on a set of common channels and react together; C_1 denotes communication actions, $chan(C_1)$ gives the channels associated with these actions, $\mathcal{C}_{N_1}$ is the set of channels defined for N_1.

The rules in the second row describe a scenario when there is no communication between nodes and only one of the two nodes reacts.

$$\frac{N_1 \xrightarrow[E_1]{O_1,C_1} N_1', \; N_2 \xrightarrow[E_2]{O_2,C_2} N_2', chan(C_1) \cap \mathcal{C}_{N_2} = chan(C_2) \cap \mathcal{C}_{N_1}}{N_1//N_2 \xrightarrow[E_1 * E_2]{O_1 \cup O_2, C_1 \cup C_2} N_1'//N_2'}$$

$$\frac{N_1 \xrightarrow[E_1]{O_1,C_1} N_1', chan(C_1) \cap \mathcal{C}_{N_2} = \emptyset}{N_1//N_2 \xrightarrow[E_1]{O_1,C_1} N_1'//N_2} \qquad \frac{N_2 \xrightarrow[E_2]{O_2,C_2} N_2', chan(C_2) \cap \mathcal{C}_{N_1} = \emptyset}{N_1//N_2 \xrightarrow[E_2]{O_2,C_2} N_1//N_2'}$$

Table 18.1: Rules for asynchronous composition

The rules for the synchronous constructs are shown in Table 18.2. A, A' are executing $RSMs$ associated with the RSM $\mathcal{A}$. Similarly, A_1, A_1' and A_2, A_2' are executing $RSMs$ for $\mathcal{A}_1$ and $\mathcal{A}_2$ respectively. Rules 1, 2, and

18.2. Semantics of CRSM

3 describe the reaction in the automaton for the three types of transitions viz., non-preempting, preempting and idling. Rule 4 describes the reaction for RSMs in synchronous parallel composition. Rules 5 and 6 describe the reaction for an RSM with local signals defined. A $Must$ and Can analysis is performed to determine the status of the local signal. The $Must$ function determines what signals must be emitted in a reaction. The status of a signal that appears in $Must$ is set to present. Can determines what signals can be emitted in a reaction. This includes signals that are emitted on a transition whose guard is undefined. The status of a signal that does not appear in Can is set to absent. Note that $Must \subseteq Can$. If a signal is present in Can but not present in $Must$, the behaviour is unacceptable and the program is rejected as invalid.

$\dfrac{(q_c, \emptyset, o, c, q_d) \in T_{NP}}{A \xrightarrow[E]{o,\{c\}} A'}$ 1. Non-preemption	$\dfrac{(q_c, i, o, \emptyset, q_d) \in T_E,\, E \to i \wedge o}{A \xrightarrow[E]{o,\phi} A'}$ 2. Preemption
$\dfrac{(q_c, i, \emptyset, \emptyset, q_c) \in T_I,\, E \to i}{A \xrightarrow[E]{\phi,\phi} A}$ 3. Idling	$\dfrac{A_1 \xrightarrow[E]{O_1,C_1} A'_1,\; A_2 \xrightarrow[E]{O_2,C_2} A'_2}{A_1 \| A_2 \xrightarrow[E]{O_1 \cup O_2,\, C_1 \cup C_2} A'_1 \| A'_2}$ 4. Parallel composition
$\dfrac{a \in Must(A, E * a^\perp),\, A \xrightarrow[E * a^+]{O,C} A'}{A\backslash\{a\} \xrightarrow[E]{O\backslash a, C} A'\backslash\{a\}}$ 5. Localization - a present	$\dfrac{a \notin Can(A, E * a^\perp),\, A \xrightarrow[E * a^-]{O,C} A'}{A\backslash\{a\} \xrightarrow[E]{O,C} A'\backslash\{a\}}$ 6. Localization - a absent

$\dfrac{A \xrightarrow[E]{O_1,\phi} A',\; A_1 \xrightarrow[E]{O_2,C} A'_1,\; q \in active(A),\; q \notin active(A')}{A[q \to A_1] \xrightarrow[E]{O_1 \cup O_2, C} A'[q \to Passivate(A'_1)]}$
7. Transition where q is the source state

$\dfrac{A \xrightarrow[E]{O_1,C} A',\; q \notin active(A),\; q \in active(A')}{A[q \to A_1] \xrightarrow[E]{O_1,C} A'[q \to Activate(A_1)]}$
8. Transition where q is the target state

$\dfrac{A \xrightarrow[E]{O_1,\phi} A',\; A_1 \xrightarrow[E]{O_2,C} A'_1,\; q \in active(A),\; q \in active(A')}{A[q \to A_1] \xrightarrow[E]{O_1 \cup O_2, C} A'[q \to Reinitialise(A'_1)]}$
9. Self transition in state q

$\dfrac{A \xrightarrow[E]{\phi,\phi} A,\; A_1 \xrightarrow[E]{O_1,C} A'_1,\; q \in active(A)}{A[q \to A_1] \xrightarrow[E]{O_1,C} A[q \to A'_1]}$
10. No explicit transition enabled in the parent automaton

Table 18.2: Rules for synchronous operators

Chapter 19

Multiclock ESTEREL

In this chapter, we discuss another paradigm called Multiclock Esterel[7, 65, 67, 66], which extends the synchronous formalisms. We show that the Multiclock Esterel paradigm[1] provides a general framework for the design of systems with multiple local clocks and the earlier paradigm of CRP (*Communicating Reactive Processes*) [13] can be obtained as an instance of the newly proposed paradigm. Furthermore, it preserves the advantages of the synchronous monoclock Esterel paradigm and thus benefits from the advantages of verifiability of specifications/models.

19.1 Need for a Multiclock Synchronous Paradigm

Before discussing Multiclock Esterel, we shall highlight the limitations of globally clocked systems (either at a logical or a meta level) and the advantages of multiple clock systems. It may be pointed out that Esterel - one of the highly developed members of the family of synchronous languages - is a monoclock system. We shall base our discussion of these aspects on an example of a simple CPU-RAM system.

Consider a simplified example of modelling a system consisting of a CPU and some RAM. Let us assume that the CPU runs at a faster clock than the RAM and that they synchronize only during data transfers between them. Modelling such a system using existing synchronous languages needs

---

[1]The notion has also been developed in G. Berry, E. Sentovich. Proc. CHARME'2001, Edinburgh, Correct Hardware Design and Verification Methods, Springer-Verlag, LNCS 2144. We describe our version developed around 1998 that considers complete impact of multi-clocks with respect to preemption and suspension completely and also shows the embedding of [13].

to analyze the following issues:

1. Global *vs.* Local Clocks: With increase in the complexity of systems, it becomes necessary and convenient to *distribute* functionality of a program. Physical distribution naturally leads to multiple clocks. For instance, in the above example, it would be nice to develop the model for the CPU and the RAM by specifying the clock of each system independently. However, if we use a global clock, we need to explicitly filter clock ticks to yield the desired clock; such a scenario will require complete re-design if we change the clock.

   Synchronous languages implicitly work with a notion of a global clock and hence, it becomes an impediment especially when independent module development is attempted. The paradigm of CRP [13] proposed to integrate a network of Esterel modules communicating over named channels provides a method of dealing with multiple clocks in a restrictive way with the drawback that synchronous parallelism and network parallelism cannot be mixed freely.

2. Preserving Modularity - In the context of the above CPU - RAM example above, independent code development for the CPU (or RAM) module cannot be done without explicit knowledge of the clock for the RAM (or CPU) module. This information would be required to build the explicit clock filters for these modules The applicability of a language to characterize and implement real systems will be enhanced if modularity of the language is not affected by the introduction of independent clocks.

   Synchronous languages, and in particular Esterel, supported the concept of modules and provided a way of composing modules to form more complex modules. Esterel however tacitly assumed that there existed a global clock in the system of interest. This limitation comes in the way of maintaining modularity when dealing with systems with multiple clocks.

3. Synchrony *vs.* Asynchrony -

   Extending our CPU - RAM example above to include *interrupts*, it becomes obvious that one needs to be able to handle asynchronous interrupts in the CPU module since external interrupts are not constrained to be synchronous with the CPU clock. Another area where synchronization comes to the fore in this example is when the CPU and RAM modules exchange data. Even though the CPU and RAM run on independent clocks, they do synchronize between themselves.

The synchronous paradigm imposed severe constraints on the kind of systems that could be effectively characterized using it. In particular, it required that input events occurred synchronously with the internal system clock. Unfortunately, several systems have asynchronous interactions with their environment. The need to deal with asynchronous events in the environment requires that reactive languages be adapted to interface to these asynchronous events. Furthermore, it would be nice to have a unified way of abstracting synchrony and asynchrony from a theoretical as well as practical perspective.

4. Verifiability - In the context of our example, we would like to be able to prove that, say, interactions between the CPU and RAM modules satisfy their design specifications. Synchronous languages supported the development of *verifiable* code. By judiciously relaxing the constraints imposed by the synchronous paradigm, it should still be possible to apply proof techniques developed for the synchronous language.

5. Retention of existing features of reactive languages - In our example, we would like to be able to model the CPU and RAM modules working in parallel in situations such as: prefetching instructions, suspension of normal operations when interrupts occur, or preemption when error conditions occur.

Synchronous languages and Esterel in particular provided certain features, like parallelism, preemption and suspension, that made them well suited to address problems in certain application areas. These features should continue to be supported in any alternate proposal to augment functionality.

19.2 Informal Introduction

Multiclock Esterel is based on the synchronous language Esterel, which in turn is based on the *perfect synchrony hypothesis*. The hypothesis can be interpreted to mean that outputs are produced synchronously with the inputs. In other words, reactions to inputs happen in *zero time* (in the sense that the time is not observable in this context). Further, there is no explicit clock associated with Esterel. Multiclock Esterel is a language designed to support the explicit specification of clocks as is usual in the specification of hardware circuits. The perfect synchrony hypothesis has been adapted to support the explicit specification of clocks in the sense that while in Esterel the reactions to external events were controlled just by the environment (which indirectly defined the "clock" of the response), in Multiclock Esterel, reactions are determined by the clocks controlling the current execution by appropriately abstracting the input from the environment and reacting to it in the form of outputs (again controlled by the appropriate clocks). With such an adaptation of linking reactions to the current clock, Multiclock Esterel can also be considered to satisfy the synchrony hypothesis.

The syntax and form of Multiclock Esterel closely resembles that of its precursor, Esterel. The general structure of a Multiclock Esterel program consists of a collection of named modules composed using the parallel or sequence operator. Each of these modules has an explicitly specified clock associated with it.

Each module in turn is built of either sub-modules or simple statements composed using either the parallel or sequence operator. Multiclock Esterel is for the most part block structured but supports explicit access control that *limits* the scope of objects. The rules for defining or accessing variables or signals or sensors, data structures and host languages follow essentially on the same lines as that of Esterel with the possibility of explicit access controls. complex ones like *structures* are not.

Multiclock Esterel supports a simple complement of data types that includes *integers*, *floating point* numbers and *character strings* in addition to *signals*, *latches*, *clocks* and *sensors*. However, complex data structures like records are not supported.

While variables of simple types like *integers* are valid only in the modules defining them, signals can be shared across modules. Signals are used as an interface to communicate with the external world. Signals are distributed using an instantaneous broadcast mechanism just as in other synchronous programming languages like Esterel. This in turn implies that the statement emitting a signal will see the signal in its current execution environment. Sensors are a special kind of signal that can be queried at any time to obtain a value. They do not contribute to the signal environment in as much as they do not generate events.

Since every statement is bound to a clock, there is obviously a need to provide some amount of limited memory in the form of *latches* to interface the asynchronous environment to the reactive core. In the sequel, we shall describe latches in section 19.2.1, and the expression that can be formed with respect to signals and clocks.

19.2. Informal Introduction

19.2.1 Latched Signals

Esterel or synchronous languages in general do not require latching of signal. The underlying model followed assumed that the system was fast enough to react to every input event. The capability of Multiclock Esterel to explicitly bind *clocks* to specific signals (including boolean functions on them) introduces certain problems. For instance, how does one treat events that occur *out of sync* with the current `tick` signal?

Example 1 *We present a typical scenario using a (simplified) real world example. Consider the example of a CPU running at a clock, clock-c, and a peripheral device, running on a different clock, interfaced to it. The peripheral requests service from the CPU by raising an interrupt and we can safely assume that a second interrupt is never generated before the first is serviced. Now assume that the CPU is capable of servicing interrupts at the beginning of any cycle of clock-c and that the CPU cannot respond to the interrupt at arbitrary points in its execution sequence. Now consider two successive points in time, t_1 and t_2 where clock-c starts a cycle. Assume the peripheral raises an interrupt at time t_3 such that $t_1 < t_3 < t_2$. The expected behaviour of the system is for the CPU to service the interrupt at t_2 and not at t_3. This indeed is how a present day CPU would respond to interrupts. We therefore require the CPU to react to the interrupt at time t_2 even though the interrupt occurred strictly before t_2. This brings us to the notion of a* latch *which can be used to store the* previous value of a signal. *Using a latch on the CPU, one could store the interrupt at t_3 to be serviced later at t_2. Again, this is conceptually how interrupts are handled in present day systems.*

In the following, we present the form of latch used in Multiclock Esterel(refer to [7] for other possible notions).

Figure 19.1 shows the relationship between a clock, a signal and the latched version of the signal as used in Multiclock Esterel.

- the waveform labeled *tick* is assumed to be the current clock. It is not necessary that the clock be periodic as shown. In fact, in the case of event driven systems this is likely to be the norm rather than the exception.

- the waveform labeled *signal s* represents an arbitrary signal occurring in the environment of a Multiclock Esterel module.

- $\hat{s}$ denotes a signal that sustains the value of *s* until the *next* clock tick.

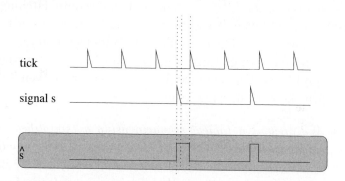

Figure 19.1: Clock, signal and latches

The interval for which $\hat{s}$ sustains the signal s *includes* the next clock *tick*. In particular, $\hat{s}$ generated for any given event will never span *two* clock *ticks*. This in turn implies that if s occurs synchronously with a clock tick, its value will not remain latched until the next instant.

Latching serves to implement *limited* memory in asynchronous environments. In particular, *latching*, as it is used in the sequel serves only to hold the *last* value of a signal until the next clock tick. This implies that, for a given set of clocks and signals, it is possible to lose all record of certain events when the clocks used are too slow for the signals being monitored. This condition is referred to as *under sampling*. As a direct consequence of under sampling, we cannot hope to distinguish between a single occurrence of an event and multiple occurrences of an event between successive clock ticks. Multiclock Esterel uses a technique similar to that used above to deal with signals that occur out of synchronization with the current clock. The use of *latched* signals makes interfacing modules/statements with different clocks easy. Signals may never be accessed using disparate clocks, but the *latched* versions of these signals can be read using any clock. Therefore parameter passing between modules with no common clock can be effectively accomplished using latched signals.

19.2.2 Expressions

Multiclock Esterel supports two kinds of expressions.

1. The first kind ranges over signals and are referred to as *clock* expres-

19.2. Informal Introduction

sions. Clock expressions are boolean functions over signals and cannot contain references to variables or sensors. They are used to specify bindings for the local clock or `tick`.

2. The second type of expression ranges over variables as well as *latched* version of signals and are referred to as signal expressions. These expressions are what Multiclock Esterel code can test for as part of its execution sequence. Note that clock expressions can only be used to bind clock signals. *Latches* of signals are derived entities. All references to signal values are implicitly made to reference the corresponding latch.

19.2.3 Multiclock ESTEREL Statements

Unlike Esterel, where there is an implicit *global* clock (the *tick*) at which the entire Esterel program makes transitions, in Multiclock Esterel modules are independently and explicitly clocked. This feature is a major deviation from Esterel and accounts for almost all the enhancements that Multiclock Esterel offers. Clocks can be specified as boolean expression over input signals.

The following two new constructs are added to ESTEREL to obtain the Multiclock Esterel.

Statement : newtick s in p end
This construct is what sets Multiclock Esterel apart from Esterel. This construct starts synchronously at the current clock and initiates execution of statement p on clock s. Statements in p do not start executing until clock s occurs. All statements in p see signals in their environment through values latched on the new clock s. The construct terminates synchronously with the first occurrence of the current clock after the termination of statement p which will in turn terminate synchronously with the new clock s. Further, statements in statement block p are insulated from any suspensions imposed on this construct. For all practical purposes, statement p can be considered an independent process.

Statement : weak newtick s in p end
This is a variant of the newtick construct introduced above. This construct starts synchronously at the current clock and initiates execution of statement p on clock s. However, statements in statement block p are *not* insulated from any suspensions imposed on this construct. The keyword `weak` is used to signify that the change of clock is not sufficient to protect the enclosed

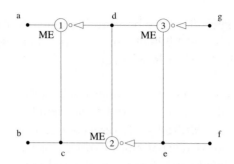

Figure 19.2: Asynchronous Pipeline

statements from suspensions imposed on the construct.

19.2.4 Informal Development of Programs in Multiclock ESTEREL

In this section, we shall illustrate the style of development of programs in Multiclock Esterel using the asynchronous system referred to as *micropipelines*, first introduced in [86] and discussed in [42].

Example 2 *Micro-pipelines* -

Let us first review the working of the circuit shown in Figure 19.2. In Figure 19.2, the circle labeled ME represents a *Mueller element* whose behavior is to set the state of its output line to that of its input lines whenever all the input lines have the same state and maintain its previous state otherwise. Points marked a and g are inputs while those marked b and f are outputs.

To start with let us assume that both inputs (a, g) are held low and points d, c and e (and hence points b and f) are also low. The outputs at all the *inverters* shown will be high.

Now consider that input point a makes a transition from low to high. The *Mueller* element labeled 1 will then drive the point c high too. This in turn will cause the *Mueller* element labeled 2 to drive the point d high. This causes the output of the inverter connected to the *Mueller* element labeled 1 to go low. Point d going high in turn causes the *Mueller* element labeled 3 to drive the point e (and therefore point f) high. This in turn sets the output of the inverter connected to the *Mueller* element labeled 2 to be driven low.

19.2. Informal Introduction

Now consider a second transition on the input point a, this time from high to low. As in the case above, point d will eventually be driven low, because the *Mueller* elements labeled 1 and 2 will allow the new state to pass through on the output line. However *Mueller* element labeled 3 will not drive the point e low because, the output of the inverter driving one of its inputs is still high. Also note that the output of the inverter connected to the *Mueller* element labeled 1 is now high (because point d is low) while the output of the inverter driving the *Mueller* element labeled 2 is still low (because point e hasn't changed state). The net result is that the second transition remains blocked at the *Mueller* element labeled 3.

Reasoning in an analogous manner, it is easy to see that a third transition on input point a will remain blocked on the *Mueller* element labeled 2 and so on.

Now consider the effects of driving point g high. This drives the output of the inverter connected to the *Mueller* element labeled 3 low. This in turn will allow the low value at point d to be gated to point e (and therefore point f). Thus the second transition on point a will now be visible at point f. Point e being driven down will cause the output of the inverter connected to the *Mueller* element labeled 2 to go high. This in turn will allow the high value at point pointc (due to the third transition on point a) to propagate until point d where it will get blocked by the *Mueller* element labeled 3.

Thus, we see that the circuit functions as an asynchronous FIFO wherein transitions on point a are eventually visible at point f so long as point g is toggled to acknowledge receipt of each successive value available on point f. Note that values propagate along the FIFO only when the previous transition has been acknowledged and that the circuit is not explicitly clocked.

The micro-pipeline of Figure 19.2 can be specified in Multiclock Esterel by building each component separately and combining them to construct the entire circuit follows from the following discussion.

```
module MUELLER :
inputs I1, I2
output O1
    newtick I1 or I2 in
        var LAST_VAL = 0, I1_VAL = 0   I2_VAL = 0 in
            loop
                await tick
                present I1 then I1_VAL = ?I1 end
                present I2 then I2_VAL = ?I2 end
                if I1_VAL == I2_VAL then
                    LAST_VAL = I2_VAL
                end
                emit O1(LAST_VAL)
            end
        end
    end
end
```

A Mueller element is a circuit that either maintains its previous state or takes on the value of its inputs *if* all its inputs have the same value. The above code models such a circuit. Note that the system will make transitions only when either input changes and remembers the previous value seen on an input.

```
module INVERTER :
inputs I1
output O1
    newtick I1 in
        loop
            await tick;
            emit O1(not ?I1)
        end
    end
end
```

The code represents a simple NOT gate or *inverter*. Note that the code makes transitions only when the input changes state. Also note that the circuit has no memory.

```
module COMBINATION :
inputs I1, I2
output O1
    signal T1 in
        run INVERTER [T1/O1] ||
        run MUELLER [T1/I2]
    end
end
```

19.3. Formal Semantics

The code above shows how Multiclock Esterel modules can be composed to give other modules. Note that the output of the *inverter* is bound to one input of the *Mueller element* through the local signal *T1*. This usage of local signals is very typical of Multiclock Esterel programming.

```
module MICRO_PIPELINE :
inputs SIG_IN, ACK_IN
inputoutput SIG_OUT, ACK_OUT
    signal T1 in
        run COMBINATION [SIG_IN/I1 T1/I2 ACK_OUT/O1] ||
        run COMBINATION [ACK_OUT/I1 SIG_OUT/I2 T1/O1] ||
        run COMBINATION [T1/I1 ACK_IN/I2 SIG_OUT/O1]
    end
end
```

The above code shows how we can specify complex behaviors in a very modular fashion using Multiclock Esterel modules bound together using local signals.

19.3 Formal Semantics

Here, we will describe in detail, the behavioral semantics of Multiclock Esterel. Being multi-clocked, execution of statements in Multiclock Esterel is initiated at every occurrence of the current local clock and therefore clock distribution forms a very important part of the execution model. We therefore first describe how statements are bound to clocks and their propagation before describing the semantic of Multiclock Esterel's programming constructs.

19.3.1 Specification of Clocks

Statements in Multiclock Esterel can be bound to different clocks but necessarily need to be bound to a clock before it can be scheduled for execution. Multiclock Esterel being a synchronous language, even termination of statements is tightly coupled to the clock in effect. In this section, we present the details of clock distribution in Multiclock Esterel. We will use the notation $stat_c$ to denote the statement *stat* running at clock c, $stat_-$ to denote that no clock has yet been specified for the statement *stat* and $_c(stat)$ to denote that statement *stat* is scheduled to terminate on clock c.

$$Statement : stat \quad \rightarrow \quad Clocked\ form : stat_-$$

This is a syntactic rule included for completion. It effectively means that initially statements are not bound to any clock.

$$\text{Statement}: (stat\_)_c \quad \rightarrow \quad \text{Clocked form}: {}_c(stat_c)$$

This rule ensures that statements that have unbound clocks get bound to the current clock before execution. Note that they are constrained to terminate on the same clock.

$$\text{Statement}: (stat1\_; stat2\_)_c \rightarrow \text{Clocked form}: {}_c(stat1_c; stat2_c)$$

This rule shows how clock bindings distribute across the sequential operator. Note that for the rule to be applicable both components of the compound statement must be free from any clock bindings. Each component is then bound to the clock c. Also note that the whole construct is constrained to terminate on clock c.

It follows that any two statements composed by a *sequence* operator will be bound to the same clock. This helps in ensuring the synchronous semantics of the sequence operator whereby the initiation of the second component is to be synchronous with the termination of the first.

Example 3 *This example serves to illustrate how the rules related to clock distribution and the sequence operator can be used in a recursive manner to distribute clocks over arbitrary sequences of statements. Consider*

$$stat1 \rightarrow stat2 \; ; \; stat3$$
$$stat3 \rightarrow stat4 \; ; \; stat5$$

and that statement stat1 *is to be run on clock* c. *Applying the relevant rules to* stat1 *results in*

$$stat1_c \rightarrow {}_c(stat2_c \; ; \; stat3_c)$$

Statement stat3 *in turn will expand as given below.*

$$stat3_c \rightarrow {}_c(stat4_c \; ; \; stat5_c)$$

Note that at each successive application of the rule results in a growing sequence of statements each of which are bound to the same clock c.

$$\text{Statement}: (stat1\_ \| stat2\_)_c \rightarrow \text{Clocked form}: {}_c(stat1_c \| stat2_c)$$

19.3. Formal Semantics

The rule shows how the clock distributes across the parallel operator. Note that for the rule to be applicable both components of the compound statement must be free from any clock bindings. Here again, each component is bound to the clock c. Further, the entire construct is constrained to terminate on clock c.

It follows that any two statements composed by a *parallel* operator will be bound to the same clock. This helps in ensuring the synchronous semantics of the parallel operator whereby termination of the whole construct is synchronous with the termination of the later of the two branches.

$$Statement : (\texttt{loop } stat\_ \texttt{ end})_c \quad \rightarrow \quad Clocked\ form :\ _c(\texttt{loop } stat_c \texttt{ end})$$

If a `loop` construct is bound to a clock c, then the statement block within its scope gets bound to the same clock c. Also, the whole construct is constrained to terminate on clock c.

$$Statement : (\texttt{abort } stat\_ \texttt{ when } S)_c \quad \rightarrow$$
$$Clocked\ form :\ _c(\texttt{abort } stat_c \texttt{ when } S)$$

This rule implies that statements inside the scope of an `abort` construct bound to a clock c is bound to the same clock c and is also constrained to terminate on clock c.

$$Statement : (\texttt{weak abort } stat\_ \texttt{ when } S)_c \quad \rightarrow$$
$$Clocked\ form :\ _c(\texttt{weak abort } stat_c \texttt{ when } S)$$

This rule implies that statements inside the scope of a `weak abort` construct bound to a clock c is bound to the same clock c and is also constrained to terminate on clock c.

$$Statement : (\texttt{signal } S \texttt{ in } stat\_ \texttt{ end})_c \quad \rightarrow$$
$$Clocked\ form :\ _c(\texttt{signal } S \texttt{ in } stat_c \texttt{ end})$$

The `signal` construct serves to limit the scope of a signal. This construct is not strictly an executable statement but is included here for convenience. As in the cases above the clock is bound to the statement within the scope of the construct and the whole construct is constrained to terminate on clock c.

$Statement$: $(\text{present } S \text{ then } stat1 \text{ else } stat2 \text{ end})_c \quad \rightarrow$
$Clocked\ form$: $_c(\text{present } S \text{ then } stat1_c \text{ else } stat2_c \text{ end})$

This rule governs how clocks are distributed to components of the **present** construct. Notice that both *stat1* and *stat2* are bound to clock c, irrespective of the condition being tested for. The whole construct is also constrained to terminate on the same clock.

$Statement$: $(\text{newtick } S \text{ in } stat \text{ end})_c \quad \rightarrow$
$Clocked\ form$: $_c(\text{newtick } S \text{ in } stat_S \text{ end})$

The **newtick** construct is one of two constructs that can explicitly bind statements to specific clocks. Note that the rule above causes statement *stat* to be bound to the clock S though the **newtick** construct itself is bound to clock c. Also note that the entire construct is still constrained to terminate on clock c.

$Statement$: $(\text{weak newtick } S \text{ in } stat \text{ end})_c \quad \rightarrow$
$Clocked\ form$: $_c(\text{weak newtick } S \text{ in } stat_S \text{ end})$

The **weak newtick** construct is the other construct that can explicitly bind statements to specific clocks. Note that the rule above causes statement *stat* to be bound to the clock S though the **newtick** construct itself is bound to clock c. Also note that the entire construct is still constrained to terminate on clock c. Note that their behavior *vis a vis* clock distribution is identical.

$Statement$: $_c(\text{nothing}_c) \quad \rightarrow \quad Clocked\ form$: nothing_c

This rule differs from the rules presented above in that it deals with synchronization of statement termination. This rule implies that a **nothing** construct bound to clock c and constrained to terminate also on clock c is equivalent to a **nothing** construct bound to clock c. This rule ensures that an extra tick of clock c is not consumed upon termination of the construct.

$Statement$: $_c(\text{nothing}_s) \quad \xrightarrow{\frac{S,0}{E_c \cup \mathcal{L}}} \quad Clocked\ form$: nothing_c

This rule too deals with synchronization of statement termination and can be applied *only* when clock s is present. This rule implies

19.3. Formal Semantics

that a **nothing** construct bound to clock s and constrained to terminate on clock c is equivalent to a **nothing** construct bound to clock c (after clock s occurs). This rule ensures that the construct terminates on clock c.

From the above rules we see that

- the execution clock for a given statement or block of statements is inherited from the enclosing block, unless explicitly reassigned by a **newtick** statement,
- statements are constrained to terminate on the clock they started on, and
- the execution clock distributes over the sequence and parallel operators.

Now that the rules regarding clock propagation have been dealt with, we will discuss the semantics of the individual statements in Multiclock Esterel.

1. **nothing**:
$$nothing_c \xrightarrow[E_c \cup \mathcal{L}]{\phi, 0} nothing_c$$

This rule specifies that the **nothing** construct does not alter the environment in any way and terminates instantaneously, transforming itself into yet another **nothing** construct that will behave similarly.

2. **halt**:
$$halt_c \xrightarrow[E_c \cup \mathcal{L}]{\phi, 1} halt_c$$

This rule specifies that the **halt** statement never terminates and does not contribute to the signal environment in any way. Notice that its termination status in 1.

3. **emit**:
$$emit_c S \xrightarrow[E_c \cup \mathcal{L}]{S, 0} nothing_c$$

This rule specifies the behavior of the **emit** construct. It simply adds signal S to the environment and terminates, transforming itself into the **nothing** construct.

4. *Sequencing Rule 1*:
$$\frac{stat1_c \xrightarrow[E_c \cup \mathcal{L}]{E', 0} c(stat1'),\ stat2_c \xrightarrow[E_c \cup \mathcal{L}]{E'', b} c(stat2'_d)}{stat1_c;\ stat2_c \xrightarrow[E_c \cup \mathcal{L}]{E' \cup E'', b} c(stat2'_d)}$$

This is one of two rules that define the behavior of the sequence operator in terms of the behavior of the individual statements it composes sequentially. Here we deal with the case where the first statement (*stat1*) terminates as is evident from the preconditions specified. Here the second statement (*stat2*) commences execution in the same instant. The termination status of the construct is that of the statement *stat2* while the contribution to the signal environment is the union of the individual contributions of the two transitions.

5. *Sequencing Rule2*

$$\frac{stat1_c \xrightarrow[E_c \cup \mathcal{L}]{E',b} c(stat1'_b) \quad b \neq 0}{stat1_c; stat2_c \xrightarrow[E_c \cup \mathcal{L}]{E',b} c(stat1'_d); stat2_c}$$

This is the second of two rules that define the behavior of the sequence operator in terms of the behaviors of the individual statements it composes sequentially. Here we deal with the case where the first statement (*stat1*) does not terminate as is evident from the preconditions specified. Here the second statement (*stat2*) is not even scheduled for execution as the first component has not yet terminated. The termination status of the construct is that of the statement *stat1* and the contribution to the signal environment is that made by statement *stat1*. Also note that the construct itself has retained its form while the first statement has been transformed into *stat1'*.

6. *Paralle Rule1*

$$\frac{stat1_c \xrightarrow[E_c \cup \mathcal{L}]{E',b'} c(stat1'_d), \quad stat2_c \xrightarrow[E_c \cup \mathcal{L}]{E'',b''} c(stat2'_e)}{stat1_c \| stat2_c \xrightarrow[E_c \cup \mathcal{L}]{E' \cup E'', b' \vee k''} c(stat1'_d) \| c(stat2'_e)}$$

Here we present one of the rule that govern parallel composition in Multiclock Esterel. The precondition specifies that neither of the constituent parts terminate. The transition rule then specifies that each of the constituent branches transform independently contributing to the common signal environment. Note that the contribution of the construct to the signal environment is the union of the contributions of the constituent branches. Further the rule specifies the termination status of the construct to be the maximum of the termination statuses of the individual branches. This in turn implies that the parallel construct terminates only when both the branches terminate. Also note that the construct has remained the same while each of its constituents have transformed independently.

7. *Parallel Rule2*

$$\frac{stat1_c \xrightarrow[E_c \cup \mathcal{L}]{E',0} c(stat1'_d), stat2_c \xrightarrow[E_c \cup \mathcal{L}]{E'',b} c(stat2'_e)}{stat1_c \| stat2_c \xrightarrow[E_c \cup \mathcal{L}]{E' \cup E'',b} c(nothing_c) \| c(stat2'_e)}$$

This rule specifies that a terminating branch of a parallel construct transforms itself into a **nothing** construct. The addition to the signal environment is the union of the contributions of the individual components and the termination status is the maximum of the termination status of the individual branches. The **nothing** construct ensures that the parallel construct does not terminate unless *both* its branches do.

8. *Terminated Paralle Branches*:

$$nothing_c \| nothing_c \rightarrow nothing_c$$

This rule specifies that a parallel construct both of whose branches are **nothing** constructs with identical clocks, transforms itself into a **nothing** construct on the same clock. Note that this is a syntactic rewrite and does not constitute any real execution.

9. *Loop*:

$$\frac{stat1_c \xrightarrow[E_c \cup \mathcal{L}]{E',b} c(stat1'_d)}{loop\ stat1\ end_c \xrightarrow[E_c \cup \mathcal{L}]{E',b} c(stat1'_d); loop\ stat1\ end_c}$$

This rule describes how the **loop** construct is unfolded for execution in the Multiclock Esterel environment. Note that the **loop** construct can nevel terminate. See also that the loop involves restarting statement *stat1* every time the statement *stat1* itself, or its derivative, terminates.

10. *Selection Rules*:

$$\frac{\langle exp \rangle \xrightarrow[E_c]{} true, stat1_c \xrightarrow[E_c \cup \mathcal{L}]{E',b} c(stat1'_d)}{if\ exp\ then\ stat1\ else\ stat2\ end_c \xrightarrow[E_c \cup \mathcal{L}]{E',b} c(stat1'_d)}$$

The `if-then-else` construct is one of the ways in which choice or selection is implemented in Multiclock Esterel. This rule covers the case where the expression (*exp*) being tested for is true. In this case, the statement behaves exactly as though it were statement *stat1*. The termination status as well as the contributions to the signal environment are identical to those of statement *stat1* executed in the same environment.

11. *Selection Rules*:

$$\frac{\langle exp \rangle \xrightarrow[E_c]{} false,\ stat2_c \xrightarrow[E_c \cup \mathcal{L}]{E',b} c(stat2'_d)}{if\ exp\ then\ stat1\ else\ stat2\ end_c \xrightarrow[E_c \cup \mathcal{L}]{E',b} c(stat2'_d)}$$

This rule covers the case where the expression (*exp*) being tested for is false. In this case, the statement behaves exactly as though it were statement *stat2*. Both the termination status as well as the contributions to the signal environment are identical to those of statement *stat2* executed in the same environment.

12. *Present Rule1*

$$\frac{S \in E_c,\ stat1_c \xrightarrow[E_c \cup \mathcal{L}]{E',b} c(stat1'_d)}{present\ S\ then\ stat1\ else\ stat2\ end_c \xrightarrow[E_c \cup \mathcal{L}]{E',b} c(stat1'_d)}$$

The `present` construct is another way of implementing choice or selection in the Multiclock Esterel environment. It differs from the `if-then-else` construct in that it tests the presence of signals in the environment while the latter tests for state associated with variables. Note that it is the *latched* value of the signal which is being tested. As is evident from the preconditions, this rule covers the case where the signal being tested for is present in the environment. In this case, the whole construct behaves exactly as the statement *stat1* would in the same environment.

13. *Present Rule2*

$$\frac{S \notin E_c,\ stat2_c \xrightarrow[E_c \cup \mathcal{L}]{E',b} c(stat2'_d)}{present\ S\ then\ stat1\ else\ stat2\ end_c \xrightarrow[E_c \cup \mathcal{L}]{E',b} c(stat2'_d)}$$

This rule specifies how the `present` construct behaves when the signal being tested for is absent in the current environment. Note that it is the *latched* value of the signal which is being tested. As is clear from the rule above, it behaves exactly like statement *stat2* would in the same environment. Both the termination status as well as the contributions to the signal environment are identical to those of the statement *stat2* executed in the same environment.

14. *Preemption Rules*:

$$\frac{present\ S\ else\ abort\ stat1\ when\ immediate\ S\ end_c \xrightarrow[E_c \cup \mathcal{L}]{E',b} c(stat1'_d)}{abort\ stat1\ when_c\ immediate\ S \xrightarrow[E_c \cup \mathcal{L}]{E',b} c(stat1'_d)}$$

This rule describes how *strong* preemption is implemented in Multiclock Esterel. It says that in the absence of the signal *s* in the environment, it behaves like the **abort** construct while if the signal *s* is present, the whole construct terminates. But this definition is recursive in its statement and will not serve to specify an operational semantics for the construct. We therefore provide the following two rules to specify the behavior of this construct.

15. *Preemption Rules*:

$$\frac{S \in E_c, stat1_c \xrightarrow[E_c \cup \mathcal{L}]{E',b} c(stat1'_d)}{abort\ stat1\ when_c\ immediate\ S \xrightarrow[E_c \cup \mathcal{L}]{\phi,0} nothing_c}$$

This rule describes the behavior of the **abort** construct when the signal being watched is present in the environment. The trasition rule states that the entire construct is transformed into a **nothing** construct. Note that the modification that statement *stat1* would have made to the environment are discarded.

16. *Preemption Rules*

$$\frac{S \notin E_c, stat1_c \xrightarrow[E_c \cup \mathcal{L}]{E',b} c(stat1'_d)}{abort\ stat1\ when_c\ immediate\ S \xrightarrow[E_c \cup \mathcal{L}]{E',b} abort\ c(stat1'_d) when_c\ immediate\ S}$$

The above rule governs the behavior of an **abort** construct when the signal being watched for is *not* present in the environment. The behavior specified by the rule is to execute exactly as statement *stat1* would. Note that the construct remains unchanged while the enclosed statement *stat1* has transformed into statement *stat1'*.

17. *Preemption Rules*

$$\frac{S \notin E_c, stat1_c \xrightarrow[E_c \cup \mathcal{L}]{E',0} c(stat1'_d)}{abort\ stat1\ when_c\ immediate\ S \xrightarrow[E_c \cup \mathcal{L}]{E',0} nothing_c}$$

The above rule governs the behavior of an **abort** construct when the signal being watched for is not present in the environment and the statement within its scope has terminated. The behavior specified by the rule is to execute exactly as statement *stat1* would. Note that the construct has transformed itself into a **nothing** construct. The difference with respect to the previous rule is that in this case *stat1* has terminated.

18. *Preemption Rules*:

$$\frac{stat1_c \xrightarrow[E_c \cup \mathcal{L}]{E',b} c(stat1'_d)}{abort\ stat1\ when_c\ S \xrightarrow[E_c \cup \mathcal{L}]{E',b} abort\ _c(stat1'_d)when_c\ immediate\ S}$$

The above rule governs the behavior of an **abort** construct when the **immediate** modifier is not present. The behavior for the first instance, as specified by the rule, is to execute exactly as statement *stat1* would. Note that the construct has changed into the **immediate** variant of the **abort** statement while the enclosed statement *stat1* has been substituted by statement *stat1'*.

19. *Suspend Rules*:

$$\texttt{suspend}\ _c(stat_{d_u})\ \texttt{when}_{c_u}\ \texttt{immediate}\ s \to\ _c(stat_{d_v})$$

This rule captures how the **immediate** variant of a **suspend** statement modifies the clock of a given statement. Effectively, we are re-assigning a new clock derived as a function of the existing clock d_u and the signal s to the statement block *stat*. Note that we have decorated the clock expression with state variables, u and v, which we term *suspension contexts*. In this case the suspension context u and the signal s are used to derive a new suspension context v which controls the execution of the statement

19.3. Formal Semantics

stat. Informally, a function of the suspension context is used to gate the clock to the statement block within the scope of the suspend statement. Further note that the suspension context is normally inherited from the parent statement though this is not shown in the rules above. Details regarding the exact mechanism adopted are not discussed here; the interested reader is referred to [7]. The rule for this statement cannot be modeled in terms of the rules for suspend in Esterel.

20. *Suspend Rules*:

$$\frac{stat_c \xrightarrow[E_c \cup \mathcal{L}]{E', b} c(stat'_d)}{\texttt{suspend } stat \texttt{ when}_c \ s \xrightarrow[E_c \cup \mathcal{L}]{E', b} \texttt{suspend } c(stat'_d) \texttt{ when}_c \texttt{ immediate } s}$$

This rule captures how a suspend statement is treated in Multiclock Esterel. The construct behaves like the statement within its scope and then transforms into the immediate variant of the suspend statement. Note that for this transition to be enabled the statement within the scope of the suspend statement (*stat*) should not terminate at the first instance.

21. *Suspend Rules*:

$$\frac{stat_c \xrightarrow[E_c \cup \mathcal{L}]{E', 0} c(stat'_d)}{\texttt{suspend } stat \texttt{ when}_c \ s \xrightarrow[E_c \cup \mathcal{L}]{E', 0} \texttt{nothing}_c}$$

This rule captures how a suspend statement is treated when the statement block it encloses terminates in the first instance. Note that the whole construct transforms into the nothing construct.

22. Exit:

$$exit_c \ T \xrightarrow[E_c \cup \mathcal{L}]{\phi \cup \mathcal{L} \cup T, b} halt_c$$

This rule describes how the exit statement works in Multiclock Esterel. It does not contribute to the signal environment but adds to the set of labels that maintain state about the weak suspension contexts in effect. Note that the construct does not terminate. Instead, it is transformed into a halt construct. This is the mechanism used in Multiclock Esterel to raise an exception condition to abort normal control flow.

23. *New tick Statement*:

$$newtick\ S\ in\ stat\ end_{c_u} \xrightarrow[E_c \cup \mathcal{L}]{\phi,b} c(stat_{s_\phi})$$

The `newtick` construct is the only construct that can explicitly alter the binding of clocks to statements. Note that the rewriting is merely syntactic in form and does not contribute to the signal environment in any way. The rule states that the execution of statement *stat* will be carried out on clock *s* while termination of the whole construct will still be synchronous with clock *c*. Note also how the `newtick` construct resets the suspension context of the statement block *stat* to ϕ, thus insulating it from suspensions triggered from enclosing blocks. The exact mechanism used to manipulate suspension contexts will not be discussed here and the reader is referred to [7].

Example 4

```
newtick C0 in
    emit S1
    newtick C1 in
        emit S2
    end
    emit S3
end
```

The above code ensures that signal S1 *and signal* S3 *are synchronous with clock* C0 *and that signal* S2 *is synchronous with clock* C1. *On execution, even though there are no explicit* await *statements, this code snippet will* not *terminate instantaneously unless clocks* C0 *and* C1 *occur simultaneously in which case a single event containing all three signals* S1, S2 *and* S3 *will be observable. If clocks* C0 *and* C1 *do not share any instant, then three distinct events will be visible, each characterized by the presence of one of signals* S1, S2 *or* S3. *The third case occurs when initially clock* C0 *occurs in isolation while the second occurrence of clock* C0 *coincides with that of clock* C1. *In this case, two distinct events are visible, the first characterized by the presence of signal*

19.3. Formal Semantics

S1 *while the second event will contain both signal S2 as well as signal S3.*

24. *Newtick statement (weak):*

$$\text{weak newtick } S \text{ in stat end}_{c_u} \xrightarrow[E_c \cup \mathcal{L}]{\phi, b} c(\text{stat}_{s_u})$$

The **weak** variant of the **newtick** construct differs from strong version in that the suspension context of the enclosed statement block is *not* altered while the clock is switched. Again the rewriting is merely syntactic in form and does not contribute to the signal environment in any way. The rule states that the execution of statement block *stat* will be carried out on clock *s* and with the inherited suspension context *u*.

25. *weak abort:*

$$\frac{S \in E_c, \text{stat1}_c \xrightarrow[E_c \cup \mathcal{L}]{E', b} c(\text{stat1}'_d)}{\text{weak abort stat1 when}_c \text{ immediate } S \xrightarrow[E_c \cup \mathcal{L}]{E', 0} \text{nothing}_c}$$

This rule describes the behavior of the **weak abort** construct when the signal being watched is present in the environment. The transition rule states that the entire construct is transformed into a **nothing** construct. Note that the modification that statement *stat1* made to the environment are preserved. However the termination status of the statement *stat1* is discarded.

26. *weak abort rule2:*

$$\frac{S \notin E_c, \text{stat1}_c \xrightarrow[E_c \cup \mathcal{L}]{E', b} c(\text{stat1}'_d)}{\text{weak abort stat1 when}_c \text{ immediate } S \xrightarrow[E_c \cup \mathcal{L}]{E', b} \text{weak abort } c(\text{stat1}'_d) \text{ when}_c \text{ immediate } S}$$

The above rule governs the behavior of a **weak abort** construct when the signal being watched for is *not* present in the environment. The behavior specified by the rule is to execute exactly as statement *stat1* would. Note that the construct remains unchanged while the enclosed statement *stat1* has transformed into statement *stat1'*.

27. weak abort rule3

$$\frac{S \notin E_c, stat1_c \xrightarrow[E_c \cup \mathcal{L}]{E',0} c(stat1'_d)}{weak\ abort\ stat1\ when_c\ immediate\ S \xrightarrow[E_c \cup \mathcal{L}]{E',0} nothing_c}$$

The above rule governs the behavior of a **weak abort** construct when the signal being watched for is *not* present in the environment *and* the statement within its scope has terminated. The behavior specified by the rule is to execute exactly as statement *stat1* would. Note that the construct has transformed itself into a **nothing** construct. The difference with respect to the previous rule is that in this case *stat1* has terminated.

28. *weak abort rule4*

$$\frac{stat1_c \xrightarrow[E_c \cup \mathcal{L}]{E',b} c(stat1'_d)}{weak\ abort\ stat1\ when_c\ S \xrightarrow[E_c \cup \mathcal{L}]{E',b} weak\ abort\ _c(stat1'_d)\ when_c\ immdediate\ S}$$

The above rule governs the behavior of a **weak abort** construct when the **immediate** modifier is not present. The behavior for the first instance, as specified by the rule, is to execute exactly as statement *stat1* would. Note that the construct has changed into the **immediate** variant of the **abort** statement while the enclosed statement *stat1* has been substituted by statement *stat1'*.

29. Trap Statement:

$$\frac{stat1_c \xrightarrow[E_c \cup \mathcal{L}]{E' \cup \mathcal{L} \cup \mathcal{T}, b} stat1'_c, b == 0\ or\{T\} == \mathcal{L}}{trap\ T\ in\ stat1\ end_c \xrightarrow[E_c \cup \mathcal{L}]{E' \cup \mathcal{L} - \{T\}, 0} nothing_c}$$

This rule governs the behavior of a **trap** construct when either the enclosed statement *stat1* terminates, or this instance of the **trap** construct is the top most one for which an exception is pending. Under both these conditions, the **trap** statement is transformed into a **nothing** construct. As can be seen from the rule, changes made to the environment by statement *stat1* are preserved. Further, note that T is not a signal but a *trap* label that is used to identify the **trap** statement that is being activated *via* an **exit** statement.

19.3. Formal Semantics

30. **Trap Statement Rules:**

$$\frac{stat1_c \xrightarrow[E_c \cup \mathcal{L}]{E' \cup \mathcal{L} \cup \mathcal{V}, b} {}_c(stat1'_d), \{T\} \notin \nu}{trap\ T\ in\ stat1\ end_c \xrightarrow[E_c \cup \mathcal{L}]{E' \cup \mathcal{L} \cup \mathcal{V} - \{T\}, 0} trap\ T\ in\ {}_c(stat1'_d)\ end_c}$$

This rule covers the behavior of the **trap** construct when the enclosed statement block has raised an exception or has not terminated. Further, if an exception has been raised, the precondition states that this is not the outer most **trap** construct. The behavior then is to remove from the set of labels, the label corresponding to this instance of the **trap** construct and continue execution as shown above. Note that the termination status of the construct has been reset to 0. Actual termination will occur when the enclosing **trap** statement that has been triggered here actually preempts all the enclosed blocks. Here again, T is not a signal but a *trap* label that is used to identify the **trap** statement that is being activated *via* an **exit** statement.

In the multiclock environment, we also need to consider the issues of latching relative to preemptive and suspend features. theses aspects are treated in the next section.

The use of latches raises some subtle issues when considered in the context of features in Multiclock Esterel. We shall not go into details; the reader is referred to [7].

The following theorems can be established using the semantics rules.

Theorem 1: With the restriction that output signals are not used in clock expressions, the clock propagation rules provide a unique non-cyclic binding of clocks for the statements and the process of clock propagation terminates.

Theorem 2: If there is no explicit clock i.e., no **newtick** statement used in the program the semantics coincides with the classical semantics of Esterel.

Theorem 3: If the given Multiclock Esterel program is non-causal (in the sense of the notion of Esterel) and the clocks are not cyclic (verifiable by the simple restrictions mentioned earlier), then the program is executable ignoring *metastability* issues due to the density of clocks.

An interesting question to ask is:
Is it meaningful to have a translation of Multiclock Esterel to Esterel ?

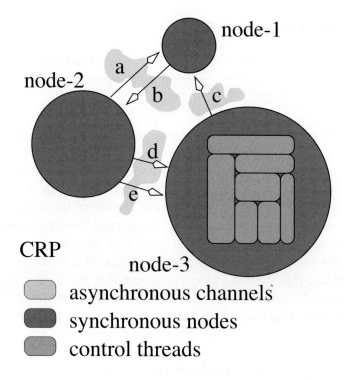

Figure 19.3: The *CRP* Environment

The answer is Multiclock Esterel program can be translated Due to the process of synchronization of the asynchronous behaviour, one loses the modularity. In fact, some of the variant notions of suspend that have strong hardware annotations are not possible in Esterel. Further, the suspend construct as it exists in Esterel itself again is not modular.

19.4 Embedding CRP

In this section, we shall show how CRP can be seen as a special case of Multiclock Esterel .

A *CRP* program essentially *CRP* is a program consisting of a network $M_1 \parallel M_2 \parallel M_n$ of Esterel reactive programs or *nodes*, each having its own input/output signals and its own notion of an instant. Embedding CRP in Multiclock Esterel involves (i) controlling the visibility of the channels as required and (ii) the protocol for implementing the rendezvous and the guarded choice.

19.4. Embedding CRP

First, let us consider access control in Multiclock Esterel . In addition to normal block structured scoping, Multiclock Esterel permits the use of declarations to *restrict* the visibility of objects. This feature does not modify any of the underlying concepts involved in latching and clocking modules.

This is a generalization of the *CRP* scenario (Figure 19.3) where Esterel nodes had explicit names and channels declared between nodes were visible only to the nodes they connect.

Example 5 *The ability to arbitrarily restrict the visibility of objects is a prerequisite if we are to correctly implement CRP programs within the framework of Multiclock Esterel because CRP programs involve the existence of named channels that are private to the nodes connected by them.*

Now, let us turn to protocols required for implementation. The general framework for the implementation would involve implementing each *CRP* node as an independently clocked Multiclock Esterel module and using signals (which are automatically latched) to communicate amongst them. Private channels are implemented by restricting the scope of the signals constituting the channel.

Considering the configuration given in Figure 19.3 we could have the following partial implementation.

```
module node3 :
input d, e;
output c visible only to node1
    newtick clock3 in
        statement
    end
end
```

Note that the code for node node-3 *is free to execute on its own private clock* clock3. *This code segment however does not realize* rendezvous *as defined by the CRP paradigm. This example only provides the necessary framework to implement* rendezvous.

We now extend Example 5 to implement *rendezvous* as defined in *CRP* on the lines of the implementation described in [8, 64]. Note that we follow the synchronization protocol as given in [8].

Example 6 *We give below code snippets that implement the* rendezvous *protocol of CRP. The code is divided into* sender *and* receiver *components.*

```
01 module sender :
02 input rcpt, rabrt, labrt;
03 output data, conf, sabrt, success, fail;
05    present labrt else
06       emit data;
07       await case
08          labrt :  emit sabrt
09                   emit fail
10          rcpt  :  emit conf
11                   emit success
12          rabrt :  emit fail
13       end
14    end
15 end
```

The sender module above works by first emitting the signal data and then waiting for either an rabrt or rcpt signal to arrive from the receiver. On receipt of the rcpt signal, the sender confirms the rendezvous via the conf signal. If on the other hand, the sender is locally preempted using the signal labrt it responds by emitting the sabrt signal and terminates. Receipt of signal rabrt also causes unsuccessful termination of the rendezvous. Note that the sender module has not defined an explicit clock and will run at the default one. Further note that preemption at the initial instance precludes the emission of signal data. A successful rendezvous is characterized by the presence of signal success at termination.

```
01 module receiver :
02 input data, sabrt, conf, labrt
03 output rcpt, rabrt, success, failure

05    present labrt else
06       await case
07          labrt :  present data then
08                      emit rabrt
09                      emit failure
10          end
11          data  :  emit rcpt
12                   await case
13                      labrt :  emit failure
14                      conf  :  emit success
15                      sabrt :  emit failure
16                   end
17       end
18    end
19 end
```

19.4. Embedding CRP

The receiver module given above works by waiting for a data *signal to arrive from a sender module and then acknowledging it by emitting a* rcpt *signal. It then awaits the arrival of a* conf *signal which will indicate successful termination. Note that preemption at the initial instant is transparent to the sender whereas preemption simultaneous with the receipt of the* data *signal causes the emission of the* rabrt *signal. Note also that preemption occurring after the* rcpt *signal is emitted will not prevent the sender from treating the* rendezvous *as complete. As in the case of the sender module, no explicit clock has been specified.*

Example 6 above provides an overview of how Multiclock Esterel could be used to implement a *CRP* style *rendezvous*. However, this alone does not suffice to implement the generic *CRP* paradigm wherein *guarded choice* could be involved in *selecting* a particular *channel* from amongst many possibilities. The following example outlines how this could be achieved.

Example 7 *We present an example of how* guarded choice *as in the CRP paradigm could be implemented in Multiclock Esterel. For the sake of brevity we consider only two* rendezvous *in each guard.*

```
01  module receiver :
02  input dataA, sabrtA, confA,
          dataB, sabrtB, confB, labrt;
04  output rcptA, rabrtA,
           rcptB, rabrtB, success, failure;

07      present labrt else
08        await case
09          labrt : present dataA then
10            emit rabrtA
11          end
12          present dataB then
13            emit rabrtB
14          end
15          dataA : emit rcptA
16            await case
17              labrt : emit failure
18              confA : emit success
19              sabrtA : emit failure
20            end
21          dataB : emit rcptB
```

```
22      await case
23          labrt  : emit failure
24          confB  : emit success
25          sabrtB : emit failure
26      end
27    end
28  end
29 end
```

The code for a receiver module above works by making a choice on which of signals dataA and dataB to respond to and then behaving like that was the only rendezvous being attempted. As a consequence of the deterministic nature of Multiclock Esterel, the implementation above is constrained to select signal dataA whenever both signal dataA and signal dataB occur together. Also note that the decision to implement choice in this manner precludes the possibility of allowing mixed guards (i.e. mixed input and output channels) as this could lead to implementation induced deadlocks.

```
01 module sender :
02 output dataA, sabrtA, confA, dataB,
03        sabrtB, confB, success, failure;
04 input rcptA, rabrtA,
05       rcptB, rabrtB, labrt;
06   present labrt else
07     emit dataA;
08     emit dataB;
09     await case
10         labrt : emit sabrtA
11           emit sabrtB
12         rcptA : emit confA
13           emit sabrtB
14           emit success
15         rcptB : emit confB
16           emit sabrtA
17           emit success
18         rabrtA : present rabrtB then
19            emit failure
20         else
21            await case
```

19.4. Embedding CRP

```
22              labrt : emit sabrtB
23                 emit failure
24              rabrtB : emit failure
25              rcptB : emit confB
26                 emit sabrtA
27                 emit success
28            end
29         end
30         rabrtB : present rabrtA then
31            emit failure
32         else
33            await case
34               labrt : emit sabrtA
35                  emit failure
36               rabrtA : emit failure
37               rcptA : emit confA
38                  emit sabrtB
39                  emit success
40            end
41         end
42      end
43   end
44 end
```

The structure of the sender code above implementing guarded rendezvous *makes it amply clear that it depends on the receiver to limit the choice. The sender emits both signal* dataA *and signal* dataB *and awaits a response of either signal* rcptA *or signal* rcptB. *Receipt of either one of these signals guarantees that the* rendezvous *can now successfully terminate or will be locally preempted, in which case, it is acceptable to issue an abort on the other channel. Note that receipt of an abort message from a receiver causes the sender to await a response from the remaining receiver unless there already is an abort message from it too.*

It is obvious that in both the sender and receiver modules presented, only one rendezvous *can terminate successfully. It is also easy to see that this implementation does not introduce any deadlock.*

In the above, we have illustrated that the framework of Multiclock Esterel embeds the CRP as an instance. Since the framework does not need to distinguish various levels of concurrency and also the constraints of causality of Esterel (due to the underlying asynchronous interfaces), it can be generally used the specification and verification of a hierarchical network of processes.

19.5 Modelling a VHDL Subset

Here, we sketch how Multiclock Esterel can be used to provide a rigorous semantics for VHDL subsets.

VHDL uses two distinct notions of time, real or macro time and delta or micro time. Macro time, measured in units as small as femto seconds define points in time where observations about the state of the simulation can be made by an external observer while micro time deals with the succession of strictly synchronous events that occur internally to the simulator while computing the next observable state from the current one. Intervals between point in delta time have no significance and cannot be measured. Further, there is no *a priori* limit on the number of micro time points that can exist between successive macro time points.

In contrast, Multiclock Esterel admits only one notion of time, that defined by a succession of external events where the interval between any two successive events has no significance. Nevertheless, the Multiclock Esterel engine does use an implicit notion of *micro time* to execute sequential statements. This makes for a very convenient embedding of micro time in VHDL into a similar notion in Multiclock Esterel. Another significant difference is that VHDL can specify delays in realtime while Multiclock Esterel cannot make explicit references to elapsed time. Further, Multiclock Esterel can not express any condition involving the (bounded) future while VHDL can. We model these aspects using a event-scheduler shown in Figure 19.4.

To every output signal that will be involved in delayed updates, we associate a driver. Further, we associate an *event scheduler* with the execution environment for the Multiclock Esterel program. The entire configuration is depicted in Figure 19.4. The function of the event scheduler is to implement delays outside the Multiclock Esterel environment. Delayed updates to a signal are posted as event requests by the Multiclock Esterel module to the event scheduler. After the specified delay period has elapsed, the event scheduler generates a *trigger event* in response to which the signal driver synchronously emits the signal with the updated value. Using such a scheme, we can model the timing, reactive and delay features of VHDL. While discussing the development of programs in Multiclock Esterel using

19.6. Discussion

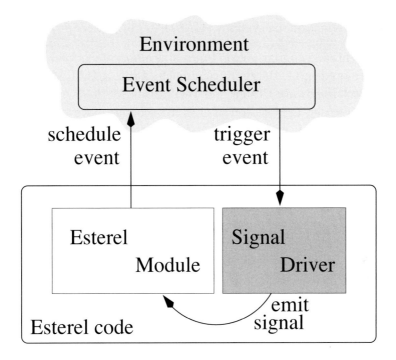

Figure 19.4: Event Scheduling

micropipelines, we have partly illustrated the modelling of operations and modules. For details the reader is referred to the [65].

19.6 Discussion

Multiclock Esterel provides:

1. a multi-clock generalization of Esterel. Such a generalization eliminates shortcomings of the classical monochronous Esterel such as weaknesses of module definitions, parameterizing clocks (or tick of modules), context-dependent suspension operators etc.

2. a unification of synchrony and asynchrony. This in turn leads to modular specification of asynchronous systems as well as systems with multiple clocks.

3. a clean model for VHDL/VERILOG features.

4. a formal methodology for the modelling of Globally Asynchronous and Locally Synchronous systems (GALs).

As highlighted, a similar notion but not as elaborate as we have discussed has been explored in G. Berry, E. Sentovich. Proc. CHARME'2001, Edinburgh, Correct Hardware Design and Verification Methods, Springer-Verlag LNCS 2144. Further exploration of clocking schemes have been explored in L. Arditi, G. Berry, M. Kishinevsky, and M. Perreaut. Proc. Designing Correct Circuits DCC'06, Vienna, Austria. The area is challenging from various perspectives of hardware, parallel computing through phase synchronization etc. These aspects will not be explored here.

Chapter 20

Modelling Real-Time Systems in ESTEREL

In the modelling of real-time systems, specification of various temporal relations between occurrences of events and interrupts plays an important role. Common examples of temporal relations required are:

- Maximal separation between events.
- Minimal separation of events.
- Exact distance between events.
- Periodicity of events.
- Bounded response of events.

The broad needs for real-time programming taking into account the temporal specification needs along with interrupt handling needs are described below:

1. *Specifying Periodic activities with deadlines:* Some components of the system may have to be executed periodically with some other components having deadlines. Additionally, we need to specify:

    - Termination of periodic activities on receiving certain interrupts.
    - Error handler on timeout.

2. *Specifying Guaranteed Activities:* We have to ensure that certain activities complete once started.

ESTEREL does not have any implicit clock. If we have to use references to clock values, we have to treat it as a sensor or an external signal. In the following, we shall discuss how the notion of a clock can be interpreted through the `exec` construct. Some of the real-time specifications are taken from [81].

20.1 Interpretation of a Global Clock in terms of `exec`

Consider a task CLOCK which accesses a global clock and sends the alarm signals at the times requested. Declaration of the task CLOCK takes the form:

```
task CLOCK(d) return alarm ({real})
```
Now, an alarm after ℓ units can be instantiated by

```
exec CLOCK(ℓ)
```
Since the `exec` statement is not instantaneous, it is necessary that $\ell > 0$. The semantics of `exec` permits the use of multiple instantiations on the same and different nodes. This feature makes it possible to use CLOCK as a global clock for different components. That is, different components can instantiate CLOCK to give them alarm at appropriate times without any interference. Note that the notion of global clock is very essential in the context of specifying hybrid systems [82].

20.2 Modelling Real-Time Requirements in ESTEREL

In this section, we shall illustrate how the various requirements of real-time programming can be modelled in ESTEREL.

20.2.1 Deadline Specification

Consider the specification of an air-traffic control system which should provide final clearance for a pilot to land within 60 seconds after clearance is requested. Otherwise, the pilot will abort the landing procedure. Assuming that there is no global clock, the program to achieve the above activity is given below.

```
emit req_clearance;
abort
```

20.2. Modelling Real-Time Requirements in ESTEREL

```
       trap T in
         [exec CLOCK(60)
       || await get_clearance; exit T];
       end trap
     when time_up
     timeout abort_landing
     end
```

where the asynchronous task CLOCK is declared as follows:

```
       task CLOCK(ℓ) return time_up;
```

with the interpretation that the return-signal time_up will be sent from the asynchronous medium after ℓ units of time.

Assuming that there is a global clock which sends Ctick signals at appropriate settings, the program takes the form shown below. Note that the clearance if not received within 60 ticks of the global clock signal Ctick, it is aborted (indicated by abort_landing)

```
       emit req_clearance;
       abort
             await get_clearance
       when   Ctick(60)
       timeout abort_landing
       end
```

20.2.2 Periodic Activities

The periodic activities can be naturally expressed in plain ESTEREL [12]. For example,

```
       every S do  stat  end
```
which expands to
```
       await S;
       loop
         do  stat  upto S
       end;
```

corresponds to waiting for the occurrence of signal S and then starting the body *stat*; the body is restarted afresh at each occurrence of the signal.

Consider a telephone network in which the switches periodically monitor other switches to detect their failures. Each switch sends an *I am alive* message to a subset of switches in the network. This subset is referred to as *cohorts* of a switch. If a switch does not receive an *I am alive* message once every period, of duration p seconds, from each of its cohorts, it suspects that the cohort may be down and initiates fault detection and recovery. If, for any reason, a switch is shutdown, a `SHUTDOWN` message is sent to all its cohorts. Each switch creates asynchronous tasks, one per cohort, to monitor the cohorts. In the code segment given below:

- Lines 4-10 depict the code for the process looking for a cohort message (task created corresponding to each switch is the one shown between lines 5-9) for every p secs; if it does not arrive in p secs, then it exits the trap which comes under the outermost abort statement for the SHUTDOWN while it emits SHUTDOWN).

```
1  abort
2     await p;
3     trap T in
4        loop
5           abort
6              exec cohort(id);
7           when p
8              timeout exit T;
9           end %abort
10       end %loop
11    end %trap
12    emit "SHUTDOWN";
13 when SHUTDOWN
14 end %abort
```

where emitting p corresponds to the cycle given by,

```
every p_secs do
   emit p
end
```

the asynchronous task `cohort` is given by

```
task cohort (id) return "I AM ALIVE";
```

whose task is to send the return signals periodically.

Before discussing the specification of guaranteed activities, we discuss the formal semantics of the **rendezvous** discussed earlier.

20.2.3 Guaranteed Activities

In this section, we shall give a series of examples that would highlight how the various of real-time specification such as maximal, minimal specification, duration and priority can be integrated through the rendezvous of the CRP.

Consider the realization of the rendezvous. The rendezvous can be realized using the following four input/output signals:

20.2. Modelling Real-Time Requirements in ESTEREL

- sL is an output signal signaling the request for starting the rendezvous.

- s_r_L is an input signal emitted by the asynchronous task as soon as the partners of the rendezvous have agreed to start the rendezvous. This could be declared even in the declaration of the task.

- L is the final input signal sent from the asynchronous medium indicating the completion of the task.

- kL is the kill signal as detailed earlier.

A simple guaranteed activity [81] on a rendezvous can be described as follows: wait for the actual start of the rendezvous; once it starts, we could guarantee the completion of the task for a period of time fixed a priori. This example demonstrates the a strict duration specification (essentially a watchdog timer) Assuming that once the rendezvous is started the completion is guaranteed in the given deadline, and that an alternate action is possible only if it can start before the end of t seconds (defined through the clock Ctick), the code fragment for the task is described below:

```
[       abort
            exec L:P
        when kill
        end
   ||
        abort
            await s_r_L;
        when Ctick(t)
        timeout emit kill; ALTERNATE
        end
]
```

where tick is the global clock described earlier.

In the following example, we shall illustrate how nondeterministic choice can be specified. In the program the alternative rendezvous are simultaneously initiated and whichever comes first is accepted. Note that the channels are mutually exclusive and hence, only one return signal can be received at an instant. Once one rendezvous is complete, it aborts the other rendezvous by emitting the signal kill. As there cannot be more than one return signal at an instant, the priorities as specified by the await-case do not apply.

```
[       abort
            exec L1:P1; emit kill;
        when kill
        end
```

```
    ||
         ⋮
    ||
         abort
            exec Ln:Pn; emit kill
         when kill
         end
    ||
       abort
        await
           case s_r_L1 do ;
              ⋮
           case s_r_Ln do ;
         end
       when Ctick(t);
       timeout emit kill; ALTERNATE
       end
]
```

Assuming that from the start of the actual rendezvous, at least one instant is required for completion of the rendezvous in any asynchronous task, say i, the signal `kill` will not be simultaneous with its return signals `Li` and hence, the program will satisfy the intended requirements. However, if that is not the case, then the expression `when kill` in task i would have to be replaced by `when kill and ¬(Li)`; the additional test for the absence of its own return signal at the instant `kill` could be generated will allow the completion of the task when both the signals arrive at the same instant (note that `abort-when` is a strong preemption construct).

Consider the program given below which that describes the following demonstrates how alternative action can be enforced when the normal action is not satisfying the timing constraints. This program models a simple railroad controller that controls a signal to stop or let go a train over a particular track. This controller has to determine whether the track will be clear when a train is expected to reach the track. It has to determine this early enough so as to give itself enough time to stop the train if required. Suppose, the train will not reach the track before d seconds and it takes at most s seconds to stop the train where, $s < d$. Recollect that `?request_track` gives the value of the signal at that instant.

```
    [
         await request_track;
         abort
            exec check_clear;
```

20.2. Modelling Real-Time Requirements in ESTEREL

```
            when Ctick(?request_track - s)
            timeout stop
            end
        ||
            await control;
            emit request_track(d)
            await
                case stop do APPLY_brakes;
                case clear do PASS;
            end;
    ]
```

where the `check_clear` is declared as follows:

   task check_clear return {stop, clear}

Note that when signals `stop` and `clear` arrive simultaneously, the priority is for `stop` and hence, the corresponding action of `APPLY_brakes` takes place. It is also possible to have nested priorities. An effective use of priorities in achieving predictability is illustrated by the following simple model of an autonomous guided vehicle controller.

The main components of this controller has the following functions: The sensors provide data about the vehicle's position and environment. The higher-level control system represents the land-based computer system and the on-board smoothing. It is responsible for accepting high level plans and generating points along the path which the vehicle is required to follow under normal circumstances. These points are produced more or less continually at regular intervals.

The emergency avoid system, however, would normally be in an idle state in which it monitors the vehicle sensors. If a collision appeared imminent, the module switches to an active state and provides points along some alternative path until the danger of collision has been avoided, then returning to its idle state.

A multiplexor provides a link between the higher level control and the emergency avoid process and directs their output to a buffer. It relays data from the higher level control system to the buffer until a toggle signal is received from the emergency system. It then relays points from the emergency system until another toggle is signaled. In addition, the buffer is cleared whenever the state changes. The behavioural specification requirements are:

1. Continuously get points from the higher-level control and passes it to the point buffer.

2. Once an emergency system starts, the multiplexor should:

Chapter 20. Modelling Real-Time Systems in ESTEREL

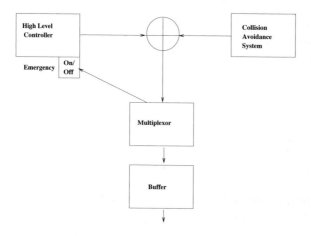

Figure 20.1: Multiplexor - Collision Avoidance

- Clear the buffer and get the points from the collision avoidance system until the collision is avoided.

Figure 20.1 depicts a schematic diagram for the same.

In the following, we describe an ESTEREL specification of the multiplexor. In the specification of ESTEREL program shown below, IN_1 and IN_2 denote the inputs the multiplexor receives from the high-level control and emergency system respectively. Note that from the requirement specification, it follows that EMERG_START has priority over the normal signals. this is reflected in the specification below; the `immediate` in the first case of the `await` reflects that it is watching the immediate instant as well. Further, EMERG_OVER has priority over the normal START; this does not play a role in this program; in fact, it could be interchanged as well (note that ?IN_2 gives the value of the signal at that instant. Also note that we assume that EMERG_START and EMERG_STOP (assume that they are separated at least by one instant) do not happen simultaneously.

```
BUFFER := NULL;
loop
  await
    case immediate EMERG_START
         abort
          await IN_2;
          emit buffer(?IN_2);
         when EMERG_OVER;
         Timeout BUFFER:=EMPTY
```

```
              end:
     case EMERG_OVER
          abort
           await IN_1;
           emit BUFFER(?IN_1);
          when EMERG_START;
          Timeout BUFFER:=EMPTY
          end:
     case START
          abort await IN_1;
           emit BUFFER(?IN_1);
          when EMERG_START;
          Timeout BUFFER:=EMPTY
          end:
  end
end
```

Chapter 21

Putting it Together

Language methodologies for specifying and analyzing complex real-time systems has been a challenging issue for quite some time. There have been several approaches for the same. In this monograph, we have primarily focussed on one of the most successful approaches for the design of complex reactive systems: the synchronous approach to reactive/real-time systems.

Synchronous approach provides an elegant and powerful abstraction of real-time enabling rigorous reasoning and efficient implementation of real time systems. This approach has resulted in many different styles of programming embedded systems, three of which were discussed in this monograph. Using this approach, several languages and associated tool chains have been developed. Two prominent languages of the family ESTEREL and Lustre based on the imperative (control) and the dataflow paradigms respectively have been adapted significantly in industries. Two distinctive features of these two languages are their amenability to verification and the tool environment provided by them for the design and analysis. The tool chain includes environments that support debugging, simulation, verification and validated code generation etc. The tools developed have been extensively used by the academic community and researchers. The tool chains discussed in this monograph have been integrated into a single commercial programming environment called SCADE. SCADE is marketed by ESTEREL Technologies and have found wide acceptance in the aerospace, process control and hardware industries. Some of the companies that use SCADE tool chain widely are aerospace companies like Aerospatiale, the European Aero space Agency and Rockwel-Colins; the other industries that are interested in synchronous approach include Schneider Electric, Dassault Aviation, ST Microelectronics, Intel and Texas Instruments. While StateCharts is one of the most widely used industrial formalisms for reactive systems (automobile, avionics etc), the synchronous approach scores over the formalism in terms of verifiability and modularity. It must be noted that scalability with complex data structures is still a challenge. This is one of the major thrusts of research.

As our focus has been on languages founded on pure synchrony hypothesis, we have not discussed other languages such as SIGNAL, Reactive C, Reactive Java etc that have also been in wide circulation in academia or industry. We have some aspects in our historical perspective discussion earlier while discussing ESTEREL .

The designers using SCADE can build their models in a mix of three different styles: state machines, data flow and imperative programs. The state machines are called Synchronous State Machines which is a synthesis of Argos and ESTEREL . Lustre is used for data flow style programming while ESTEREL is used for imperative style. The SCADE environment includes a powerful code generator that can generate DO-178 compliant code which is a requirement for aerospace software; a verification engine is also part of the tool chain and observer based verification that we discussed in this monograph is used. One of the recent extension of SCADE is the Matlab/Simulink Gateway. This enables the conventional control system designers who use Marlab/Simulink tool chain to make use the efficient and quality code generation capabilities of SCADE.

The synchronous approach has also contributed significantly to synchronous circuit design. The rich control constructs of ESTEREL have attracted the attention of many researchers. The original efficient implementation of ESTEREL was derived from a hardware implementation. Further, ESTEREL has also been widely accepted in CAD industry. It may be noted that SystemC is another language widely used for SoC (system on a chip) that has several features borrowed from ESTEREL . A foundational semantics and verifications are some of the fertile areas of research [85, 25]. ESTEREL framework has lot of potential challenges in terms of hardware/software co-design. Edward [27] have been investigating efficient software implementation of ESTEREL . Code generation of synchronous languages is quite challenging and can benefit from hardware optimization techniques [28, 62]. Specialized hardware that can directly implement ESTEREL constructs is another exploration that is being pursued [76].

Having described the foundations of classical synchrony, we have looked at the need of integration of synchrony and asynchrony. CRP was the first serious attempt towards such a rationale by us jointly with Gerard Berry. One of the issues of CRP has been restriction of asynchrony at limited levels. This limitation has been overcome through Multiclock Esterel paradigm that showed how the synchrony and asynchrony can be unified at a fine grain level. The paradigm analytically has shown succinct representations of an asynchronous network of hierarchical synchronous systems, reactive embedded systems (quasi-synchronous systems) time-triggered protocols etc. There are still a lot challenges from the perspective of relating the paradigm to synthesizing protocols compositionally, synthesizing asynchronous and synchronous hardware design and in general co-design. One important challenge will be to relate to real-time verifications in a compositional and a scalable way. One issue in these formalisms has been sensitivity due to latencies. In [21], protocol for latency-insensitive design has been proposed. It is really a worthwhile idea to integrate in a general asynchronous (which itself is elastic in a sense) framework.

Model based development using high level models have become common in the embedded system world. Matlab/Simulink, UML and Statemate are some of the modeling languages used in embedded system development. But one aspect that distinguishes synchronous approach from these methods is its rigor and mathematical semantics. The latter features are important pre-requisites for safety-critical embedded applications, like aerospace, nuclear and automotive control systems. In fact, it is a users dream to have real-time verification incorporated into UML tools from IBM Rational. There has been initial efforts done at Esterel-Technologies[37] towards such a framework through Scade and UML. One of the authors [83] has explored the integration of synchrony in the UML framework. Such environments are dreams for any embedded system industry. As ESTEREL and Lustre are input nondeterministic and output deterministic, it is interesting to see the applicability to fault-tolerant systems. An initial study was done on a fault-tolerant gyroscopic system [32]. By careful modelling, we could develop a working version of a fault tolerant Lustre program. Many questions such as timing requirements of the code and the requirements, impact of multi-rate system on the algorithm, formulating and establishing properties of un-reachability, relevance of fault modelling along with probabilities of inputs from a reliability analysis etc need a deep exploration.

A large number of control applications are being implemented in distributed architectures. for instance, future automotive control systems implementation platforms are distributed platforms with multiple Electronic Control Units (ECUs), interconnected with time triggered buses, like Flexray. Multiple control functions are spread over multiple ECUs and their implementations from high level languages is a challenge facing automotive system developers. Applications to automobile arena is one of the fertile applications of these languages.

While the languages like ESTEREL , Lustre and Argos could be useful for uni-processor implementations, the other languages CRP, CRSM and multiclock ESTEREL will be intrinsically amenable for distributed applications. The technology, the methods and tools for uni-processor implementations of synchronous languages are well-developed and being used in the industries. For distributed applications, research is underway to extend the uni-processors technologies to distributed platforms. We believe and hope that the foundational principles presented in this monograph would enable the researchers and engineers to develop future technologies, methods and tools for distributed implementation of complex control applications.

Bibliography

[1] F. Boussinot and R. de Simone . The Esterel language. *Proceedings of the IEEE*, 79(9):1293–1304, September 1991.

[2] A. Bouali and R. de Simone. Symbolic Bisimulation Minimisation. *Proceedings of CAV 92*, 1992.

[3] Charles André. SyncCharts: A Visual Representation of Reactive Behaviors. Technical Report RR 95-52, I3S, Sophia-Antipolis, France, 1995.

[4] M. Antoniotti, A. Ferrari, A. Flesca, and A. Sanjiovanni-Vincentelli. An esterel-based reactive java extension for reactive embedded system development. In *Kluwer Academic Publishers*, The Netherlands, 2004.

[5] R. Bagrodia. Synchronization of asynchronous processes in csp. *ACM Trans. Program. Lang. Syst.*, 11(4):585–597, 1989.

[6] J. Barnes. *High Integrity ADA*. Addison Wesley, New-York, 1997.

[7] Basant Rajan. *Programming Languages: Specification & Design of Multiple-Clocked Systems*. PhD thesis, Tata Institute of Fundamental Research, 98.

[8] Basant Rajan and R.K. Shyamasundar. An Implementation of CRP. In *IASTED*, Singapore, 97. (Also TIFR/TCS-95/7 Bombay, India).

[9] G. Berry. Real-time programming: General purpose or special-purpose languages. In G. Ritter, editor, *Information Processing 89*, pages 11–17. Elsevier Science Publishers B.V. (North-Holland), 1989.

[10] G. Berry. Preemption and concurrency. In *Proc. FSTTCS 93*, Lecture Notes in Computer Science 761, pages 72–93. Springer-Verlag, 1993.

[11] G. Berry and G. Gonthier. The Esterel synchronous programming language: Design, semantics, implementation. *Science Of Computer Programming*, 19(2):87–152, 1992.

[12] G. Berry and G. Gonthier. The Esterel Synchronous Programming Language: Design semantics, Implementation. *SCP*, 19(2):87–152, Nov 92.

[13] G. Berry, S. Ramesh, and R.K. Shyamasundar. Communicating reactive processes. In *Proc. 20th ACM Conf. on Principles of Programming Languages, Charleston, Virginia*, 1993.

[14] G. Berry and E. Sentovich. Multiclock esterel. In *CHARME 2001, LNCS 2144*, Edinburgh, 2001. Springer-Verlag.

[15] A. Bhattacharjee, S.D. Dhodapkar, R.K. Shyamasundar, and S. Seshia. A graphical environment for the specification and verification of reactive systems. *Proc. 18th Int. Conf. on Computer Safety, Reliability and Security*, pages 431–444, SAFECOMP'99, Toulouse, France. LNCS vol. 1698 Sept. 1999.

[16] G. Boudol, V. Roy, R. de Simone, and D. Vergamini. Process calculi, from theory to practice: Verification tools. In *Workshop on Automatic Verification Methods for Finite State Systems*, Grenoble, June 1989. LNCS 407, Springer Verlag.

[17] G. Boudol, V. Roy, R. de Simone, and D. Vergamini. Process calculi, from theory to practice: Verification tools. In *Automatic Verification Methods for Finite State Systems*, pages 1–10. Springer-Verlag, LNCS 407, 1990.

[18] G. N. Buckley and A. Silberschatz. An effective implementation for the generalized input-output construct of csp. *ACM Trans. Program. Lang. Syst.*, 5(2):223–235, 1983.

[19] C. Puchol et al. A Formal Approach to Reactive Systems Software: A Telecommunications Application in Esterel. April 1995.

[20] P. Caspi, D. Pilaud, N. Halbwachs, and J. Plaice. **LUSTRE**: A declarative language for programming synchronous systems. In *14th ACM Symposium on Principles of Programming Languages, Munich, Germany*, January 1987.

[21] Jordi Cortadella and Mike Kishinevsky. Synchronous elastic circuits with early evaluation and token counterflow. In *DAC 2007*, pages 416–419, 2007.

[22] Robert de Simone. Higher-level synchronising devices in meije–sccs. *Theoretical Computer Science*, 37, 1985.

[23] E. W. Dijkstra. *Discipline of Programming*. Prentice Hall Int., New-York, 1981.

[24] L. Doldi. *Validation of Communications Systems with SDL: The Art of SDL Simulation and Reachability Analysis*. John Wiley & Sons, New-York, 2003.

[25] F. Doucet, R. K. Shyamasundar, I.H. Kruger, S. Joshi, and R. Gupta. Reactivity in systemc transaction level models. *HVC 2007, LNCS*, 4899:34–50, 2007.

[26] D. Drusinsky-Yoresh. A state assignment procedure for single-block implementation of statecharts. *IEEE Transactions on Computer-aided Design*, 10(12):1569–1576, 1991.

[27] S. A. Edwards. An esterel compiler for large control-dominated systems. *IEEE Transactions on Computer-Aided Design of Integrated Circuits and Systems*, 21(2):169 – 183, 2002.

[28] Stephen A. Edwards and Jia Zeng. Code generation in the columbia esterel compiler. *EURASIP J on Embedded Systems*, 31, 2007.

[29] E.M. Clarke et al. Verification of the Futurebus+cache coherence protocol. *Proceedings of the Eleventh Int. Symp. on Computer Hardware Description Languages and their Applications*, April 1993.

[30] F. Boussinot. Reactive C: An extension of C to program reactive systems. *Software Practice and Experience*, 21(4):401–428, 1991.

[31] Florence Maraninchi. Operational and Compositional Semantics of Synchronous Automaton Compositions. *Proceedings of CONCUR 92*, 1992.

[32] S.A. Dahodwala C. Parent D Merchat Florence Maraninchi, R.K. Shyamasundar. A case study with the lustre programming environment: A fault-tolerant gyroscopic system. Indo french promostion for advanced research study report (also at synchrone 2002), TIFR, Mumbai, 2002.

[33] G. Berry. The constructive semantics of pure esterel. *http://www-sop.inria.fr/meije/esterel/esterel-eng.html.*

[34] G. Berry. The esterel v5 language primer version v5-91. *http://www-sop.inria.fr/meije/esterel/esterel-eng.html.*

[35] G.Berry. Preemption in Concurrent Systems. volume 761 of *LNCS*, pages 72–93. Springer-Verlag, 93.

[36] D. Gries. *Science of Programming.* Prentice-Hall Int., New-York, 1983.

[37] Alain Le Guennec and Bernard Dion. Bridging uml and safety critical software. In *ERTS*, January 2006, Toulouse.

[38] P. Le Guernic, Albert Benveniste, Patricia Bournai, and Thierry Gautier. Signal, a data flow oriented language for signal processing. In *IEEE Journal on Acountics, Speech and Signal Processing, ASSP-34(2)*, pages 363–374, 1986.

[39] N. Halbwachs. *Synchronous Programming of Reactive Systems.* Kluwer Academic Publishers, Dordrecht, 1993.

[40] D. Harel. Statecharts: A visual formalism for complex systems. *Science of Computer Programming*, 8(3):231–274, June 1987.

[41] D. Harel. Statecharts: A visual formalism for complex systems. *Science of Computer Programming*, 8(3):231–274, June 1987.

[42] Scott Hauck. Asynchronous design methodologies: An overview. *Proc. of the IEEE*, 83(1):69–93, Jan 1995.

[43] H.Kopetz and G.Grunsteidl. Ttp - a protocol for fault-tolerant real-time systems. *IEEE Computer*, 27(1):14–23, Jan 1994.

[44] C. A. R. Hoare. *Communicating Sequential Processes.* Prentice-Hall, 1985.

[45] C.A.R. Hoare. Communicating Sequential Processes. *CACM*, 21(8), Aug 78.

[46] S. Ramesh J. Hooman and W.P. de Roever. A compositional axiomatization of statecharts. *Science Of Computer Programming*, 101(2):289–335, 1989.

[47] C. B. Jones. Specification and design of (parallel) programs. *IFIP Congress*, pages 321–332, 1983.

[48] H. Kopetz. Real-time systems: Design principles for distributed embedded applications. In *The Kluwer International Series in Engineering and Computer Science, Kluwer Publishers*, 1997.

[49] R. Koymans, R.K. Shyamasundar, R. Gerth, W.P. de Roever, and S. Arun-Kumar. Compositional semantics for real-time distributed programming languages. *Information and Computation*, 79(3):210–256, December 1988.

[50] E. Madelaine and D. Vergamini. Auto: A verification tool for distributed systems using reduction of finite automata networks. In *Proc. FORTE'89 Conference, Vancouver*, 1989.

[51] Zohar Manna and Amir Pnueli. *The Temporal Logic of Reactive and Concurrent Systems Specification*. Springer-Verlag, 1992.

[52] F. Maraninchi. Argonaute, graphical description, semantics and verification of reactive systems by using a process algebra. In *Workshop on Automatic Verification Methods for Finite State Systems*, Grenoble, June 1989. LNCS 407, Springer Verlag.

[53] R. Milner. *Communication and Concurrency*. Prentice-Hall Int., New-York, 1989.

[54] Robin Milner. Calculi for synchrony and asynchrony. *Journal of Theoretical Computer Science*, 25:267–310, 1983.

[55] Lionel Morel. Efficient compilation of array iterators in lustre. *ENTCS*, 65(5):19–26, July 2002.

[56] C.C. Morgan. *Programming from Specifications*. Prentice-Hall Int., New-York, 1990.

[57] E.-R. Olderog. Towards a design calculus for communicating programs. In *Proceedings of the CONCUR '91, Vol. 527, LNCS*, pages 61–72, September 1991.

[58] J. Ostroff. *Temporal Logic for Real-Time Systems*. Advanced Software Development Series. John Wiley, New York, 1990.

[59] P.K. Pandya, Y.S. Ramakrishna, and R.K. Shyamasundar. A compositional semantics of esterel in duration calculus. *2nd AMAST Workshop on Real-Time Systems: Models and Proofs*, June 1995.

[60] S.R. Phanse and R. K. Shyamasundar. Application of esterel for modelling and verification of cachet protocol on crf memory model. *14th Int Conf. on VLSI Design*, pages 179–188, 2001.

[61] A. Pnueli and E. Harel. Applications of temporal logic to the specification of real time systems. In M. Joseph, editor, *Symposium on Formal Techniques in Real-Time and Fault-Tolerant Systems*, volume 331 of *LNCS*, pages 84–98. Springer-Verlag, 1988.

[62] Dumitru Potop-Butucaru, Stephen A. Edward, and Grard Berry. *Compiling Esterel*. Springer-Verlag, 2007.

[63] W.Wood P.Place and M. Tudball. Survey of formal specification techniques for reactive systems. Tech. report cmu/sei-90-tr-5, Software Engineering Institute, Carneige Mellon Uty., Pittsburgh, 1990.

[64] B. Rajan and R.K. Shyamasundar. Networks of preemptible reactive processes: An implementation. In *Int. Conf. on VLSI Design*, New Delhi, India, Dec 1995.

[65] B. Rajan and R.K. Shyamasundar. Multiclock Esterel: A reactive framework for asynchronous design. In 13th *Intl. Conf. on VLSI Design*, pages 76–83, Calcutta, India, Jan 2000.

[66] B. Rajan and R.K. Shyamasundar. Modelling distributed embedded systems in multiclock esterel. In *Forte/PSTV Conference*, pages 301–320, Pisa Italy, October 2000.

[67] B. Rajan and R.K. Shyamasundar. Muliticlock esterel a framework for asynchronous design. In *IPDPS*, pages 201–209, Cancun, Mexico, May 2000.

[68] S. Ramesh. A new efficient implementation of csp with output guards. August 1987.

[69] S. Ramesh. Efficient translation of statecharts into hardware circuits. *Proc. of 12th Int. Conf. on VLSI Design*, January 1999.

[70] S. Ramesh. Implementation of communicating reactive processes. *Parallel Computing*, 25(6), 1999.

[71] S. Ramesh, S. Sonalkar, V. D'silva, N. Chandra, and B. Vijayalakshmi. A toolset for modeling and verification of gals systems. *Proc. of Computer Aided Verification, CAV 2004*, July 2004.

[72] Bernhard Steffen Rance Cleaveland, Joachim Parrow. The concurrency workbench. In *Proceedings of the international workshop on Automatic verification methods for finite state systems*, 1990.

[73] W. Reisig. *Petri Nets*. Eatcs Monagraphs, Springer Verlag, 1985.

[74] T. Pitassi R.K. Shyamasundar, K.T. Narayana. Semantics of nondeterministic asynchronous broadcast networks. *Information and Computation*, 104:215–252, Jun 1993.

[75] R.K.Shyamasundar, Sophie Pinchinat, and Eric Rutten. Taxonomy and Expressiveness of Premption: A syntactic Approach. In *LNCS*, pages 125–141. Springer Verlag, 1998.

[76] P. S. Roop, Z. Salcic, and M. W. Sajeewa Dayaratne. Towards direct execution of esterel programs on reactive processors. *Proceedings of the 4th ACM International Conference on Embedded Software (EMSOFT '04)*, pages 240 – 248.

[77] V. Roy and R. de Simone. Auto and Autograph. In R. Kurshan, editor, *proceedings of Workshop on Computer Aided Verification*, New-Brunswick, June 1990.

[78] John Rushby. An overview of formal verification for the time-triggered architecture. In *Formal Techniques in Real-Time and Fault-Tolerant Systems, Lecture Notes in Computer Science*, volume 2469, pages 83–105, September 2002.

[79] S. Seshia, R.K. Shyamasundar, Anup Bhattacharjee, and S.D. Dhodapkar. A translation of statecharts to esterel. *Proc.1st World Congress on Formal Methods (FM'99), Toulouse, France*, LNCS, 1709:983–1007, September 1999.

[80] R. K. Shyamasundar. Multi-clock esterel: A framework for gals. Invited paper, September, Pisa, Italy 2003.

[81] R.K. Shyamasundar. Specifying dynamic real-time systems. *IFIP Congress*, pages 75–80, August 1994, North Holland Publishing Co.

[82] R.K. Shyamasundar. Specification of Hybrid Systems in CRP. In *Proc. of AMAST 93*, Workshops in Computing Series, pages 227–238. Springer-Verlag, Dec 93.

[83] R.K. Shyamasundar. Towards synchronous rsd (rational system developer) for embedded system design. In *Unpublished Report, TIFR*, September 2005.

[84] R.K. Shyamasundar and J.V. Aghav. Validating real-time constraints in embedded systems. In *IEEE PRDC*, pages 347–355, Seoul, South Korea, December 2001.

[85] R.K. Shyamasundar, F. Doucet, R. Gupta, and I.H. Kruger. Compositional reactive semantics of systemc and verification in rulebase. *Proc. Workshop on next generation Design and Verification Methodologies for Distributed Embedded Control Systems*, Springer-Verlag:227–242, 2007.

[86] I.E. Sutherland. Micropipelines. *Comm. of the ACM*, 32(6):720–738, June 1989.

[87] M. Y. Vardi and P Wolper. An automata-theoretic approach to automatic program verification. In *Proceedings of the 1st Symposium on Logic in Computer Science*, June 1986.

[88] Jean Vuillemin. On circuits and numbers. Technical report, Digital Paris Research Laboratory, Paris, France, November 1993.

[89] N. Wirth. Program development by stepwise refinement. *CACM*, 14:221–227, 1971.

[90] N. Wirth. Toward a discipline of real-time programming. *CACM*, 20(8):577–583, 1977.

[91] J. Woodcock and J. Davies. *Using Z Specification, refinement and proof*. Prentice-Hall Int., New-York, 1996.

[92] J. B. Wordsworth. *Software Engineering with B*. Addison Wesley, New-York, 1996.

[93] N. Raja and RK Shyamasunda, Web-scripting Languages for free, International Conference on Software Engineering Applied to Networking and Parallel/Distributed Computing SNPD'00, May 18-21, 2000.

[94] H. Kopetz and G. Grunsteidl, TTP - A protocol for fault-tolerant real-time systems. *IEEE Computer*, 27(1):14–23, Jan 1994.

Index

CRP, 213, 215
    channel selection, 215
    deadlocks, 216
    program, 212
    receiver, 213
    sender, 213

access
    restriction, 213
Asynchronous
    Ada, 151
    CSP, 151
    Occam, 151
asynchronous interaction
    exec, 67
asynchronous interaction
    task, 67

banker teller example, 157
bisimulation, 133
block
    enclose, 201, 211
    structure, 213

causal, 45
channels, 217
    input, 216
    named, 188, 213
    output, 216
    private, 213
    selection, 215
clock synchronization, 113
clocks
    explicit, 214, 215
    independent, 213
    private, 213
collision avoidance, 228
compiler
    Esterel, 47
    open source, 48
complete, 11
consistent
    inconsistent, 11
CRP, 151
CRSM, 181

dataflow paradigm
    Lustre, 95
deadline, 6
    hard real-time
        soft real time, 7
deterministic, 45

embedded systems, 3
encapsulation, 14
expressions
    clock, 206

feedback, 5

Graphical formalism
    SyncCharts
        Esterel, 128
graphical reactive formalism
    Argos, 95
guaranteed activities, 224

guarded choice, 215
guards
    mixed, 216

interactive programs, 5

label
    trap, 210, 211
liveness
    safety, 11
LTS, 183

modules, 33
Multiclock Esterel
    deterministic, 216
multiform notion of time, 27

observation equivalence, 137

perfect synchrony, 152
perfect synchrony hypothesis
    synchrony hypothesis, 26
periodic activities, 223
protocol
    futurebus, 71
    time triggered, 111

reactive
    non-reactive, 46
reactive kernel, 25
reactive programs, 5
refinement, 9
rendezvous, 214, 216
    CRP, 213
    Multiclock Esterel, 215
    complete, 215
    guarded, 217
    successful, 214
    termination, 214

safety
    liveness, 11

Scade, 97
semantics
    Exec, 90
    interleaved, 20
simulation
    Xes, 49
specification
    requirement, 11
    system, 13
Statecharts
    visual reactive formalism, 95
statement
    rendezvous, 156
statements, 34
    block, 199, 207, 211
    control, 35
    data handling, 35
    derived, 41
    instantaneous broadcast, 45
    reactive, 36
    signal handling, 37
synchronous
    languages, 197
    semantics, 198, 199
synchronous language
    Lustre, 97
synchronous language
    Argos, 123

task
    declaration, 68
temporal relations, 221
termination level, 80
time triggered protocol
    bus guardian, 114
timing requirements
    deadline, 222
transformational programs, 4
TTP
    fault tolerant average, 117

verification
    abstraction, 136
    atg, 52
    context filtering, 139
    first-order based, 143
    hiding, 136
    observer based, 141
    temporal logic, 140

verification environment
    Xeve, 52

watchdog timer, 155

zero delay hypothesis, 20